AT
THE
SHARP END

Paul Nunn

UNWIN

HYMAN

LONDON SYDNEY WELLINGTON

First published in Great Britain by Unwin Hyman, an imprint of Unwin
Hyman Limited, 1988.

UNWIN HYMAN LIMITED
15–17 Broadwick Street, London W1V 1FP

Allen & Unwin Australia Pty Ltd
8 Napier Street, North Sydney, NSW 2060, Australia

Allen & Unwin with the Port Nicholson Press
60 Cambridge Terrace, Wellington, New Zealand

British Library Cataloguing in Publication Data

Nunn, Paul, 1943–
At the sharp end
1. Mountaineering
I. Title
796.5'22

ISBN 0–04–440138–8

Set in 10 on 12 point Plantin by Nene Phototypesetters Ltd, Northampton
and printed in Great Britain at The University Press, Cambridge

CONTENTS

Where is the Menu?   *page* 1

THE PEAK

Two Great Climbs, Two Great Crags   5
In the Peak – The 1960s from the late 1980s   7
An Age of Aid?   9
Incident   10
Bastion Route – High Tor   11
Stoney Middleton at the Change of Life and After   13
Sirplum, Cheedale, Derbyshire   19
Dovedale and Manifold – The End of a Last Quiet Corner   22
Grades and Climbs   25
The Gritstone Rim   27
Kinder Scout Plateau   27
Clubs and Climbers   29

GWYNEDD

Black Wall   31
Llanberis 1964   33
The West   33
The Black Cliff   37
Western Gully – Ysgolion Duon   39
Anglesey – Gogarth Climbers' Guide   43
Quo Vadis Bergsteigerland?   44
Helyg   48

THE LAKE DISTRICT

Will Ritson of Wasdale Head   50
Napes Needle and Needle Ridge (Great Gable)   53
Engineers' Slabs (Gable Crag, Great Gable)   55
Central Pillar (Esk Buttress, Eskdale)   57
New Guides for Old   58
Rock Climbing   61
'The Other Side of the Historical Coin'   63
Steep Ghyll, Scafell   64
Pat Fearnehough   66
A Hundred Years of Rock Climbing in the Lake District   69

Contents

ANOTHER DIMENSION – SCOTLAND

Observatory Ridge (Ben Nevis)   73
Filming *The Bat and the Wicked*   77
Far Far Away Land   82
Emerald Gully (Beinn Dearg, Northern Highlands)   84
Foinaven Saga – The Cnoc and The Maiden   86
Tom Patey is Dead   91
One Man's Mountains   94
Millennium (Foinaven, 1982)   96
Scottish Guides   103
Polyphemus Gully (Lochnagar)   103

THE ALPS – DOLOMITE DREAMS

Tofana – Pilastro de Rozes   106
Civetta (1987)   107
'One of these old classics . . .' – The Bonatti Pillar, 1964   108
The Capucin   110
The Alps and Alpinism   112
A New Direction – The Alps in Winter   114
Roger Baxter Jones (1950–85)   116
Albigna Interlude (1987)   118

A GLOBAL SCALE

A Dream of Ushba   122
Asgard Outing   125
Pamir Postscript (1981)   129
Latok – Karakoram   132
Latok 2 Again, 1978   137
Baleful Barnaj – Jammu Kashmir   141
Dr Pete Thexton   147

MIRRORS ON MEN AND EVENTS

Angles on Reinhold Messner   150
Restating Tradition – A Comment on Wilfred Thesiger   153
The Six Mountain Travel Books   154
Two generations   156
Smythe's Mountains: The Climbs of F. S. Smythe   157
The White Death and *Fifty Years of Alpinism*   157
High Drama   159
The Next Horizon   160
The Shining Mountain   162

Everest the West Ridge   165
Tim Lewis – Editor of *Mountain*   166
Abode of Snow   168

FILM ILLUSION

Fred Zinnemann's *Five Days*   171

BACK TO THE HILLS

Into the Gasherbrum Cockpit – The Scottish Expedition to
   Gasherbrum III (1985)   176

AROUND EVEREST

Kingdoms of Experience; Everest the Unclimbed Ridge   183
K2 Tragedy – A Postscript   184
K2 – The Savaged Authors   186
Conquistadors of the Useless   192
Forward Communication   198

Index   199

This book is a personal comment on climbing and its writing over three decades. For most of that time I have written historical, critical and reflective pieces about this obsessive passion. Many were originally published in magazines and the book is essentially a personal commentary. It is not autobiography, which smacks of confessions.

PN
9 February 1988

WHERE IS THE MENU?

At the opening of the Sheffield reference library dedicated to the memory of Al Rouse, Sir Jack Longland conspired with almost unlimited white wine to raise the spirits of the climbers, dignitaries and media representatives assembled.

'These climbers', he said. 'The Library really does not know what it is taking on. They write and they write and they write, far more than in any other sport. They will demand ever more shelves and storage space, pushing all else aside and may be a threat even to Sheffield's town hall itself. Now for all their writing I don't know who reads it all.'

It was a timely caution for someone who has written a lot. Yet thirty years of active climbing and frantic scribbling seems to deserve a moment of reflection. So much time and energy has been expended in such curious ways. Though most things prove senseless at root, a residue of curiosity remains.

It began in the Peak. I shall never forget the thrill of seeing Hen Cloud and the Roches glowing in the spring sun: the look of the place drew me back there within weeks, before my thirteenth birthday. Soon, with a few friends from Macclesfield, I had climbed some of the classics. On Sundays and school holidays celebrating saints' days we came near to Heaven, solo climbing Bachelor's Buttress and Black and Tans and numerous others, walking wearily home via Wincle. Real climbers were not always impressed by our untutored antics; we slyly spied on their practices, read a few books and improved. An older cousin from the Royal Marines demonstrated 'their' abseiling by leaping

From Cluelow Cross to the future – in the western Peak District.

in one great swoop over the massive roof of the Sloth. The rope running under each arm didn't look too secure; his hands and wrists looked sore, though he didn't complain much, but we didn't consider doing the same.

In a few adolescent years gritstone was the focus of almost all my energy – cycling, swimming, Boy Scouts faded. My hands were raw every Monday morning, barely recovering before the next foray. At home, beside the little catechisms which described the climbs, were others by Guisto Gervasutti, André Roche, Gaston Rebuffat and above all Hermann Buhl. Hugh Merrick's translation of Buhl's *Nanga Parbat Pilgrimage* (Hodder and Stoughton, 1956) became a Bible. Within a year or two of his ascent of Broad Peak with Kurt Diemberger and his death attempting Chogolisa my ideas were fully formed, a seamless web and progression, from the Roches to the Himalaya.

Few of my early friends were so fanatical; apart from Dave Peck, who shared the daily school train to and from Manchester, most fell away. First visits at fourteen and fifteen to the Lake District and Snowdonia were more or less alone, though a friend came for part of the three-week hike round Cumbria and did one or two climbs. I ran into older climbers, some very kind: Brian Wright adopted me for at least one day on the Napes of Great Gable, persons unknown let me climb Hope on the Idwal Slabs with them, and others on the Milestone. From it came no long associations, but much enjoyment and a lone walker's knowledge of most of the main peaks and valleys in many moods. Characteristic was the Snowdonia trip. It began from and returned to Colwyn Bay on foot, via most tops, in a week.

Lone exploration did not continue long, though I retained a need to keep my own company. The established climbing clubs, whether local or quasi-national like the Climbers Club, were remote from my experience and anyway would have looked askance at a fourteen-year-old. I read widely, avidly devouring guidebooks, maps, biographies and expedition books. After discovering the Rucksack Club Section in the Manchester Central Library I crept in there rather than getting on with school work. Some time in late 1958 I met Alan (Richard) McHardy at the Roches, and he persuaded me to join him and his friends on Stanage the following weekend. I had been before with school friends, going on foot from Chapel-en-le-Frith via Kinder and Win Hill, doing fifty climbs and walking home to Macclesfield via Buxton on the Sunday, but this was different. Richard was a member of the new Alpha Club, Manchester based; already some members had climbed in the Alps and others were doing new routes every day on the less-frequented parts of Stanage. There were several 'extreme' leaders, some of whom had already had broken ankles. Some people even owned motorbikes and most were three or more years older than I.

They treated my peculiarities with amused indulgence. They loved a good argument but were good friends to me and to each other. Most met up one night in the middle of each week at Richard's house in Droylsden, to gossip and plan where to go next weekend. The high point of the evening was Richard's mum's cow pie, baked in a very deep washing-up bowl. Richard apart, the whole family had already eaten from it, yet more than three-quarters still remained to feed

Type, Male. Mesamorph – Richard beckons.

Hen Cloud Eliminate and Bachelor's Left Hand.

Doug Scott and Terry Bolger on the first ascent of Limelight, High Tor, Matlock, November 1968. *Photo by Bob Holmes.*

Jack Street on Dead Banana Crack, Stoney Middleton. *Photo by R. Keates.*

eight or twelve hungry youths. Richard doled out the portions with a vast spoon, pressing the choicest morsels on those most favoured. For me there followed a dark bus journey to the (now) Piccadilly Station, and a walk home through Macclesfield streets an hour later. A few hours afterwards I was back in Manchester at school. When I completed my homework I have no idea, though I did well enough at school. Probably I was helped by a sage of the crags who took me up a couple of routes I had found intimidating at Windgather, and warned me of the consequences of not paying alimony: 'Prison isn't so good, and you had better concentrate on your "O" levels.'

Either from ignorance or a blind eye the school encouraged climbing. Somehow I seemed to miss games for years, taking instead to my push bike to reach the crags. Perhaps my one denunciation and caning by the head was a reminder of an authority more aware than we thought. Yet when we were bouldering on a brick wall with tiny holds, Brother David the head teacher caught us. Instead of a reprimand he announced that he had not done this since he climbed Gimmer Crack with the Bishop of Lancaster. Later the whole school stood in mourning at assembly for a sixth former who was killed with his girl friend in the Karwendel Range in Austria.

The Alpha Club never stuck to climbing one crag. The Peak, Wales, Lakes alternate, with odd visits to Yorkshire, Skye and Chamonix. Motor bikes were the key and, in 1959, my grandmother played a master stroke: she bought me a 250cc BSA.

Barely sixteen, at least I had ridden many thousands of miles on push bikes, at first with my father who remained keen on long rides well into his fifties and then with other friends. The last of the bikes was sold to a school pal from Buxton who won races as I moved into another game.

In the home of Reg Harris this was another apostasy!

THE PEAK

All my life I have lived within it, or within a very few miles of its borders. I met an old lady a few days ago, systematically combing the blackberry bushes of Robin Hood's Stride in the razor-edged light of early evening. 'Having much success?' I asked, as unnecessary a question as could be, as I could see there were few in her little pan. 'Not a lot,' she said. 'Are you here on holiday?' An innocent question so often asked, which rarely fails to throw me into confusion even outside the Peak. But here! 'No, I live near here,' came the answer. Then we went our opposite directions, she ferreting through the undergrowth for more berries, me stroking the pink boulders with chalky fingers and floppy old Firés. What a relief not to be asked where I live, not because I am ashamed of the bright woods and moors of Hallam, but because 'home' is vaster than that.

Two Great Climbs, Two Great Crags

Central Climb, Hen Cloud, Staffordshire; Suicide Wall, Cratcliffe Tor, Derbyshire

Hen Cloud is the king of all those North Staffordshire Clouds, the sentinel of the south-west Peak, marking the border to the wild country and the wild hill folk of Flash and Goldsitch Moors, sneering down on the lush green pastures of Meersbrook, and across, with even greater disdain, at a miscellany of redundant Leek factory chimneys clustered protectively in the near distance. In the greater distance, a haze of atmospheric grime mercifully conceals an insane menagerie of twisted pylons and 'post office' towers, sky-probing Jodrell Bank saucers and pottery pit heaps.

In the evening sun, Hen Cloud is rosy, a split pyramid, formed almost entirely of rounded, sand-hued, rough gritstone. The pebbled grit holds the lichen, which invades the bloody wounds of jamming scars and colonizes them, delaying recovery to the next weekend or beyond. Unlike the nearby Roches crags, the rock is undisguised by trees and seems exposed, mountain-like. On wet winter days, the wind howls round the upper turrets where the vertical fissures cut through the summit, and thin mists frequently cling to the rocks. There is an air of repulsiveness about the holdless, slimy chimneys and cracks, reinforced by closer inspection.

There are great climbs of all standards, though the classics have to follow lines of least resistance amid the formidable rounded walls. Central Climb is one of the greatest natural lines, a fault of almost 100ft, which just fails to reach the base of the crag. There is a natural direct start, but it is an inhumanely hard crack, and steep as a way to what is obviously a more amenable route of ascent. Before the First World War, pioneers were forced into a steep, wide, 25ft crack, a little to the right of the groove, and still problematical enough to demand respect. This crack repulsed a good number of pioneers, before being climbed by John Laycock in 1909. Unfortunately his second, A. R. Thomson, was unable to climb it as 'he was handicapped by a congenital disability which made all climbing a matter of heroic endeavour'! Laycock continued, but was overtaken by nightfall below the top of the crag and was rescued after several hours by a sturdy chauffeur. He later confessed: 'Not everyone has been benighted on gritstone and, though one ought to be ashamed of want of prudence, the episode is delightful to me in retrospect; gritstone has a romance no less than granite.'

The initial crack demands a deep probe into its innards at mid-height, and some knee-jamming technique. Its polished holds smack of the greatest antiquity and many a sweaty palm. Once underway, a glacis and large ledge are welcome below the main corner and the most difficult section is over. The next crack requires a degree of shuffling expertise to reach a ledge on the right, and short grooves end on the great field which can be used for a bivouac, or as an escape route. There remains a fine groove of massively composed gritstone, and a steep section to the summit nick. Scope exists for a little individual variation. Beyond is the twisted mass of Ramshaw Rocks and the boggy acres of Goldsitch, stretching away northward towards Axedge and the Peakland core. One can teeter here between the remains of two cultures and in the reality between two climates, as the clouds sweep in from the west laden with the next deluge of rain.

Suicide Wall, Cratcliffe Tor, Derbyshire

Unlike most gritstone edges in Derbyshire, Cratcliffe Tor is isolated and compact, the largest of a series of romantic, tree-studded tors of massive bouldery gritstone which outcrop west of the Derwent. The steep, clean-topped walls are shrouded in trees below and characterized by a blocky structure that creates long horizontal creases and wiltingly blank interior walls. Hidden behind an ancient yew, a hermit's cave is ill protected by a rusting metal fence, and the south-easterly aspect of the place makes it both pleasant and somehow warm and intimate.

A 100ft wall dominates the east end of the cliff. Plumb-vertical, sprouting hardy trees at its base and a pattern of awkwardly distributed cracks above, for many years this wall was the outstanding challenge of the crag. A narrow crack escapes from the trees and leads diagonally to the Bower, a shelf below a beetling overhang. The Bower sports a massive tree, which has seen countless abseil retreats. No crack escapes direct from there to the cliff top; instead, a fierce flake descends the upper wall to fade out a few feet away in an apparently smooth short section of grainy gritstone.

The Bower was reached by a Severe route as early as 1922 by Fred Pigott and Morley Wood of 'Cloggy' fame. Above, the overhang blocked all access to the upper wall, while the horizontal crack leaving the Bower's easy corner offered few holds and less apparent possibility of progress. Doubtless others looked, but Frank Elliott, leader of the nearby Unconquerable, top-roped the exit from the Bower in 1933. It appears that this bold pioneer was unprepared to lead it, and it was not until 1946 that Peter Harding led the wall after a top-roped inspection and some gardening. He was accompanied by Veronica Lee, who must have been a considerable female gritstoner for those days.

Suicide Wall remains a serious undertaking, especially if the lichen, stimulated by mist or rain, makes the usually rough rock at all slippery. A gritstoner's climb *par excellence*, it is varied, steep, strenuous and unrelenting, and yet never outstandingly difficult. A deceptive tree-swarm over the initial bulge leads to a niche below more serious climbing. A running belay here might prevent impalement on the barer branches of the gnarled trees below. The narrow, slanting crack above is a hand-grinder and lacks footholds, so that it frequently draws blood. It leads quite quickly into the edge of the Bower, which provides a belay and a good place to recoup one's energy for the rigours of the upper wall. It also enables the leader to reassure doubting seconds, for the wall above is entirely out of sight round the overhang to the right.

The shelf is left by a swing on horizontal hand-jams, placing the climber in a bridged position below the smooth section which cuts him off from the cracks above. A delicate and perhaps committing step up is not so difficult as it appears, but in summer nettles growing from an exiguous crack could end up in the leader's face. Above, a sharp flake is best taken boldly on jams and layaways until a central niche is attained. A dwarfish resting position becomes possible here.

The final flake looks formidable and, by rapidly widening beyond jamming width, prevents aged gritstoners from avoiding abhorrent laybacks. Again, a quick bold approach is probably preferable in order to reach excellent jams and jughandles like battlements, which allow an exhilarating final swing over the top for those with remnants of energy. Most climbers accept such gifts gratefully, as arms tire, ropes begin to snag and the second snoozes indifferently, neutralized and blinkered in the Bower below. But, then, his or her turn is yet to come!

In the Peak – The 1960s from the late 1980s

In the early 60s able young climbers and veterans were legion in the Peak. Spurred on by Eric Byne's proposed new guides, activity spread far and wide: typical examples were Fern Groove at Stanage (Fearnehough) and the Brush Off at Rivelin (Crew). Between 1963 and 1966 the number of climbs on the unfrequented edges of Kinder and Bleaklow doubled and even trebled. Simpkin's routes at Tintwistle Knorr, some of the newer routes higher up in Longdendale, and the best of the Kinder climbs, all compared favourably with the best grit at the time.

From the mid-60s a spate of climbs began more fully to exploit the magnificent Roches area, including Walleroo, Elegy and the fierce Encouragement. Gosling's addition, The Swan, used a peg for aid, was criticized and eventually done free.★ Though all these climbs were done by the Black and Tan Mountaineering Club, the North Staffordshire Mountaineering Club and Martin Boysen were also active.

At Millstone Edge and Birchwood Quarry the pegging mania wilted and free ascents of climbs like Plexity and Lyon's Corner House ushered in a new era. Modern climbs like Green Death (Proctor and Myhill) or Xanadu (Myhill and Evans) continued to demonstrate the potential. Elsewhere results were similar – aid cut and great routes unearthed – but different people were involved, like Tony Howard and the Rimmon club in Saddleworth-Chew.

Once Derbyshire meant gritstone, but the 60s will always be associated with limestone. In 1960 Gray West was a bearded eccentric battling away in obscurity at miles of virgin limestone. At best he attracted tolerant scepticism from the rock climbing establishment. But the best cliffs in Derbyshire are built of this fickle, charming, rock. Today the most reputable limestone climbs are free, including one-time aid climbs like Big Plum and The Prow.

West's death in 1963 deprived the Gritstone Club of their most ardent pioneer. In the Wye Valley his mantle fell on Tony Howard who for a time produced many routes, some classic (Chicken Run). In South Derbyshire, Steve Read and Doug Scott were very active during the early 60s, producing good climbs of every type and grade. In the Manifold, Nat Allen and Derek Burgess broke new and terrific ground with climbs like Cummerbund and Central Wall. In 1963 Pete Williams found John Peel, which long held its reputation as Dovedale's best climb.

Another active group was Sheffield University Mountaineering Club (SUMC). Barry Webb, Bob Dearman, Rod Brown and Alpha climbers Oliver Woolcock and myself produced routes on most limestone cliffs. Alan Clarke, another active member on both grit and limestone, produced a spate of routes at Stanage, Millstone and elsewhere. Webb started a trend at Stoney with Brown Corner, Compositae Groove, Pology Wall and Mortuary Step. Dearman extended it with his activities on Windy Ledge, before going on to do Derbyshire's then most exposed free climb – Sirplum – with Rod Brown.

Dearman owed much to his association with the Cioch Club, a very different group of limestone-orientated and competitive climbers. Chris Jackson discovered the delectable Armageddon and Chee Tor Girdle and later opened up the central face of High Tor to free climbing with Debauchery. At Stoney, Jack Street was the most prominent of a dynamic group. Jasper, Hex and Dead Banana Crack took Webb's tradition further and formed the basis for Tom Proctor's futuristic horrors of the decade from 1967–1978. Not only were Our Father and Pickpocket very hard, they are good climbs of a type which later became widespread. In a sense they are the product of a competitive environment, unlike that which until then had been usual in the limestone valleys.

★All of these were eliminated later, as free-climbing standards improved and protection was revolutionized.

To new route seekers, outlying and once inferior cliffs have assumed great importance. Time will judge their relevance. To do new routes, a computer-like brain is not always necessary, but one cannot help feeling it would help!

Thus was 'Gary Gibson' prophesized. *Rocksport* (1968).

In fact the early 70s were to mark a breakthrough, contributed to by improved equipment for protection, increased preparation of new routes by cleaning from abseils and even altering the rock to provide holds, use of chalk, like many other ideas arriving from Yosemite, and an emphasis on technical difficulty which took bouldering standards on to the crags to a greater degree than before. Later came an emphasis on training, use of climbing walls and improvements in protection, footwear and a change in attitudes. These two bursts of change are firstly associated with John Allen and Steve Bancroft, Pete Livesey and Ron Fawcett, and secondly with the free ascents of routes on Raven Tor Miller's Dale, or on gritstone the transition from London Wall to Beau Geste and its successors. Interestingly, Tom Proctor, who with Jack Street, Keith Myhill and Ed Drummond had done so much to raise standards in the late 60s, continued to climb at a very high standard with Circe's first free ascent in 1978 (E5 6b). Similarly Ron Fawcett and John Allen made major contributions in the Peak in the 80s, though arguably these did not quite stay with the standard of Johnny Dawes's top climbs like Gaa at Black Rocks, or Andy Pollitt's ascents on Ravenstor.

An Age of Aid?

Reading these old fragments recalls first flush enthusiasms and regrets for the loss of innocence. Climbing on limestone in the early 60s was not a social activity except at Stoney Middleton. At Beeston Tor, Chee Tor or in Water-cum-Jolly one rarely saw another climber. After Clive Rowland had led the Black Flake finish to Chicken Run first ascent in November 1964, we were amazed to see two climbers on Chee Tor Girdle. They were Joe Brown and John Amatt, probably on the second ascent. Alpha Club 'meets' on such crags usually resulted in a new route or two, and were the rare occasions on which a few people congregated in the same place. Most of the climbing was free, then as now, though arguably less aid was used on many of these routes despite primitive gear than on almost any ascent of a modern, top-standard, technical climb of a protected nature. Of course the routes ranged from VS to E2, with 5c as the usual top technical standard. Cynically Pat Fearnehough would refer to the new nut protection, unsophisticated as it was, as 'nut-pegs', and the reputation of late 60s pioneers was reduced temporarily when they were observed to spend many hours hanging on nuts trying to work out what to do next. Both protection and the pioneers, or some of them, eventually improved – perhaps the latter were bored by not getting very far very fast. Of course, for most of us, swarming up the aid of Mecca in February 1961 was soon forgotten in ascents of the Comici and Cassin routes on the North Faces of the Tre Cima in July. Likewise a solo aid ascent of Bastion Wall occurred a week or two after the Badile North East Face, East Face of the Capucin and a retreat through injury with Les Brown from the West Face of the Dru. Limestone was almost a private playground, whether in the Pennines, Avon or elsewhere, and remained so in some cases, until for example Cheddar Gorge, the early 70s. This heightened the affinity between the heretics that were hooked. In 1963 Oliver Woolcock and I were greeted with such enthusiasm by the local limestone climbing group in Bristol that we were prevented from reaching our intended destination. Perhaps that was the intention.

Incident

SUMC Journal *(1961–2).*

There can be little to better a fine sunny Saturday in November and this one seemed ideal for an artificial climb, quite cold enough to be uncomfortable on gritstone but really suitable for limestone climbing, strenuous hammering and swinging around in etriers. The prospect of pegging without the misery of sitting on some ledge with freezing water trickling down one's neck was truly inviting – especially so since the chosen climb had occasioned far too many unpleasant days in the winter of 1960. We intended to do Behemoth, a route in Miller's Dale, a climb I had previously ascended half-way rather too often.*

The road snakes down into the drab grey scar of the Dale, with all the usual terrors for pillion passengers – 'Mind that grit' or 'Is that a patch of ice?', all the while never daring to speak for fear of the dreadful label, 'back seat driver', though Al Parker and I were less 'macho' than most.

The river was its usual mediocre grey self but it asserted itself by enforcing a walk back to Litton Mills in order to cross dry-shod, for the old log bridge had been swept away. A fearful and hesitant shuffle along a narrow water pipe solved that problem. Eager to get at the crag we rushed across the scree and scrambled up to the base of the buttress.

The rucksacks were upended and out poured a mound of hopelessly tangled slings, ropes, pitons, karabiners and etriers, a heap of expensive and beloved paraphernalia. Thirty steel karabiners (Stubai), runged etriers, wooden-handled Stubai hammers, four No. 2 laid ropes, No. 2 and 'quarterweight' rope slings, forged Stubai and ex-military pitons, blade and channel 35, wooden wedges – three thick, three thin. There followed the frustration of untying dilapidated slings to separate them from the clinging mass of karabiners and other slings. Soon a piton rang home, a sign of security, amid too much instability, as muscles relaxed in the comforting rungs, trembling a little from an excess of effort. The crag is imposing despite a height of little more than 150ft but it looked short. Surely this ascent would not take long?

*First ascent B. Ingle, B. Barlow, P. Nunn (third on rope caught in dark, fell into space when peg came out depegging) (December 1960).

Ropes were knotted, all prepared. The jangling equipment is always more of a nuisance than is anticipated. An arm pull and a few steps upwards, one or two surprisingly difficult moves that jog an inefficient memory and a peg was inserted while in a bridged position. This was restful as long as the footholds remained part of the cliff. A fumbling hand grasped a piton, teeth held it for a moment and then in it went with a blow or two, a long horizontal Stubai, reliability itself. A shiny Allain karabiner from the chaos of gear and the rope snapped in. 'Tension.' Bliss: at last the ground had been left behind and the human fly stepped ambitiously into the second rung. Surely, by hooking a foot over the top rung and bracing a heel against the second, greater height would be achieved and one peg less used? Yes! By leaning right out and boldly standing erect another piton could be crashed into the magnificent horizontal crease in the edge of the black groove over the bulge. A classic position was therefore adopted with one foot braced on the black pineapple-shaped rock of the bulge. Onward! A glorious and furious communion with the rock.

How weak is the perception of man's mind, how frail and futile his ambition, and how those bloody ankles ached (by far the most important)! Surely the Dale could not be oblivious to the events so reaffirming its sense of superiority.

'Are they broken?' asked a sympathetic voice.

'Which café are we going to?' was the speedy reply.

The treacherous piton slid nonchalantly, on the karabiner, down the rope, to clank insultingly on the white rock of the ledge.

Bastion Route – High Tor

SUMC Journal *(1963–4)*.

One September morning I felt an itch to do some climbing, but I was at home in Macclesfield and there seemed to be no one available. I put a few pegs and etriers in my rucksack, picked up two dusty old ropes and roared out to Derbyshire on the 'Gold Flash'.

After Buxton the Wye Valley attracted, but I did not stop at the Big Plum as I had half thought I might. Once I had reached Bakewell, High Tor seemed to be the only possibility. In a few minutes I was there. The white rectangle of limestone dominates the road between Matlock and Matlock Bath, emerging from a steep jungle slope and lunging almost 200ft skywards.

It was a silent still day; all distant views were obliterated by warm brown mists and the sky was a hazy blue, the sun rarely blinking through the vapour masses. The air felt thick.

My ancient 80ft rope lay uncoiled on the grass, a knot decorating one end to prevent it unravelling. Fifteen or twenty pitons, a dozen karabiners, the inevitable spiked hammer and three etriers were all fastened to a complicated harness of ex-army webbing and rope which combines support round the thighs, waist and shoulders. Blue *PAs*, unusual here, gave me a sense of serenity. It seemed strange to set off on a limestone climb in shirt sleeves and the sun after so many wet winter epics.

The first pegs were shiny new and unnecessary and I removed them in passing. There was one disconcerting move to reach the ledge, using an old rusty peg. Above, a bulge blocked the way, but to my surprise and great pleasure, numerous pitons indicated the route above. By fastening myself to two, three or four of these on almost all moves I felt secure enough to continue in etriers. But it curdles the stomach at first, swinging in etriers alone on two or three pegs. Above the bulge I made slow progress, removing about half a dozen good pegs, some of which came out with only a couple of hammer blows.

At 3pm, after three hours' climbing, the worst was above – a loose bulge below the second ledge. I had just been in a horrifying tangle from using too much protection and had gone to the opposite extreme. I stood in an etrier fastened to a peg having removed everything below. There were about 10ft of powdery rubbish, with no places for really secure pegs. I climbed it free, protected by a loop back to the peg, and using a hand-inserted piton behind a tottering block, and grasped an old 'Gray West' peg. Even now I did not feel too secure. The ropes hung down behind, parallel blue and grey. Below was the river, a long way.

Not putting too much weight on this fat little piton I produced my secret weapon, 13in of channel piton won with labour from Kilnsey only a week before. It was slammed into a narrow crack until only the ring was in sight, peeping out from below an overhang. Blood from my knuckles dripped red down the white stone as I slumped back on its security.

Two faces appeared, stared from above, said not a word and disappeared. Perspiration soaked my clothing, my arms ached and my load of pegs felt heavier and heavier.

As the day wore on the top still seemed quite distant. Straight up a crack bristling with pegs, fastened to two and removing everything within hammer range, hanging upside down, adjusting the prussiks. It broke my heart to leave a shiny 'Charlet' when time seemed short, for the light was getting worse. There was a last sticky bit, just above an old bolt, where flakes adhered to the wall like plates and pitons were placed between them. A 'Cassin', firm but not deeply placed in an independent pocket above, eased my nerves. Then while resting I glanced for a second time at the river, and at four spectators. They were all wearing the habits of a religious order.

It was gripping almost to the end, when a big wedge appeared and eased a section that looked abominable, and I knew it was done, with care. I staggered over the top, half expecting to meet the man asking for money, but fittingly there was no one in sight. Dirty, animal sweat dripped from my face, which was plastered in grit. Behind me dragged a mass of equipment, my shoulders felt cut to the bone with the weight and a gum of saliva and limestone clogged my mouth with the worst taste I have ever yet experienced. My muscles quivered as a feeling of relief and exultation surged up inside. The sun was already a yellow glow behind the opaque evening clouds as I coiled the ropes and collected my pitons from the pile. The desire for a drink soon drove out every other feeling or instinct, including the immediate pleasure of success.

Stoney Middleton at the Change of Life – and After

Mountain 9. (1970).

The Dale will never free itself of the brands seared by the Industrial Revolution. Narrow and confined in character, it has been rocked and shaken by high explosives, torn asunder and thoughtlessly wrecked by successive generations of quarry companies. Ashen dust coats the greenery with funereal drabness, giving the trees an eerie half-dead appearance. Blasting continues to devour the south side of the valley, threatening to turn it into a twentieth century limbo. Already, there are the characteristic scars, the rusted tin shanties sporting gaping holes in their roofs, the stagnant fetid pools. Wild life retreats, vegetation becomes sparse. The valley is picked to its geological bones. Years would be needed for regeneration if the limestone gluttony stopped tomorrow. It makes a mockery of the grandiloquent but piecemeal and penny-pinching legislation which purports to protect our most scarce of valuable resources – natural beauty.

The climbing cliffs in Stoney were once quarried. Sir Francis Chantrey's illustration of 1818 shows the Tower of Babel and Windy Ledge Buttress, with clouds of smoke billowing from lime-burning on the Promenade, but the old quarry activities were relatively small in scale and disturbed the underlying strata far less than modern methods. As a result, the wounds have healed on the north side of the A66.

Despite the dirt and starkness of the quarries, the valley retains some of its essential charm. The village, standing astride the entrance to the narrow defile with the cliffs pressing on the crowded low buildings, has a close, warm and intense atmosphere. Every amenity, except for adequate car-parking space, is available within 100yds. There awaits the best big cup of tea in Derbyshire, itself worth a pilgrimage. There are pubs, closely conditioned by the climbing atmosphere, with the inevitable highly competitive dartboard, flung jargon, ribaldry, and juke-box sounding in the background – never noticed except when silent. This warmth and convenience, and the ease of approach by bus from the east, must certainly have attracted those regular weekend habitués who set up their abode at the end of Eric's café in the mid-60s. The closeness and intensity of the place came to be reflected in their activities.

Since so many of the prettier limestone valleys are awkward to reach by public transport and, once reached, require a hike before climbing is possible, since they often seem to lack a convenient pub or café, and since one's friends will not be there anyway, it is little wonder that Stoney attracts the carless. Probably, it is when the long day is over that the area's advantages come into their own.

The cliffs have many charms. They catch whatever sun is available in the long winter months, and the temperature is tolerable when north-facing crags demand the most spartan efforts. There is less rainfall here than further to the west in the Peak. Snow rarely lies long. The sight of Windy Ledge Buttress catching the sun against a brilliant backcloth of blue sky is immensely stimulating after a drab early morning drive from grey industrial towns. Although the east wind may chill one's enthusiasm for the exposed walls of that formidable crag, the complex of quarried bays to the west is so sheltered that only heavy rain can make climbing in them intolerable.

Within less than ten minutes of cake and tea, one can be climbing on grand exposed rock. With stamina, one can remain until ten minutes before the last bus.

Before the 50s, a few stabs were made at the immense possibilities. Frank Elliott, the bold Nottingham climber, made the most significant of pre Second World War routes in his ascent of the Great Ridge (Aurora). This was a VS climb at that time – steep and serious in the conditions under which it was ascended. Elliott's achievement was overshadowed by the death of a friend who fell on a subsequent attempt. The tragedy lent ammunition to those who claimed that limestone was unsuitable for climbing and even bad for technique: 'The style of the scrambling is dreadful to watch,' they said. What is remarkable is that most climbers agreed with them. Apart from semi-speliological scrambles and a few easy climbs in prehistoric times by Puttrell and Bishop, and others in the 30s by Byne and Clifford Moyer, Elliott's climb remained the only pre-war route of importance. The change in attitudes following the Second World War prevented the wholesale acceptance of theories prevalent before it: climbers became more numerous and more active, while their contact with tradition was greatly weakened.

Limestone climbing became usual in a number of places between 1945 and 1955, but Stoney had its special attractions. Like High Tor, it was easily reached from much-frequented local grit edges, and the A66 was commonly used by itinerant climbers. Parties from the Valkyrie, and later the Rock and Ice, were lured on to the crags, battling their way through ivy and jungle using much artificial aid. This was the beginning of a slow and cautious process of development which ended in the early 60s. The climbs were really only an extension of the idea behind the ascent of the Great Ridge, for although Sin, Glory Road and the Golden Gate seemed somewhat harder, pegs were used on them. A rather exaggerated idea of their difficulty remained in people's minds as a result of the unfamiliar nature of the rock, the initial looseness and, above all, the vegetation which choked corners and grooves. Vegetation was so pervasive that some post Rock and Ice climbers came to believe that their ascents of earlier climbs were the first, rather than repetitions of routes done half a decade or more earlier.

The apparent slowness of development here, as on mountain limestone in general, was in part due to the great concentration on the traditional medium – the gritstone edges. These continued to yield some of their finest and most difficult problems in the 50s, usually without extensive gardening. There was fierce competition on gritstone, while limestone was irrelevant. Nat Allen, Joe

Brown, Don Whillans and Ron Moseley were among those who climbed on it, but their activity was skimpily recorded and frequently regarded as training for greater things rather than an end in itself. Limestone, like many of the gritstone quarries, had to await people who would see its inherent qualities.

From around 1957, a trend developed in that direction. SUMC climbers began to climb here regularly. The group included people like Dave Gregory and Jack Soper (who was to be very active at a later stage on 'Cloggy'), but the man who concentrated on limestone, and particularly on Stoney Middleton, was Dave Johnson. At that time, it was accepted that pitons were 'a natural resource', and one is occasionally amazed at the low level of competence exhibited in their use in that era. Kingdom Come, on Windy Ledge Buttress, was regarded as the hardest of the cliff's routes, a stiff A3. As a peg climb, it could never have been of a very high standard. This is no criticism of Johnson, for even the specialists in artificial climbing in Britain – Biven, Peck, Moseley and Gray West – all appear extraordinarily slow by modern standards. Their gear was primitive, their use of it often heroic! Climbs like Kink were approached with trepidation for years – even those bold enough to tackle limestone often feared instant death under a rapidly descending pile of rubble.

Despite the neuroses, the pegs and the panics, Stoney Middleton came of age by the end of the 50s. The classics of the cliff were established. Johnson had led the impressive Windhover, the bold central arête of Windy Ledge Buttress. On the same buttress were other possibilities for the future. Climbs like Aurora, Sin, Glory Road, Froth and Wallop, Golden Gate, Minestrone, the Pearly Gates and the cracks of the Tryglyph were all ascended regularly by a small band of enthusiasts. People kept on discovering Stoney, only to find that it had all happened before. Many learned limestone techniques in this valley.

In the meantime, the emphasis of Peak development had switched to limestone. Eric Byne had urged Gray West and the Manchester Gritstone into their great Wye Valley campaign. There were miles of virgin crag. Gray West's 1961 guide* was, for many, as much a pointer to possible routes as an indicator of realized ones. Yet this was not an especially active period in the Stoney area. Relatively little was done, but it was excellent. Barry Webb, then a member of the SUMC, made four futuristic ascents. He was a climber of undoubted brilliance and inconsistency, lightly built, phenomenally agile, and determined – when the day and his mood coincided. In a few months, in 1960–1, Webb found Compositae Groove (an excellent open book corner east of all the existing climbs), free-climbed the steep wall of Padme, found the then much more difficult Mortuary Steps, and capped it all with his ascent of the ferocious Brown Corner. As was not unusual in the late 50s in the Peak, it was rumoured that Joe Brown had ascended this climb, although there was no evidence that he had done so. Webb's approach was typical, composed of great dash and aplomb, and indifference to surrounding circumstances and established traditions. He

Rock Climbs on the Mountain Limestone of Derbyshire; Cade & Co Ltd and the Manchester Gritstone Climbers Club, 1961.

and Charles Curtis approached the climb after a few pints of excellent bitter, whose influence might explain the severity of several of Stoney's climbs. The gloomy, rank, quarried corner was at least as formidable as Cenotaph Corner★ before Brown's ascent. Loose rock and jammed blocks abounded, held together by earth and foul vegetation. The corner is steep and sustained; three pitons were used for aid at the bulge before a neck-stretching layback up the long upper corner. Today, with all the filth removed, the climb remains strenuous and formidable. At the time it was a *tour de force*.

One climb at Stoney competed with it. Medusa, the great crack left of the Golden Gate, should have been a gritstoner's glory, yet it was years before a lead took place. Len Millsom led the crack in 1961, after a number of top-roped ascents had been made. Similar to Webb's climbs in overall difficulty, it took the centre of the quarried wall which had previously been ignored.

Stoney Middleton. *Photo by Tony Riley.*

All these developments occurred before Stoney Middleton really became a major climbing ground. It was, after all, less impressive than High Tor, and little more developed than a number of similar alternatives. Great climbs and hard climbs were no more plentiful than elsewhere. In the 60s, however, there was a shifting of the balance. Why was it that so many came to Stoney to climb? That Geoff Birtles published a guide in 1966 was not a sufficient explanation.

★Cenotaph Corner, Dinas Cromlech, Llanberis.

Stoney forced itself on one's attention; newcomers always wanted to sample its routes. One thing should be made clear in that it is not the raw material that was so special; the rock is not as good as much in the South Derbyshire area, and is not really much more varied than other major limestone cliffs. Yet there is a concentration of most of the hardest limestone climbs in the Peak, unrivalled elsewhere in the area. If the rock is not so special, the lines not intrinsically so fierce, the intensity of development could only have been the result of the intensity of attention. Stoney Middleton Dale became a forcing ground, yielding especially hard routes as a result of attention more intensive than that paid to any other Derbyshire limestone cliff. The source of this intensity came after 1961, although there were signs of it among the earlier SUMC pioneers.

The essential impetus came from the Cioch Club. Just as Froggatt and Curbar Edges were once the province of the Rock and Ice, Stoney Middleton came to belong to this group. Feudally and safely installed in their hut at the end of Eric's café, inward-looking for years, fairly localized in origin, they were inordinately jealous of their stamping ground. In the middle and late 60s, little of importance was done here by others, who frequently went elsewhere and fell behind as the Stoney routes were hatched, rarely to catch up again. The Cioch was represented here every weekend, when Cloggy, Anglesey, Pillar Rock and the Eastern Fells, or Chee Dale, High Tor, Dove and Manifold were being exploited.

Most of the Cioch group were in their teens in 1963. Naturally, they suffered from lack of transport, and Stoney benefited from its natural advantages. Most of the members came from Sheffield or the Chesterfield area and were unusual in that most of them had started on limestone or had taken it up early in their climbing careers. At a time when gritstoners were brought up in the long-armed and long-toothed mythology of the Rock and Ice, this was no bad thing for climbers operating on a new medium. They made their own standards for their own activity, which initially included more pitons than the gritstoner likes, although in the long run this helped the evolution of their attitudes to the rock.

Weekend in, weekend out, for perhaps three or four years, the Cioch came to Stoney. They soon ran out of routes, but instead of going elsewhere they started finding their own. Bob Dearman, a technician at Sheffield University, battered his way up a number of routes on Windy Ledge Buttress and elsewhere. Among them was the Great Flakes left of Windhover, an obvious link between the latter climb and Kingdom Come. His climbs generally required artificial aids but, as in the case of Windhover, once the barriers of the unknown were down freer moves were interjected until the pitonage faded away. The increase in knowledge of Windy Ledge Buttress enabled Brian Moore and Dearman to traverse from Aurora to Kingdom Come. The crossing of the Scoop Wall area was so loose that difficulty was experienced even though pegs were used. Some of these were so bad that there seemed to be only marginally greater virtue in avoiding their use. There were many such sections in the new-look Stoney climbing, some of the new free routes being in places frequently dismissed even for aid climbing in earlier periods. The Alcasan traverse, done in June 1964, was

17

climbed increasingly free and extended by other Cioch members, Chris Jackson and Brian Moore, in the same year. It remains one of Stoney's foremost climbs, alternating strenuous and delicate climbing in an unrelentingly exposed situation.

Another good traverse had already been found by Moore, with P. Fieldsend, in the previous year. The buttress near the garage had yielded the Pendulum, first climbed artificial with several falls. Local concentrations resulted in this, too, being done with less aid by Jack Street and Jackson. Meanwhile, the long traverse idea spread rapidly to other suitable limestone cliffs. There, too, they have come to rate among the best of Derbyshire's climbs.

The members of the Cioch Club were an extremely competitive group, both internally and externally. They subjected unfortunate 'outsiders' to a psychological onslaught even more raucous than that of either the local crows or the Sassenach-baiters of Glencoe. Though there were exceptions to the general rule of noisiness – including the genteel traverser and discoverer of the delectable Armageddon, Jackson – the tone was set by the more clamorous. The brothers Street were regulars. One could never be quite sure whether or not they owned shares in the local hostelries. Their forceful personalities made them prominent in the group, Jim Street being a formidable deterrent to all but the most drunk on a Saturday night, and his younger brother Jack excelling on the rock. For a considerable period, Jack was the star, though many others also did new climbs. A carpet fitter from Sheffield, his finger-strength has become legendary which even compelled alien photographers to be finger-conscious. His climbs were power climbs, notable for their reliance on small and dubious holds in which the quarried bays abound. Climbs like Jasper, the Hex, John Peel and the less fearsome Dead Banana Crack followed the Webb tradition and extended it. The steepness was too great for the delicate fumblings of more traditional limestone routes. Not only strength, but great push, was required; in this, Street's climbs pointed towards the even greater horrors yet to come.

Fortunately for some, delicacy could still just pay off. The general opening up of Garage Buttress fell into this category. Climbs like Rippemoff, Evasor and Aquiline were traditional-style limestone climbs never so prohibitively strenuous as to force the leader into reckless speed. Even the lower traverse, Atropos, belatedly discovered by Jackson, was of this type.

There was a great burst of concentrated climbing in the mid-60s before an uneasy lull in 1966–7. Already, the hardest climbs approached or equalled the hardest limestome routes elsewhere, but the real pay-off came in a final feverish spurt of activity in 1968–9. One of the old Cioch members, the flamboyant, dandyish Geoff Birtles teamed up with a very active young climber, Tom Proctor of Chesterfield. Proctor did most of the leading and they created a new generation of super severe problems, some being traditional artificial routes done free and others being quite novel and difficult throughout. The approach to these climbs must be dynamic; the standard is as high as anywhere else. Despite looseness and steepness, whatever holds there are must be used. To dally is almost certainly to fail for all but the strongest. Gritstoner's dynamism must combine with the limestoner's psychological ruthlessness with self. Protection is usually adequate, but very enervating to arrange. The Pickpocket, a vertiginous wall right of Medusa, typifies the less frightening of the new genus. The route up the right wall of Scoop Wall, Our Father, is one of the fiercest: strenuousness and looseness, small holds, advanced layback and delicacy, small runners and an occasional piton all combine to make this a climb requiring a concentration of superlative effort. For a safe ascent, it requires leadership of the most mature kind, recognition of the margin without weakness. Possibly, no such ascent has ever been made. Only those who have done it really know!

It is concentration which has produced the elixirs of effort that have made Stoney Middleton magnetic. Even inveterate limestone-haters deign to come occasionally, disguising their disgust to ascend Sin or, more recently, Medusa, the Flakes, and Pickpocket. Now, they pick at the base of Our Father, preparing for a necessary act of faith and hope, to ensure that they are still up with the times. The concentration has produced tradition where once, little more than a decade ago, there was none. The traditions have been forged by the untraditional, above all by the Cioch group, and Stoney rules are more rigid now than those of extensive, distant, mysterious and rhubarb-ridden Chee. They are close to nearby grit in their puritanical absolutism; enraged moralizers now abound in the valley's society. The Cioch hut, and even the club as such, has gone, but there are still regulars who, like the gritstoners of the late 50s, are somewhat overshadowed by the group which made the place its own. Stoney traditions are now exported to High Tor, Dovedale and Priestcliff. Problems of definition, especially on aid, still remain to be finally sorted out for initiates: 'What is aid is aid is aid is . . .' Perhaps successive generations will become more and more severe in interpreting the strictures of their predecessors. This has happened elsewhere (on gritstone, on 'Cloggy', and especially in Anglesey).

Meanwhile, Stoney settles down to a comfortable and revered middle age. From the grey-green, gentle hills of the White Peak, it smiles – as a successful upstart at its precursor – at the grim uncompromising walls of Curbar Edge, where an earlier generation of innovators expended themselves, succeeded and failed, before dispersing to the ends of the earth. The comfort is half illusory, however, for as transport becomes nearly universal, Stoney becomes increasingly a staging post, a place to call and taste the tea and the atmosphere before departing for valleys less developed and less spoiled.

Sirplum, Cheedale, Derbyshire

K. Wilson (Ed.) Hard Rock, Hart-Davis, MacGibbon, 1974.

Cheedale's cliffs remained almost unexplored until the late 50s. Harold Drasdo had climbed the gritstone-like crack of Stalk, on Plumb Buttress, but most of

Bob Dearman – far from the madding crowd near Cape Wrath. *Photo by Tony Riley.*

Adjudicator Wall meets Pete Livesey. *Photo by Bob Dearman.*

the subsequent climbing had been unambitious. There was a certain wariness about bigger, steeper bits of limestone, particularly after Gordon Mansell's spectacular fall when he was attempting the unclimbed bulge that later became the Big Plum. In this atmosphere, Gray West's ascent of Big Plum seemed like a breakthrough, although it was really only a matter of catching up with normal limestone practice elsewhere. For a time it seemed that Plum Buttress would remain a pegger's paradise, and subsequent climbs like Tony Howard's Victoria served to emphasize the fact.

Yet many a nosy climber, groping his way along the bisecting rake below the overhangs, must have cast his eyes across the bulging wall on the right, where black roofs meet the vertical in a jumble of small overhangs and undercut grooves. Images of that wall when it was virgin include not only these long-familiar features of an impressive climb, but also a black-cowled, 6ft flake, poised in the very middle, ominous in its obvious insecurity. Not that most climbers were likely to have gone so far as to imagine themselves clinging to such a tottering missile, for the wall itself appeared so steep and fierce that it did not require this stern guardian to give it a nightmare quality.

By dint of persistence, a little ambivalence of mind regarding the extent to which it would go free, and that subtle mixture of myopia and imagination which first ascensionists of hard climbs require, Bob Dearman sorted it out; and the vogue for Sirplum swept through local habitués as a natural aftermath to the intrigues which always surrounded new climbing activities in those times. Only the sourest of critics could carp at the excellence of the route and the boldness of its first ascent.

Grass and wild flowers creep across the promenade, which was once a railway through the Wye Valley. It is a reversion symbolic of new priorities and characteristic of the double-edged nature of so-called progress. The dodging of trains was the most death-defying feature of climbing in this area until the late 60s; tunnel-walking escapes, when the valley path flooded on winter nights, provided the pinnacle of sensation, as one leapt from the path of an oncoming monster in complete blackness, or cowered, nose in water, between the sooty walls and the roaring wheels. That excitement has now gone, and one can only conjure up the spooks of trains and tunnelling navvies on black night retreats. At the same time, this once noisy valley has reverted to the peace lost during the last century. And yet, as one walks into Chee from the west, the gargantuan and irremediable destruction wrought by the quarrying companies, carving out a wasteland of dust, mud and ugliness from a gentle, rolling limestone upland, is so painfully apparent as to make anyone who has known this country well retreat into despair. The peace of the Wye and the minor modifications brought about by the railway companies seem both Lilliputian and fragile in contrast.

The transition from mass peggery to quieter, athletic free-climbing seems a suitable accompaniment to the locomotives' retreat. Sirplum once looked as if it should be an aid climb, but it never became one despite the four or five pegs originally used as aid or protection. As for the climbing, it works a gentle and tantalizing escalation on the aspirant. Relatively solid, white, lower walls provide alternative routes to the rake, where one can be weakened not only by a large block behind which a supposed leader may attempt to hide his shame-filled face but by the lateral rake, which offers an enticingly easy and flower-strewn route to the pub and *ennui*, a variation which may seem singularly attractive on closer inspection of the steep black bulge above.

Confidence alone is hazardous here; the incautious leader, anxious to dangle the statutory 20ft of rope before his first runner, could miss a rusty piton about which a small loop may be draped. Although no longer respectable as aid, this is useful as a runner. A few grasping arm pulls, some swinging up and shuffling of the feet, and one is led to the first frieze of jugs and a protection piton.

Seductive jugs lead left, with an occasional rattling complaint, to the plinth from which the guardian flake was once levered, groaning and crashing into space. It provides a pleasant chapel of rest, with runners above. Stepping out and up, over the big overhangs below, can be alarming if one looks before making the bold moves which lead apparently to even less friendly territory. At this point the climb begins to give a little, providing a man-thickness thread which could be embarrassing to the short sling brigade. With that in place, any climber worth his salt and capable of getting there is immortal; he has the choice only of groping on, up and round the bulges, steep grooves and terrifying grasses above, or of falling clear and clean into the ample space below. There is exultation in that finality, despite aching arms, for beyond that thread Sirplum has only its excellence to give.

Dovedale and Manifold – The End of a Last Quiet Corner

Rocksport (*February–March 1971*).

One of the Peak District's better guarded secrets is out at last. The beautiful Dove and Manifold Valleys are destined to increased popularity with climbers following the publication of the *Southern Limestone* guidebook.*

Lying on the borders of Derbyshire and Staffordshire, this area has long been popular with tourists and fishermen, but by contrast for the best part of two decades it has been a haven for climbers seeking seclusion. Today it is still quiet for climbing, especially in the winter months, but one is beginning to see other climbers. It bodes ill for the future, and already connoisseurs are complaining in anticipation of the evil days to come.

The history of climbing in the area has been spasmodic, although as long ago as the nineteenth century there were experiments in climbing here. Prior to 1960 a few plums were picked by people like Sumner, Leeming and other Derby–Nottingham climbers and the old Rock and Ice. But there was no concentrated development in that period, which nevertheless provided such classics as Venery (Raven Crag – Hard VS), West Window Groove (Thor's Cave – Hard VS) and above all, The Thorn (Beeston Tor – VS). The last of these is still one of the area's best and longest climbs.

A few pitons were used on some climbs done in this period and, in an excess of modesty, there was a tendency to record climbs done with one or two pegs for aid as if they were artificial routes. This practice led to much confusion when, in 1961, Gray West published his guidebook. Some climbers came to believe that they had free-climbed old aid routes, only to discover later that their performance had been little different from that of the original authors of the climbs. Of these early climbs, artificial routes like Ilam Rock's White Edge were very popular in the early 60s.

Modern developments seem to have begun about 1963. In that year Pete Williams discovered John Peel (Hard VS) at Tissington Spires and a number of less important routes. John Peel is still one of the finest routes in the area, and it pointed towards the kind of excellent free climbs that have become most characteristic of the area. Tony Howard also snooped around, doing, among other routes, Snakes Alive (Dovedale Church) and Dr Livingstone. The latter name typifies well the problems associated with early pioneering on the more vegetated crags of the area. Meanwhile, the old war horses of the 50s were stirred into action again and Harry Smith made an aidless ascent of Venery (one or two wedges had been used originally) and made Phil's Route at Dovedale Church 'Go' with only one point of aid at Hard VS (there have been several subsequent claims†).

Above all, these areas demanded sustained effort from would-be pioneers. Many of the climbs on the slabby faces of Tissington Spires, Pickering Tor Area

The Southern Limestone Area. Compiled by Paul Nunn. Climbers Club, 1970.
†Graded E2 5c, 1987, free.

and the Manifold Crags required gardening of the kind most usual ten years ago on Tremadoc and Goat Crag. Ideally, a small band of dedicated fanatics was needed, and the Derby–Nottingham nexus provided such a group. They were near enough for this area to be evening country and there was a continuity of interest among them which was lacking in others. In a large number of visits in the mid-60s they gradually picked clean the ivy-cloaked walls of Tissington Spires, behind Pickering Tor and elsewhere in Dovedale and discovered clutches of new climbs. This donkey-work has probably been underrated by some of the less appreciative recent pioneers. They discovered climbs of all standards, with a bias towards Severe or harder but also including some easier climbs. In the same period Bob Hassall and others found the Claw (Hard VS) on the Baley Buttress in Dovedale. It appears that some aid was used at first, but it was soon eliminated.

The Derby–Nottingham group's greatest contribution of all was in the almost untouched Manifold Valley. There it was a question of turning cliffs with either one good climb or none at all into major climbing grounds. The group included veteran cheer-leaders Nat Allen, Derrick Burgess and Derek Carnell, who between them compiled the area guide, and a group of specially bred apprentices, notably several of the dwarfs in which the Rock and Ice put its faith, Terry Burnell, Speedy Smith and Dez Hadlum.

The old and the new proved to be valuable in combination. The cave face of Thor's Cave gained four great new climbs, two of which are now undoubtedly Derbyshire classics (Starlight, VS and Lightning, Hard VS). At nearby Ossam's Crag the oldies did that fine route Cummerbund (VS) which followed the only real break, diagonally up the cliff. At Beeston Tor, which previously only boasted a couple of routes, they climbed almost every major feature and left only a handful of more esoteric routes. Climbs like Central Wall (VS) and West Wall Climb (VS) are as good as any classic limestone climbs in the Peak. One can only be amazed that they were left in cold storage for so long.

Beeston Tor is one of Derbyshire's highest cliffs. It faces south and its limestone is better than on most others. What more could a climber want? The network of climbs there now includes half a dozen VS/Hard VS climbs of high quality and a number of less difficult climbs on the cliff's extremities. There seem to be no poor climbs, while Beeston Eliminate, a short but excellent traverse, is a delectably exposed quality climb at Hard VS.

Despite the crowds attending the Dovedale Dashes of the early and mid-60s, few foreigners penetrated the jungles of Dovedale or climbed more than The Thorn on a rare visit, but since then the first wave of overspill has slopped over from the more populous regions. Those ex-denizens of Stoney Middleton and other stateless persons like Tom Bolger, Jeff Morgan, Mick Guilliard and myself have come to this area in the relentless pursuit of new and/or different climbing.

In Dovedale, Jack Street, with a characteristic and studied indifference to all that had gone before, found an alternative (i.e. harder) start to The Claw, a good twin crack to Venery (Parrott Face) and another climb on the middle section of

Raven Crag, Dovedale. The latter route, Aquarius, is an excellent and difficult free route which supersedes an older piton climb. Next to this Tom Proctor climbed a twin thin crack line, Central Wall. Street also pure-minded his way up a route on the Watchblock Tower, puritanically dissecting existing climbs to create a new Extreme, Adjudicator Wall, which seems to be both very good and very hard.* He has done two more climbs of late with Alan McHardy, Harold Wilson (Hard VS/XS) on the Pickering Walls and a free ascent of the groove on the south face of Ilam Rock. Street has also free-climbed the Girdle of Dovedale Church at Hard VS. It seems likely that some of these climbs may be a bit stiff for their standard and they may need cautious handling.

Other activists concentrated on cleaning up whole areas of rock which until then had been little explored. At Raven Crag, Tom Bolger and a friend did Vex (Hard VS) to the left of Venery. On John Peel Wall, Jeff Morgan and I did two new climbs cutting directly up the wall (Yew Tree Wall, VS and Black Flip, Hard VS†) and free-climbed George at Hard VS. The latter climb again requires the attentions of some looting purist as it has since been repegged. On the lower buttress of the same wall a VS has recently been found (Mandarin, Nunn and Jones). Not far away and alongside a good old VS crack climb Silicon, Guilliard has made two new climbs which seem likely to make the old peg route Blockhole Wall redundant (Tormentor, Hard VS and Deflector, VS). Guilliard has also been up to peculiar antics in Reynard's Cave – The Flying Circus (A3, fourteen pegs and no bolts).

In the Manifold Valley there are similar tales to be told of recent activities. At Ossam's Crag the vegetation had been left to posterity (or next winter) by Nat Allen and his group. Then, between 1967 and 1970, seven new climbs were discovered on its Cummerbund face. All of them involved a measure of excavation. Aperitif (VS) began with an ascent by Pete Maddocks and Ted Howard up the slabby right wall of the crag to the break of Cummerbund and was finished much later up a loose pitch on the upper nose, at the cost of one perlon rope, by a large party *en route* to a dinner (Nunn, Rowland and Morgan). In the last year there has been a spurt of new climbs, all of them of some interest – Conventicle (Hard VS, Nunn and Toogood), Barquintine (Hard VS, Richardson and Rowland), Steerpike (Hard VS, Nunn and Richardson), The Ballad of Bilbo Baggins (VS, Evans and partner), Mardi Gras (Rowland and Nunn) and Moss Slab (Severe, Allen and Burgess).

At Beeston Tor, Jeff Morgan plugged away at a devious but interesting non-line between Patience and The Thorn and was rewarded with The Beest (220ft, Hard VS). Though it remains something of an unknown quantity for the present, it is undoubtedly a good climb on generally excellent rock.‡ Also at Beeston, Nat Allen and Bob Dearman have excavated more climbs during the

---

*E3 5c, 1987. One piton was used on the first ascent with Geoff Birtles.

†Yew Tree Wall: E1 5c 4c; Black Flip: E4 5a 6a (Direct), 1987. Two points of aid were used on the latter's top pitch eventually.

‡E3 6a 5c, 1987, free.

past year. Commendations flash round on the relative efficiency of different gardeners!

Two new roof climbs are of note. The Bat at Doveholes, Dovedale, is a worthy addition to the local repertoire, a big roof but not too hard with the bolts in place (A3, Haslam and Evans). Thor, which takes the roof of Thor's Cave, seems to be a different kettle of fish, with many loose pegs and one would-be leader fallen (A3, Dearman and Morgan). It also has a VS free pitch above the overhang in a fine exposed situation. The Beeston Roof (A3, many bolts, Moore and party) seems to be spectacular but not very difficult.

There are, of course, other crags in the area, less large and less important, and this article has only been an attempt to point to the main trends. The character of the area is determined by the scattering of the cliffs, their sheltered situations and the lack of uniformity in the rock, which demands a variety of styles of climbing.

If the publication of *Northern Limestone** is anything to go by, there will be many more new climbs in future months. Climbers new to the area should note that the local landowners and tenant farmers could be much less accommodating than they are at present. In particular, the National Trust, which has been prickly in the past in its reactions to climbers and which owns much Dovedale land, should be treated with respect. It would be all too easy, especially in doing new climbs, to precipitate a ban on climbing for the reason that climbers are befouling an area of outstanding natural beauty.

These are reasonable thoughts to entertain when one begins to contemplate the inevitably greater number of visitors that this area will have. As a climbing ground this area is unique in the Peak, if only because of its large number of necessary abseil descents from the Dovedale Pinnacles. Already old hands are beginning to complain that new climbers coming to the area will remove old pegs which have been left in specifically for abseils or belays, despite their lack of value for any other purpose. Here too the acquisitive will need to think again. Fixed pitons are present in some climbs simply to preserve them. They must be treated with care, just as the cliffs must if climbing here is to continue.

Grades and Climbs

For some time there was discussion of grading on a numerical system like that at Helsby in Cheshire. There, 5c was the living end, so logically we used 5c in that way and worked downwards. Pete Crew did this with his 'Cloggy' guide of 1963, and Martin Boysen was familiar with numerical grading from High Rocks and Harrisons; some of us thought in such terms when doing routes such as Brush Off or on limestone. This made nonsense of the unwillingness to grade above VS

---

*The Northern Limestone Area. Compiled by Paul Nunn. Climbers Club, 1969.

Jack Street's Claw – Left Hand Route, Ravenstor, Dovedale. *Photo by R. Keates.*

Nice face, mean grader – Steve Bancroft. *Photo by Chris Griffiths.*

on climbs such as Malham right wing. Most of my best climbing friends climbed everywhere that was worth bothering with if possible, so there was a good deal of knowledge of standards, whatever the local eccentricities like the Scottish unwillingness to grade above VS. When Martin Boysen and I climbed in the Civetta in 1963, Alan Austin and Eric 'Matey' Metcalfe were there representing Yorkshire, and Dave Gregory, Clive Rowland, Oliver Woolcock and Jerry Rogan Sheffield, with Dave Potts and his mate Lew as the Oxford University contingent. Munich was represented by Klaus Werner and Pit Schubert, both major figures. The latter, a Whillansish character, has been much involved in gear testing and improvement since, including the introduction of the Sticht plate. Everybody was climbing around the same standard, and made comparisons. Eventually it was formalized in the Peak, with a list of grades published in *Rocksport* the book, 'Rock Climbing in the Peak District' and Steve Bancroft's pamphlet on new climbs generalizing what had been specialized and slightly esoteric knowledge. In part numerical grading was a stir. Interestingly, Steve Bancroft kept on with 5c as the living end – but since then writers have been more flattering. Almost all his technical grades have gone up, and the E grading system has become mightily confused. I never took grades seriously, but it is nice to find the odd E3 to one's credit, even if there had been a little aid. After all there were no Rocs, no Friends, no chalk, no sticky boots, no training and in many cases no abseils or gardening from above, and at times the formidable obstacle of a night out with Jack Street.

The Gritstone Rim

There is much more to the Peak than its rocks. For me much of its appeal is in the high moors, the changes of colour and mood, the seasonal extremities. I can still recall the magic of the Dane Valley and Three Shires Head, an eight-year-old walking from Wincle with my mother and her friends from the picking room in Kershaw's Mill. Their perceptions were steeped in the Brontës. My early life was coloured by the light and shade of tragic romanticism. It made sense of lives otherwise too hard-working and humdrum.

Later the high moors took on an added attraction. In winter they could become very hard. How often as kids after pushing on through the sleet and wind all Sunday on Kinder, we would drag ourselves back through the dark lanes above Kettleshulme. The stone at Saltersford, recording the death of a local man in a blizzard and the discovery of a woman's footprint by his body, provided an excuse for five minutes' rest. In spirit it bound us to another age.

Now the Peak often seems at its best when snow closes almost all the roads and wardens wisely broadcast warnings to eschew the hills. Sliding on skis from the Flouch to Moscar as the wind whips spindrift across the sastrugi, swooping on an ever-changing surface in a great arc from Margery Hill into Abbey Brook, ever conscious that one must not break a leg, no one else is to be seen. Then there is the long puff on skins up towards Derwent Edge, with scarcely a square foot of rock discernible through the drifts. And what paradox, when at 5.10pm at Cut-throat Bridge an empty bus comes Marie-Celeste-like out of gathering gloom to deposit me outside a favourite bar just as the doors swing wide.

Kinder Scout Plateau

Mountain 34. (1974).

Most hills have moods, subtleties and nuances, whose scope is too diverse to be absorbed in a single day's experience. Kinder Scout is no exception. This ambivalent plateau, as large in area as many a Monro, is a hub of the northern Peak District, claiming the admiration and fascination of thousands of visitors. Its hulking, complex, fickle mass is undivided by roads or even by real paths. Kinder's attractions are its own, distinct even from those of its near neighbour, Bleaklow, which is fittingly divided from the Kinder massif by the Snake Road, itself perforated by a stark black line of gibbet-like posts and haunted by tales of Satanic pursuit.

Least forbidding are the southern slopes of Edale, plunging steeply into the natural centre. But even here an ill-defined sombreness reigns except on golden summer mornings: then, the groughs run dry and dust rolls off the plateau lip in tiny swirls; the sun bakes into the bracken-covered slopes and haze blurs the cone of Win Hill. On such occasions the south-facing gritstone attains a golden-brown hue and for a little while climbing on the Tors or Crowden

Clough Face can be idyllic, though the temptations of an afternoon snooze are likely to prove overpowering.

The northern edges are craggy, remote, black and windswept. From Blackden to Mill Hill, the lichenous gritstone stares into the north over an endless vista of untamed moor and bog. Clinging mists writhe up from the valley across the wide flats below the redoubt of Fairbrook Naze. No standing habitation remains on that jealously guarded slope. *'Les déserts anglaises'* as Katrine, a French friend, familiar with Bolivia, once opined. Even the once-sturdy cabins of the shooting fraternity are decayed and flung down. Only the bizarre shapes of the scoured boulders relieve the unbending severity of this primitive landscape. On the last toil up the seemingly endless stone wall leading to Seal Edge, after six or seven hours of a winter-day walk from Marsden, the usual reward is the ferocious blast of a sleet-filled wind, the preliminary to a last stumble through mist, groughs and darkness until, hopefully, the lights of Edale twinkle far below.

Wind and water carried from the north-west batter the Downfall Ravine. The Downfall river drains much of the plateau and provides its most frequented thoroughfare. The ravine is a jumble of cliffs, collapsed earth banks and ever-tumbling boulders. Beyond the Kinder reservoir, the chimneys, smoke and glow of the towns impinge. Though seemingly remote, they take their toll. Smoke abets tramping feet and overgrazing in denuding Kinderlow, where acres of black peat erode valleywards, leaving slab on slab of coarse gritstone bare to the sky.

Kinder Downfall in benign mood.

Guarded within these steep barriers, the plateau is a land of mercurial mood and playful chicanery. Once understood, it seems friendly, but it can be merciless to the careless. Hazy summer afternoons swiftly boil into nimbus in the west, and sudden gusts of wind carry drenching pillars of rain up the Kinder Ravine. The great sumps of the plateau secrete it greedily, allowing little to seep through to the deep peat groughs. Slowly, deviously, the water flows back to the few main cloughs. On days of thick mist and slow progress, the plateau can seem oppressive. The devil in pursuit at Doctor's Gate has his equivalent in the long walker's familiar, an inescapable presence frequently discovered after a few hours of solitary wandering.

There is no real summit to Kinder: it is all approach and no culmination. Few visitors seek the summit and probably fewer find the ill-marked cairns which grace Crowden Head in the midst of a wilderness as bleak as any in England. The plateau has a splendid air of isolation. Its sudden mists and deceptions quicken the senses into a sharper appreciation of the contrast when the ground at last falls away and green valleys replace trackless meanderings in bog and heather. In winter the transitions are more sudden, from endless ploughing through snow or dancing across the frozen cardboard of the peat, to the real focus of Kinder – the Downfall itself: the dry wadi of summer, the roaring torrent of a wet autumn, gives way to a great, hanging curtain of translucent green and blue ice. As the dazzling sun of a short winter day slides behind South Head, the ravine enjoys a final explosion of gold merging into the red sunset across the industrial plain.

Clubs and Climbers

From a review of Climb if You Will, *a commentary on the late Geoff Hayes (Beeston) and his club, 'The Oread', with a foreword by Sir Jack Longland. Compiled and edited by Jean Russell in association with Jack Ashcroft.* Rocksport *(Limited Edition) 1974.*

Mountain *35. (1974).*

Anyone ignorant of the variety and complexity of the British climbing club scene would do well to delve into this volume, which commemorates Geoff Hayes, a Midland climber killer on Dow Crag in 1971. There is more vitality displayed here, in the short, intense contributions and the varied perspectives of the attendant photographs, than is to be found in any but the rarest of the 'Senior Club' journals.

It is not usual in Britain for climbers to perform the rites of passages for dead friends in quite this way, but here it has been undertaken: a commentary on the life and times of a respected local climber, painstakingly constructed with material from his own diaries and from his friends. The account passes gracefully from the modest, intensely local man to the broader achievements of

The Climbers Club at Brackenclose, Wasdale, in the 70s. *Photo by Tony Riley.*

his club, his friends and his associates. Such a celebration may seem too sentimental, but that is how people have felt it and thought about it all, and whatever any outsider says is not worth twopence, because ultimately the account has been written for those who knew Geoff, and any other advantages are purely incidental.

Yet there are advantages, particularly in these times of hero-figures and tele-gods, in refurbishing the images of those who never sought such glories. Though 'respect' for the great lurks here and there in the concept of the perhaps now fading *tiger* and in the presentation of the glories of the harder climbers of the club, it is the life of the group and its self-sustaining quality which shines through.

In fact, it is not just the Oread that has been fêted: it is the North Midland climbing fraternity, an intensely local yet highly active and even cosmopolitan element in the British climbing scene, secure in its deep roots. If not all the text is burnished to the PR man's image of mountaineering greatness, if plain men's ways of seeing the world seem indiscreet, then all the better, for to whom else is it dedicated? Those who doubt may best take time to analyse their own cultural deprivations.

GWYNEDD

In the 1960s many of my friends went to live in Wales. I doubt if I could unless forced by dire necessity. Yet it is a hate-love relationship: Wales has the climbs, but also melancholy. Each year many visits are required, foot down along the newish Cheshire motorway, Friday night through the magnificent expanses of Clocaenog Forest, with luck a view across the Currig y Druiden straights to Snowdonia. Always there is hope of a fine tomorrow. Almost every mile of the journey has been the setting for some past motoring alarm – this was where Al Parker turned his Morris van on its roof, that was where Alan Clarke did the same, producing a fortunately harmless mixture of scrambled eggs, wife and child in the back. That is where Barry Ingle was momentarily silhouetted in sparks as the motorbike hit the first Bettws bend, though we still did Cromlech Girdle. Here is where Hilary and I picked up Dave Cook on the Gold Flash, to go three-up twenty miles to 'Cloggy'. There the Gold Fash died, black smoke puthering from a hole made by an exploding big end, taking Pete Crew for a fast ride, and finally the last stand of the white Bonneville, an awful scream from the engine one hour fifteen minutes from Macclesfield Broken Cross. Yes, over-whelmingly, Wales makes me grieve!

For a time Llanberis was the centre of our attentions, especially in 1959 and 1960. In 1959 Alan McHardy and I retreated there from the Creag Dhu Club haunt of Jacksonville in Glencoe, after multiple falls in a streaming Raven Gully and wet times on Ben Nevis. Not that the Scots' welcome was poor. John Cunningham and John McClean invited us into their domain – but their weather was too bad, and the newspapers spoke of flag-cracking sun in the south.

Black Wall

SUMC Journal *(1961–2).*

As the motorbike crunched against the grey stones of the wall, Clive had already bounded over the gate and was striding out up the green hillside. A chill wind moaned down Llanberis and already the sun glowed only over the summits on the south side of the Pass.

Craig Ddu leers down at the narrow road, but on that day its normal repulsive appearance was mellowed by dryness, for there had been an exceptionally rainless period. Only a few surreptitious bands of moisture were seeping down. The first pitch of Black Wall was attractive, grey, solid holding rock; exposed and steep but never lacking sharp holds. Clive was outlined against the sky as his careful movements took him upwards, a classic portrait of a climber with the rope trailing away behind in a relentless wind. Soon he had belayed and the rope was quickly taken in. After drying my PAs on the inside of my breeches I followed.

The next bit looked easy – a short wall with some holds that looked good. It proved awkward, the holds sloping and slimy, and despite its shortness I was glad to pass it. One wanders about then rather alone on Craig Ddu, amid wet grass ledges and strange angled walls, past steep grooves and dripping corners, the rope dragging soddenly behind until a small black spike provides a belay.

Clive looked rather miserable, standing on the slippery ledge with water spattering down his collar and a funny brown beret crammed on to his head. Tangled ropes were freed and there was an exchange of slings so we could pass on. Above was a repulsive black corner, starting as an overhang with a crack splitting it and finishing among some frowning bulges from which issued a continuous stream of water. In the wind a karabiner swung, an ancient relic attached to a piton which must have been in for years. Already twilight had crept up, and though the sky was bright we were shrouded in gloomy shadows. We would have to be very quick to avoid the darkness.

Hand jamming in a slimy crack was followed by some steep pull-ups on good holds, a few bridging moves brought the old piton into reach; the karabiner was crusted like a link of anchor chain but there was little time to gaze at it. The wall steepened, but after a few tentative moves upwards, a cluster of slivers of shattered rock seemed the key to the exit. They were grasped, pulled up on and finally stood on. A shallow niche allowed some rest but there were further acrobatics to perform.

The only escape is by a traverse, for smooth wet bulges beetle down from above. This wall was dark, gloomy and indefinite and one had almost to feel for holds. But it is surprising what can be achieved when speed is essential and a belay was soon discovered, a sling attached and the slack hauled in. It was hard to tell that one was sitting high on a cliff, for below the shadows had so deepened that the ground was obliterated. Little lights twinkled up in the Pass and probably the balaclava-clad heroes were already recounting their epics in the Pen-y-Gwryd. But Clive was still down in the black hole no doubt saturated by now. A faint voice recalled my attention and the rope crept in foot by foot.

After an almost intolerable length of time he appeared, a dark shadow creeping along on an even darker outline, 15ft away in the blackness precariously poised on those little holds. It didn't seem to ruffle him, as the rope sneaked in. My leg was braced against a boulder, an eye checked a stalwart belay and hands grasped the rope firmly. He persevered, feeling his way across most difficult moves, then he had grasped that final superb flake.

The wind was still whining and a star occasionally showed through the scudding clouds. The moon would soon be up. Coiling the ropes in the darkness, walking down the steep grass, casting off agonizing PAs kicking up the motorbike, driving off to fish and chips; all that time we experienced that satisfaction which is the elusive Holy Grail of the climber.

It was by way of compensation for an earlier failure. Earlier that day Al Parker and I had been on Red Slab on Clogwyn d'ur Arddu. I led the first pitch wearing a duvet because of the cold, but took far too long. I could see Al's blue nose from the stance. He did not come up. Rarely have I so resented a retreat, though I could hardly feel my hands to fix the abseil. My mind had been in another time nine years earlier with bold John Streetly on his first ascent of 1952. For a few hours life was as grey as the photo of it in Wilfred Noyce's Snowden Biography. *Dent, 1957.*

Llanberis 1964

> The product of human determination awed us all,
> Though now in five years passing
> The image is blurred, the hard core does remain
> All the cursed inches of grey strontium ninety rain
> The ice and snow which made it all impregnable
> While we dreamed by firesides,
> Excessive superstitions ousted by superficiality
> Even the pitons legacy, an expensive red-browchip
> In the wrong place
> Taken to build a name which somehow never came
> For all the trouble. After all the hubbub
> Trinity of Llanberis, their sulky brother
> The quieter cliffs hiding superior virtue to the South
> Remain.
> In very little not the same
> While ladders built in the imagination
> Dissolve even for Supermen
> After very few drops of rain.

The West

Clogwyn d'ur Arddu

'Where the slabs are vertical and the walls are overhanging.' (1959 Common Adage).

Mountain 8. *(1970).*

How many climbers must have questioned the authenticity of the West Buttress 'slabs' while ascending Longland's Climb or Great Slab for the first time? All too often, the second disappear below an overhanging retaining wall, while small flakes support toe-ends; below, the space is immediate and frightening. Newcomers to Clogwyn d'ur Arddu almost always experience an impression of overwhelming exposure – as much on the West Buttress slabs as on the more vertiginous East. Yet the climbs *are* slabby: the rock frequently lies below the 70° angle. The feeling of exposure and the reality of space are both a result of the complex geological structure of the place, which makes it very easy to fall from a slab into space. All too often, the entries to climbs creep through the rare weaknesses in the lower overhangs on to the slabs themselves. Traverses such as that on to the bottom of Great Slab involve almost immediate danger; once the slabs are gained, the exposure is house-roof-like. The slabs drop away over overhangs beyond which only the distant scree and the black Llyn are visible.

Fortunately, the slabs themselves are rarely smooth and holdless. Etive-style padding, without a wrinkle to go for or a hope to descend on, is rare. The cliff is covered in holds of sorts, but they are generally small, frequently flaky, and occasionally frail. The rock varies enormously, from the red rust of Bloody Slab – a little friable, slaty-smooth and uncompromising – to the grey, bubbly, rough areas on white slab, with good friction if all else fails. One always plans one or two moves ahead on the tiny holds, and placing the feet often requires imagination. PAs are ideal for the small square holds, but other stiff-soled boots are well suited. There are large jugs, some of which provide excellent running belays. The occupational hazard of the slab climber – the unprotected run-out – does exist, but not to the same degree as on many uniformly smooth, unrelentingly slabby cliffs. The complex rock structure enables a cunning leader to protect himself on the most serious of climbs. Even Bloody Slab, West Buttress Eliminate and The Boldest are not so adamantly blank as some granite climbs.

The complex of vertical jointing gives rise to numerous lines, whose appeal is enhanced by an eccentric side-tilting. The early pitches always contain an element of mystery, of uncertainty as to what lies round the next corner. Some climbs lay themselves wide open after the lower barrier, but more often the simple line seen from a distance is found, on closer acquaintance, to be protected by subtle difficulties. In the centre of the cliffs, the slabs draw together defensively and rear up in steeper areas of rock. To avoid the inevitable difficulties of upper White Slab or West Buttress Eliminate, climbs like Sheaf are therefore forced into long, groping, striding traverses from groove to groove, before escaping on to the pastures of upper Narrow Slab.

It is this irregularity, this alternation of slabs and steeper areas, which makes the West one of the gems of modern British rock climbing. Once the obvious slabs had been ascended, lines of strength had to be attempted. The ascents of Bloody and White Slabs and Ghecko Groove came near to ending an era. The next had already been begun with Slanting Slab, in its ruthlessly logical acceptance of a little artificial aid to attain a sea of roof tiles, dropping over the cliff's largest overhangs. Other lines of strength followed, culminating in modern horrors which force their way through the overhangs to the left of Slanting Slab (Mynedd and Spartacus). The flakiness of the rock makes climbing possible on the steep walls which block progress between the slabs. Here, as elsewhere, some of the best high-standard climbing involves the transition from steep rock to slabs and back again, but in this case the transition can often be achieved with far less aid than would be necessary on most compact cliffs.

34

Al Rouse's first solo of Pete Crew's Boldest, Clogwyn d'ur Arddu.
Photos by Leo Dickinson and Ken Wilson.

Then there is the grass. Beloved of, and heavily caressed by, the early pioneers, its remnants have their uses yet. Most of the rock is naked, just as the slopes below the cliff are becoming worn by climbers' feet. The grass has genteelly retreated to the less-climbed upper areas on the western side of the buttress. There, it has its occasional advantages, or it can hide fine spikes. From it oozes the defensive wet streak on Bloody Slab.

Bounding the cliff to the east is the Black Cleft, the most fearful of 'Cloggy's' greasy corners, oozing slime and watercress from its eternal spring. There are similar but less obvious traps subtly hidden on the west. The climber can be forced into a corner as a refuge from the slab's baldness, only to find that the difficulties are greater and more frightening than those in the light and air of the exterior. After wet weather, the cliff sheds its water slowly, and nowhere is this more true than in Moss Groove and other esoteric corners of the West Buttress.

The acreage of rock is so great that, despite intense exploration in the ten years since golden 1959, under-explored areas still lurk on this cliff. With familiarity comes the surprise of emerging from some sombre steep groove on to a familiar friendly slab of well-trodden rock. The mystery of irregular features, maintained in part by the exclusive paucity of days of dry rock and sun, combined with the pure beauty of the place, explains why climbers continue to over-frequent the Big Cliff.

Clogwyn d'ur Arddu *by H. I. Banner and P. Crew. Climbers Club,*
2nd Edition 1967.

Mountain *1. (1969).*

A guidebook to a magnificent cliff has a built-in advantage: the excellence of the subject is likely to make the reader less critical of the text. The reviewer's task is thus all the more difficult.

Yet a great cliff deserves a great guide. The first edition of the CC Guide, published in 1963, ended a romantic era when route descriptions were carried on fag packets, transcribed from jealously guarded notebooks, or simply extracted from the ramblings of 'the great' in the Llanberis or Derbyshire pubs. That guide did justice to its subject and became a model.

It was rapidly outdated, as is shown by a glance at the first ascent list of the 1967 edition. The latter is no mere rehash, however, for it incorporates much new material. The historical section now includes lively reminiscences from early club journals. How gratifying it is to read that Morley Wood smiles 'a wicked smile' when passing up the cheating chockstones on the first ascent of Piggott's. It is also pleasing to find Birtwistle's ascent of the Drainpipe Crack of Vember mentioned. Kirkus's account of the Forty Foot Corner on Great Slab reveals much about the game of climbing exploration. 'The Corner was literally a twenty-foot wall of vertical grass. I made a mad dash at it. I had to climb more quickly than the grass fell down.'

Menlove Edwards's strictures against the use of pitons are omitted; instead

Harding is praised for his modernism. This seems only consistent in an age when bolts sprout on those implacable grey walls.

Technical detail is carefully revised. A few horrors should be avoided by the upgrading of Terrace Crack to VS; The Shadow, and Moseley's Variation to East Gully Wall, have also been upgraded. The occasional downgrading too seems sensible. Equally useful are one or two alterations in old descriptions, like the omission of the precise number of pitons to be used on Slanting Slab start, which has become very dangerous if done in the original manner, and the mention of the loss of the Naddyn Ddu flake.

There are plenty of new climbs, some of which have rapidly lost their aura of impossibility. Others, such as Mynedd and Spartacus, retain an air of mystery.

The overall presentation of the guide has been revised. The type is slightly larger, a good thing on a dark cliff. The diagrams are generally the same as in the first edition, with some newer climbs marked in. It is a pity that new climbs on the West Side of the West Buttress were not included in the diagram, though the new Far East Buttress diagram is excellent.

A few carping points arise. It seems surprising to find the entry into Ghecko Groove still described by the sling method when the groove has long been climbed free. There is a smack of Welsh insularity in the claim that the Great Wall is 'surely the most impressive sweep of rock in the country,'* while one wonders if a two-pitch description of the climb would not be more apt now that it is common practice to split it. But this is of minor importance. Overall this is a great guide to a fabulous cliff. Any rock climber in Britain should take pleasure in the contemplation of both.

The Black Cliff

The history of rock climbing on Clogwyn d'ur Arduu *by Jack Soper, Ken Wilson and Peter Crew. Kaye & Ward, 1971.*

Mountain 15. (1971).

There is no doubt that 'Cloggy' has a unique atmosphere. This book, which combines a closely written text with over a hundred relevant photographs, chronicles the development of the cliff and attempts to convey something of its atmosphere.

The history is lucid, fast-moving and spiced with anecdote, and participants are given a generous quotation allowance. Even the least literate, modern, seagull-eating activist shouldn't grow weary when he can travel in an hour or so from Abraham's pronouncement as to the cliff's 'manifest impossibility' to the activities of Linnell, Kirkus, Bridge, Edwards and others in the late 30s. A mere two hours more remain before the days of Al Rouse's Gemini and the most recent revamping of Wendy's Llanberis café are reached. By the end the first

*It probably is and certainly has the greatest collection of routes (1987).

ascent of Great Wall seems nearly as remote as those of Vember, Sheaf or Curving Crack, as too do the attitudes that shine through from the past – the leisurely approach of the 20s, the group consciousness and caution of the 40s, and the anti-traditionalism of the Rock and Ice. All this is far more than mere description. Old controversies are recounted, as indeed they should be in a book dealing with a cliff on which a major part of the development of British rock climbing was staged, and on which so many excellent climbers have performed. Great cliffs and interesting personalities create magnificent folklore and myth-ology, mostly generated by awe-stricken associates of first ascensionists, but occasionally produced quite consciously, though subtly, by the 'big men' themselves. Joe Brown emerges as one of the greatest and most economical myth generators in British climbing history. Indeed, those who read this book with pleasure should be thankful for the fact that information sources were fewer and less efficient prior to the 60s, for probably it is this that has done most to generate the welter of grand tales which decorate the pages of *The Black Cliff*. The clinical narrowness of the 60s technical mind did not seem to go hand in hand with a taste for apocryphal stories. Or did it?

The photographs amplify the themes. Ken Wilson's architectural pictures justify the care with which they were prepared, not least on the handsome exterior jacket. There are action pictures from many periods, and interesting group pictures from the pre-1960s. Important participants in the cliff's story are given a passport-size, pictorial *Who's Who*, which does few of them justice.* Overall, the quality of the photographic reproduction is not what it might be, given the excellence of the originals. But if there is a major criticism it is one concerned with perspective and objectivity. 'Cloggy' may, or may not, be the greatest cliff in Britain. It all depends on how closely one is involved. That its history 'epitomizes that of the sport of rock climbing' is indisputable, for it is the combination of geological excellence and sufficient concentration of human activity, rather than geology alone, that has made Cloggy pre-eminent. But the cliff's inherent *greatness* will depend on what other geological structures have to offer in the future, given equivalent quantities of effort. And yet it is this element of commitment to the place that is also the book's strength. A well illustrated history of almost clinical cleanliness, it gives a powerful impact. To create such a combination also required effort, though rather less than in the prosecution of the climbs. There may be little more to be said for years on the Black Cliff which remains a credit to the perseverance of *all* its multitude of authors.

There was of course a heck of a lot more to say! It remains the most balanced account of the central focus of Welsh rock climbing since 1945 with the possible exceptions of G. W. Young, W. Noyce and G. Sutton's Snowdon Biography. Dent, 1957, and T. Jones and G. Milburn's Welsh Rock. Pic Publications, 1986.

*Though some will say mine was flattering!

Western Gully – Ysgolion Duon

K. Wilson (Ed). Cold Climbs. *Diadem, 1983.*

In summer, Ysgolion Duon ('The Black Ladders') is not the most immediately attractive of cliffs. It is vast, lurks in a high cwm far from any road, and there is something reptilian, sinister even, about the peculiar set of its strata and drip of its moss-grown clefts. Vegetation and water, the staples of the iceman's craft, abound, and thus winter brings it into its own. For a cliff outside Scotland, the scale is startling. At its lower, left-hand end it is about 600ft high, but to the right of Western Gully it towers up to more than 1,000ft. Well up near the summit of one of the higher Welsh hills, it stretches a long way round the head of its desolate cwm. It is one of the classic seasonal cliffs, a Welsh counterpart to Creag Meaghaidh, and there has been much activity here on the part of connoisseurs over the last ten years, with surely more to come. Probably no other cliff south of the border has the same scope for hard mixed climbing.

Apart from its one outstanding classic, there are a dozen other fine lines and a host of possibilities as yet unrealized. The gullies hold snow late into the spring, and the height and aspect ensure that the cliff is frequently in condition when others are not. The layout is slightly confusing until you grasp the basic fact that Western Gully lies more or less at the cliff's centre, with the higher bastions to its immediate right. Most of the development and nearly all the summer lines, however, lie to the left. On the extreme left, the bounding feature is Eastern Gully, a pleasant Grade 2, especially good if the steeper right-hand finish is taken. Starting just right of the foot of Eastern Gully and cutting sharply back right is the well-concealed Pyramid Gully which, when climbed direct, gives an excellent ice-pitch at Grade 4, first climbed by Boysen and Estcourt in 1967. When approached from slightly higher in Eastern Gully, avoiding the ice pitch, it is much easier, but still very good. It defines one side of a pyramidal buttress, the other side of which falls into the deeply incised Central Gully, the crag's other classic Grade 2, although in sparse snow conditions it can quite easily be harder than that grade. This triangular buttress, in hard winters, shows two icefalls in its lower section, the left-hand one following the summer route of Jacob's Ladder and the other one flowing down further to the right. These have both been climbed at Grade 4, one by Fowler, the other by Boysen and Brown. Above the preliminary sections they lie back a little, but are none the less substantial 600ft buttress climbs.

Next comes the real meat of the crag. Between Central and Western Gullies sprawls the immense Central Buttress. Its western bounding rib is climbed by the esoteric but worthwhile summer route of Flanders (HVS), Crew, Lowe, Alcock, and Brown's route of 1969, which set the theme of First World War nomenclature for later routes on the crag. It is a sort of hard man's Amphitheatre Buttress. In winter, it would provide a sort of super-Eagle Ridge – if it could be climbed at all. The position in the upper reaches, on a knife-edged serrated arête above the plunging walls of the gully, is frighteningly exposed.

Black Ladders – parties approaching and in East Gully. *Photo by Ken Wilson.*

Western Gully is the best of the traditional winter climbs in Wales, and a route which can hold its own in any company. Joe Brown, of notoriously fickle memory, has a distant recollection of having climbed the route some time in the 50s – probably the first winter ascent. Putting aside the question of history, where nothing is certain, the quality of the route is beyond doubt. It has architecture as well as interesting climbing. Below the terrace at a third height, there are a couple of intricate pitches up grooves which can become very heavily iced and are often as difficult as anything above. They can be, and quite frequently are, avoided by following the summer route, which traverses in to the foot of the main gully-line along the terrace from the right. The middle section of the climb, up to the great chockstone which the crux slab avoids, has more of a massive open groove configuration than the traditional gully form, with little chockstone pitches and easier sections between. After the crux it slices back far into the mountain, great, dripping walls soaring out to the upper reaches of Flanders, before giving out into a névé basin under the summit ridge. At one time it saw as many failures as ascents, and there were tales of all-star teams fighting their way out in the dark after long hours of epic striving. It retained for many years a high reputation for difficulty, probably due to the smooth, high-angle rock walls which have to be climbed in its middle reaches. Along with such routes as Piggott's on 'Cloggy', it was something of a precursor to modern face-climbing.

The Central Buttress itself gives two superb mixed climbs. Gallipoli takes a very direct line from the foot of Central Gully, steep, mixed ground all the way and sustained at Grade 4. Passchendaele is completely different in character. It traverses a long way left from Western Gully along the obvious snow ramp (a direct start would surely be in order), climbs a short, difficult slab which may well be Grade 5, harder than the crux of Western Gully, then subsides back into easier grooves and shallow gullies veering up to the right. Both routes were climbed on consecutive days in the winter of 1972 by Dave Alcock and Martin Boysen.

To the right of Western Gully the cliff attains its maximum height, and has so far yielded up three major routes. Ypres (previously known as Gofrit), the Alcock and Anthoine route of 1968, climbs the lower icefalls of Western Gully before traversing a terrace leading out right to its end, then ascends a difficult 80ft groove (Grade 4) over a bulge into the obvious and easier gully above. Right again are two mammoth undertakings – The Somme and Icefall Gully, both routes of 1,000ft or more. The Somme saw some degree of competition for its first ascent in 1979. Rick Newcombe first tried it early in the season before its main ice pitch was fully formed, and was forced to retreat. A few weeks later, Boysen and Alcock succeeded, with Newcombe swooping in to snatch the second ascent shortly afterwards. It takes a faint series of icy grooves and slabby runnels which delineate Mid-West Buttress's black, overhanging mass on the left, and gives difficult, sustained climbing in its middle third. The highlight of the route is a magnificent pitch, a full 150ft long, of 70° ice, but its Grade 5 is probably based more on length and seriousness than on any especial technical

41

difficulty. People who have done it claim it to be one of the more important winter routes in Wales. Icefall Gully, the right-bounding line of the main cliff, was climbed by myself and Jack Street in 1968. The substance of the route in a good year lies in three or four consecutive medium-length pitches of ice with rock belays in between. The ice tends to be watery, as it forms from a persistent spring, and even in bitter weather a hefty swing of the pick can be rewarded by a squirt in the eye and soaking hands which subsequently freeze. It is quite stiffly graded at 4, and both routes are major undertakings. This is more or less the state of play – a traditional cliff transformed by a series of open and serious buttress and face climbs which, however technology develops, will always remain important and difficult winter routes, for the style of climbing offered here is on snowed-up rock rather than the straightforward ice or snow which lend themselves most willingly to the new implements.

One of my most rewarding climbs on the Ladders was when Bob Toogood and I snatched an ascent of Western Gully one March day in 1970. It was perhaps something of an effrontery on our part to start at 4pm in early March. We had earlier enjoyed a pleasant sprint up Central Gully, its only difficult pitch banked out by snow. As we passed the bottom of Western Gully, some hapless party lost a full bandolier of gear, and the prospect of booty was not to be missed. If we were quick, we might grab the gully and the gear.

Toogood fired off into the first ice-pitches, and we moved up together for a couple of rope-lengths. There were awkward bits and delicate shufflings, and we gained height quickly. Above the terrace we were forced out of the bed as it disappeared into a steep section of icicled overhangs. We were glad that the weather was clear and still as we ground to a halt at a shelf beneath snowy walls. A few old slings and pitons were mute testimony to past efforts and retreats.

Above us, grey rock showed here and there, with only thin streaks of ice. Time for gloves off and a bit of the bare-knuckle stuff, groping for rock holds in the powder and under verglas. It was painfully slow, with the agony of hot-aches to be endured, and it was an hour before I could traverse round a little corner back to where the gully reasserted itself. Here there was a cave of sorts and a bulging section beyond, where a chockstone barred the way. We had arrived at the famous crux pitch. A crack over on the right seemed to offer the best hope. One crampon scraped its way up this while the other scratched at the slab on its left and a mittened hand fumbled for rock holds. Sometimes a mittened handjam worked best, at other times a quick lob of the pick into a dribble of ice or a frozen sod. It was a style of climbing typical of the cliff's harder routes.

The approach of night brought with it a sense of urgency, and after some trouble I was relieved to get a belay and bring up Toogood. Things looked very black above, the sombre walls of huge buttresses curving round to crowd in a gleam of snow. Bob went at it very rapidly, sparks flying from his crampons in the gloom. Fortunately it was easier, and when he lit his headtorch and it glinted round the confining walls, things became easier still. At last the rope ran out and I followed. Seconding, I found it much simpler than it had looked from below. There was more mixed climbing above, but it gradually eased until eventually we emerged on to good late-winter névé in the final basin.

On the summit ridge clouds were blowing up and there was an occasional flash of moonlight which helped us as we searched out the top of Central Gully, and followed our tracks leading from here to the descent. We scuttled down the slopes to the east and loped off along the interminable valley to Bethesda. It seemed like midnight, but this was not Scotland – the pubs were open and it was nothing like so late. There was still time to bend people's ears in the Padarn Lake, and tomorrow we could look forward to a day on Holyhead's sun-warmed rock. Which all made up for not having found the gear.

Punditry brings its own rewards, and especially that of getting things totally wrong. Instead of being the end of an era as predicted, Pete Crew's guide to Anglesey marked the beginning of a new spurt of bold, hard developments on the cliff which have continued, with routes like The Cad and The Bells, The Bells, and many others. Arguably the 80s reduction of interest in Anglesey is a temporary phenomenon confined to a phase when the abolition of adventure in climbing situations has been pursued to allow concentration on the difficulty of sequences of individual moves to the exclusion of all else. The extent of interest is measured by the need for Alec Sharp's guide in 1977, a supplement in 1978 and another in 1981, with a new guide now due. How wrong can you get!

Anglesey – Gogarth Climbers' Guide

by Peter Crew. West Col, 1969.

Mountain 4. *(1969)*.

Some guidebooks help create development; others, like this one, record and terminate it. The quality, detail and comprehensiveness of this guide, despite outdating already begun, do justice to an excellent subject.

The climbs are compared with those on 'Cloggy'. The two guides may also be compared. Private production makes for a high price – even if this does include a new type of waterproof cover. There are a few misprints; standards have already allowed the expenditure of unprecedented quantities of hot air. The warning is welcome: 'It is not unusual to hear of strong parties failing or having epics on relatively easy climbs'. There seem to be Extreme HVSs, by standards elsewhere. Posterity will downgrade some of the greatest first-ascent grips in compensation.

The guide has many of the virtues of the 'Cloggy' one: a lively historical section; technical precision linked with exact description; illustrations of utility and quality; excellent photographs – occasionally difficult to interpret, but otherwise requiring no apologies. These combine to give tremendous impact for such a small volume.

Anglesey (1969) provided an icon of a great saga's end.

Quo Vadis Bergsteigerland?

Rocksport *(October–November 1969).*

A few years ago a whole edition of the German magazine *Alpinismus* posed this question. Today it is of particular relevance to English and Welsh rock climbing, which seems to be on the way to becoming a football match in reverse – all performers and few spectators.

Awakening from an afternoon siesta on a hot June day, the shouts echo round the cwm above Llyn d'ur Arddu. They are colourful adaptations of the textbook sterilities taken from the accepted climbing manuals, punctuated by the rattle of stones in the Central descent gullies. A kicker usually wears a crash hat and shouts 'Below!' after his stone has made its satisfying clatter down the Middle rock. All good textbook stuff. And there is a book to tell you where to go once you know how, and even before, if you wish.

The green turf below the East Buttress is swiftly disappearing, leaving loose earth and stones, although the faithful spring continues to refresh an increased clientele, even in drought conditions.

How many climbers are up there on a fine June Sunday? Fifty are apparent on the lower reaches of the West Buttress. There are people on most things on the East Buttress and no doubt others lurk in the East Gully and on the Far East. No one climb seems of importance. By the Llyn the sun is hot, and the isolation, once out of the grey shadow of the cliff, is splendid. There are too many up there whatever the count. The cliff has lost its impressiveness and the climbing has lost its point. Perhaps Llech Ddu is quieter, but if there is new stuff to be done and the Holliwells are doing it, that is unlikely!

How come there are so many of us? Baden-Powell's mild equivalent of the Hitler Youth introduced many to the open air life between the wars and after. Educational entrepreneurship in the new outdoor pursuits centres has augmented the movement, in size though perhaps not in quality. Schoolteachers anxious to escape on to the outcrops are probably even more culpable. It is good to see the young on the crags, though what the climbing community will do to their characters I shudder to anticipate. The chiselling of holds and names has reached new peaks on gritstone. Long established problems are destroyed, or rendered impracticable by the shelter building activities of little boys (Roches). We are back to the old problem of freedom and responsibility – Baden-Powell stressed that!

Knowledge that climbing is possible is not enough. We can afford to do it, to spend on the vehicles or travel; we can afford the energy too, though one questions this on some Monday mornings. The vehicles crowded below popular cliffs are no longer uniformly battered vans and motorcycles. Once the Honourable Rottersley's weekend excursion to Derbyshire in an E-type Jaguar caused widespread gossip. It might be less extraordinary now.

Basically we still seek the high drama, a contrast to a world where life is entirely conversation, while alternative tasks are obscured by the discipline of fulfilling a (sometimes not so) reasonable objective, and completion gives its own short term satisfaction.

Then there is the gear, attractive-looking, limited by weight, and to some degrees by accepted norms, but increasingly complex and increasingly used. Most hard climbs can be wholly or partially reduced to boulder problems. Pure practice of free climbing is widely distributed at a high standard, but the numbers of climbers resistant to new methods of protection are growing fewer. Double-think on the climber's part is probably easier than in the past, when the distinction between free and artificial was much more clear cut. Now there is less dependence on high morale and more on technology. The degree of uncertainty when entering on a big new rock climb is immeasurably reduced. It is exceedingly easy to overestimate one's abilities, particularly in the margin between pretty good and excellent. Probably there are still few of the latter, for while many climb hard routes a tiny minority innovate in boldness, as always.

GEAR: 1988

This has elaborated enormously compared to the expectations of 1969. Rocs, friends, chalk, sticky boots of various specialized designs, harnesses. Ropes have probably changed least. Sticht plates, shunts, etc. Designer clothing has crept into rock climbing and become more intrusive. In attempting to stand out expensively among the crowd clothes have become more garish and more body revealing, with a slight increase in functionality. Near windproof light tops for rock or second layer clothing are exempted from these strictures, as are some of the varieties of mountain clothing.

Ray Jardine, inventor of Friends. *Photo by Mark Vallence.*

Thus we are many and we are likely to become more. The gear sellers, the magazine producers, the manufacturers and the press, the educators and the interests of the pubs and cafés will contribute to the growth of the numbers in the future. We swarm like flies in the summer months and, at worst, climbing can become eye-jarring cartoon-like pandemonium. Some are able to operate in the week or in winter, but most will continue to depend upon the weekend, even if it becomes an extended period. One can climb in Scotland and avoid the crowd as yet – but for how long? Often it may seem scarcely worth the candle.

AVOIDING THE CROWD
This is actually easier than it used to be as so few crags are now fashionable. Conformism is so great that in any climbing area most crags are devoid of climbers, while very large numbers congregate at a few places. Most seem never to leave the ground, and very few reach the top. For the most part Scotland, protected by the small number of natives, fewer climbers, weather and distance, remains peaceful, though a large number of potential new routes once left until people could lead them have been manufactured from abseil descents, prepared and then led, so that the first on sight lead in one view should become the first ascent. Only in the winter at a few popular places like Ben Nevis are numbers a difficult problem.

The aggregation problem in climbing rock will turn many to broader mountaineering or other activities (canoeing?) which require similar psychology. A few real misanthropes may give up and take to buttering the final jugs on a Friday evening before taking grandstand seats on the Saturday. Some will be killed, especially if they continue to rain stones on one another on crowded days and if sages gaze into the Black Cleft and pronounce it authoritatively to be Longland's. But this offers little prospect of reducing the climbing population, as more women climb now. The mass is likely to increase for years with replacements outnumbering the wastage.

WOMEN CLIMBERS AND NUMBERS
With the reduction in births on the impact of feminism, climbing families do not seem usual or important in contributing to total numbers active, with the possible exception of one remarkably strong and fecund guide, Brede Arkless. The fact that one or both parents climb seems to be as likely to prevent children from doing so as to encourage them (*Pace* – Virginia Woolf). H. M. Kelly always took the view that the Fell and Rock Climbing Club (FRCC) grew faster from the 1920s simply because it had women in it (see CC, Scottish Mountaineering Club (SMC), Rucksack and Wayfarers Clubs, Yorkshire Mountaineering Club (YMC), Alpine Club). Did the Pinnacle Club stay small because it only had women in it – this is dangerous ground!

SOLO
There will be more people doing hard climbs and the innovators who always balance on a knife edge will be pushed one stage further. If climbing 'extremes'

is really easier, perhaps the rope should go too. On rock one can avoid aid, lose the enervating effects of the possibility of placing a nut every foot and being left with nowhere to put your fingers but in the slings. One can climb genuinely free at the highest level of technique.

To many people this will sound foolish but it is essentially logical. It is dangerous to a greater degree than protected leading at the same grade but this alone does not make it unjustifiable. Justification depends only upon the climber's assessment of himself, as long as he is not deranged. To solo revives the real relationship between man and rock which the insulation of protection obscures. Those who feel that modern aids are choking the sport are justified in reducing the insulation. To solo on hard climbs may be near rhetorical, but it is the most valid way of criticizing the technology which supports so many of our stuffed shirts.

Solo climbing took off and much was done, some of it very brave, in the 1970s. There were some bad accidents, like those to Cliff Philips, Alan McHardy and Angela Faller, or worse, deaths like Neil Molnar on Erosion Groove Direct, and, more recently, Jimmy Jewel in 1987.

Possibly Livesey and Fawcett were outstanding prior to Jimmy Jewel's extraordinary feats. By the nature of solo climbing many such feats remain unrecorded despite lists in Extreme Rock. *Diadem Publications, 1987. – a good thing?*

This question seems deeply involved with that of numbers. Crowds would not exist on hard climbs without the technology. It is noticeable that the leading climbers who have taken to soloing do so sometimes for immediate practical reasons, but often they do so because they are both actors in and detesters of the climbing circus. They wish both to differentiate themselves and to excel in an overcrowded atmosphere.

Innovators not taken with solo climbing will probably go further afield more often and involve themselves in mountaineering – even the biggest Scottish rock climbing seems to have slightly more *laissez-faire* rules than the English-Welsh system. For those not developing in these ways the traditional rock climbing south of the border looks increasingly sterile.

All this links with the third major problem. A few years ago the soloists would have done more new routes instead. They are still among those who do new routes, but all too often their quality is lower than the average of the early 60s. Many are banal. For those who cannot be satisfied by the odd holiday away from the stereotyped areas there may well be only one solution – emigration!

EMIGRATION

Several climbers did this, a whole colony removing themselves to Calgary and Colorado in the late 60s and insinuating themselves more or less successfully in the local climbing élites. Canada had enough British to almost form its 'national' team to climb Everest in 1982. Others have written the history of climbing in North America or greatly influenced 'down under' rock standards, like John Allan. His quiet habits were regrettably not assimilated there.

Helyg (Diamond Jubilee 1925–1985) *by Geoff Milburn*, Climbers Club, 1985.

To review a book celebrating a CC event for the CCJ smacks of incest. Yet there are things to be said, even by a supporter of the project. Possibly it is useful for someone close but yet a little apart to try to say them.

Helyg was not primarily intended for mass consumption. It was aimed at CC members, and especially at those with special attachments related to the earliest CC hut, founded way back in the 1920s. I have few such attachments and no memories, but found an interest in the ruminations of those who have.

Helyg was almost synonymous with the CC for many years. It symbolized the revival of the membership and their ascendancy. Masterminded by a small group seeking to drag the Club back from seemingly irretrievable decline after the First World War, it became a focus for members to an extent hardly conceivable even for Herbert Carr and the other founders. From it, members and their guests issued forth to rewrite the history of Welsh climbing, seemingly in a process beginning within months of its opening. Cars careered to it from Liverpool, Cambridge or London, and for decades it was the heart of Welsh climbing. Only since the 50s has its relative importance waned, as the club became richer and gained other huts, and the focus of activity shifted elsewhere. This thoughtfully edited volume allows the early story to unfold, principally by allowing the main protagonists to tell their own story. The accounts vary in intent and seriousness, with as sympathetic an ear to legend and folklore, to

Champagne at Helyg after fifty years. Seated, centre, second row, Noel Odell with Chris Bonington behind him, amid illustrious company too numerous to mention.
Photo by Ian Smith.

idiosyncrasy and even tragedy, as to great deeds. There emerges an image, in print and in photography, of an already lost world.

It was, on the surface at least, near totally male. Helyg was a last bastion in many ways to the advance of women in the CC, and jealously preserved. Not that all male comers were always welcome there in the past. For some it epitomized clubbishness at its best, while for others it implied its antithesis. But that is as much a part of CC history as many other aspects, and whatever one's personal views, it should not be written out. Here it is echoed, deeply different, somewhat austere, perhaps increasingly difficult to understand by younger generations. The Pinnacle Club or the SMC come nearest to it now.

Not all the writing is inspired or humorous, though much is both. The Club has effectively sponsored a brief history of itself in the guise of lauding stone and slates. The volume does well to celebrate the meeting of older members in 1985, and wisely records their activities, their memories, their images now and in the past. It brings together evocative photographs, obituaries of some who did not make it to the party, and some fine accounts of aged activism, as well as of deeds nearly forgotten. In an activist sport, it is easy for a club to become irrelevant to its longest habitués. In every respect *Helyg* acts as a corrective to such shortsightedness, and though those who know better than I will correct its perspectives, no future historian of British climbing will dare ignore it. (August 1987).

THE LAKE DISTRICT

Though the Peak is home, the Lakes captivated me early. I visited Snowdonia first, but never suffered from Hiraeth (longing to return to Wales). From the outset the Lakes gave me pleasures unalloyed by sadness or guilt. Wales had the climbs, many of which we did, but Alan Parker deflected us to Keswick. It was like going from Salt Lake City to Las Vegas, sybaritic in the extreme.

Will Ritson of Wasdale Head

Mountain *30. (1973).*

The fells dominate Wasdale Head as they dominate no other English mountain centre. Nowhere are the high mountain attractions closer in the brilliance of fine weather, nowhere are they more oppressive with that 'sense of something foreboding' which Guido Rey stressed, when curtain on curtain of rain sweeps up the gusted lake from the Irish Sea. It is on such days that locals make for their homes and visitors for the pub, as is always the case in mountain areas, whatever the puritans may distil as the true spirit of the hills. Once inside, the deluge provides every reason for escape into booze, conversation and, gradually and with luck, wit and pleasant competition.

Wordsworth was only one of several guidewriters to commend Wasdale: 'No part of the country is more distinguished for sublimity' (1810). By the mid-nineteenth century, the growing middle class provided a steady stream of visitors. Otley's guide of 1844 mentioned that 'a Public House is much wanted . . . it is expected that a licence to entertain travellers will shortly be obtained by one of the householders'. But the efficiency of that entertainment could scarcely have been anticipated, if indeed Ritson's Huntsman's Inn, opened in 1856, was the first at Wasdale Head.

Will Ritson was a statesman, the local equivalent of a freeholder. The Lakeland statesman was no downtrodden labourer, for he was relatively free from gentry control and seems to have enjoyed a proud independence only matched by his love of traditional sports, a liking for beer, and an ingrained though individualistic conservatism. Old Dalesmen in Borrowdale in the late nineteenth century are reputed to have refused to use the new road, preferring that on the slopes of Base Brown; furthermore, if Haskett Smith can be believed, they even insisted that their less sceptical sons did likewise.

A farmer and a keen hunter, Ritson knew the fells intimately before he extended Row Foot Farm to provide ham, eggs, beer and extra income in 1856. The enterprise appears to have been an undiluted success, to the credit of both Ritson and his hard-working wife Dinah.

It would be a mistake to see Will Ritson as a mere hotelier. He became the most expert of local fell guides, kept a pack of hounds and treated his visitors to massive doses of his humour. There can be little doubt that the unique mixture of traditionalism and opportunistic fun-loving flexibility fundamental to his nature did much to set the tone in the major seat of early English rock climbing.

He was intensely loyal to Wasdale and was quick to attack those 'southerners' who disparaged the place. Indeed, as local philosopher, it appears to have been his self-assigned duty.

'Fancy living 'ere all yer life. Why don't yer come up to Town and see the sights?' he was asked.

'There's nea occasion, me lad, for us to cum to London, cos some o't sights cums down here to see us,' Ritson replied. For those of us poor mortals who have long detested the great Wen's bloodsucking arrogance, Ritson's answer to a naïve enquiry about fishes' winter diet is even more acceptable: 'We git a terrible lot o' Londoners an they go to duck and wesh theirsels up i't ghyll. Well they're about as lousy as whelps an' t'laal fishes catches t'fleas and lives on them i't winter.'

In his younger days, Ritson often wandered with Professors Sedgwick and Wilson, and apparently with Wordsworth and de Quincey. He was in the habit, as champion Cumberland wrestler, of taking on his visitors at wrestling and jumping. 'The first time Professor Wilson came to Wasdale Head,' said Ritson, 'he had a tent set up in a field, an' he got it well stocked with bread and beef and cheese and rum and ale an' such like.' The Professor then proceeded to get some competitions going with the locals. These ended in a rowing boat trip in which the inebriated 'Prof' fell overboard and disappeared to cries of 'Mr Wilson's i't watter, Mr Wilson's i't watter.' After a few moments of alarm he popped up astern, delighted by the consternation he had caused.

Though he did some climbing, 'Auld Will' retained a healthy countryman's scepticism about its superiority to fell walking. One enquiry about crags on Gable met with the reply: '... isn't fells good enough for ye?' On another occasion, he was asked if he knew a climb right of Mickledore which had been done by George Seatree and John Wilson Robinson. 'No,' he replied, 'an' if it's the same place as ah mean, ah don't think yea've been up – nowt but a fleein' thing could git up there.' By this time Ritson was approaching retiring age and perhaps increasingly scathing about new-fangled ways. When Seatree's party climbed Pillar, Ritson said they had not gone the right way. 'Mr Baumgarten an' t'shepherds went up t'other side, but I've heard that some reading chaps had gitten up t'same way as you did.' Evidently by this time the academic reading party had begun the invasion which became an important constituent of early climbing in this area.

Ritson had good reason to laud Baumgarten's route, as he had accompanied him for much of the way, in 1859, desisting only on the final sections. Baumgarten got back safely, although he left 'his watch and his purse and a note ... if he never came back again it would be mine'. Characteristically, Auld Will mentioned also the great celebrations afterwards!

Terry Parker on The Medlar. *Photo by Bob Allen.*

Entertainment in the valley was both natural and manufactured. The parson provided one convenient butt to Ritson and Wilson. According to Haskett Smith, he wore knickerbockers and stockings of vivid scarlet, together with wooden clogs, their edges bound with brass. Living alone, he depended on the hotel for his one warm meal a day which he collected in a tiny tin vessel. Once 'someone tied a donkey by its tail to the bell rope of the little church', while on another occasion Ritson told the tale of the old parson who 'kept a churnful of sermons which he used to preach down to the bottom then turn over and begin again'. The local parson fared better than several visiting bishops, one of whom, on a guided trip up Scafell, complained at Ritson's speed. 'Well, here ye are, Mister Bishop,' said Ritson, 'as near Heaven as ye ever will be.'

As local philosopher, Ritson could pontificate with apparent authority on everything. When a young lad expounded in his kitchen on the benefits of marriage with a dowry, Will observed: 'That's the varra worst thing thou could think o' doin'. Our old Dinah there had a five pund note, an ah never 'eard t'last on it!'

New technology was treated as irreverently as new climbs. An unfortunate photographer in Keswick asked Will to smile. 'Ay, if thou fetch me a mug o' ale,' said Will. Once wetted, the smile appeared, was photographed and reburied in the glass. In the evening the camera plate was found to be fogged, for Ritson had opened it in the owner's absence. 'It was a gay good joke, for t'likeness-taker had lost both his beer and my smile.'

There can be little doubt that the Huntsman's Inn*, which eventually became the Wasdale Head, a centre for endless boozy nights and preposterous games of barn rugby a century after Ritson's lively inauguration, played a major part in the development of Wasdale Head as a leading rock climbing centre. It provided accommodation, food, beer, a warm fire, a few books and an accordion, on foul days, and above all it developed its own mythology, spun, elaborated and continually recreated by its irreverent and sparkling founder.

*Sadly, now modernised, has quite a different atmosphere.

Napes Needle and Needle Ridge (Great Gable)

K. Wilson (Ed). Classic Rock. *Diadem, 1978.*

Going away from home at Christmas for the first time created creeping guilt. The cold stars disappeared behind veils of thick, yellow fog, as the train roared past rank upon rank of Manchester 'back-to-backs'. Richard, *agent-provocateur* in this enormity, suitably attired in the black cagoule of the Munich school, waited in the gloom behind Manchester Central Library. After a few cups of tea the four-hour saga of the Keswick double-decker began.

The walk along the road to Seathwaite seemed endless, but midnight Christmas cheer stopped none of the wildly driven cars, and there were no lifts. At some ungodly hour the tent went up by Styhead Tarn, after a weary stumbling plod along the ancient packhorse trail.

Rain was the excuse for a long morning doze in which the old tent dripped, but about midday it stopped, the cloud lifted a few feet and the camping gear was stowed behind a convenient boulder by Kern Knotts. Thin sleet touched the fell tops and not a person stirred. A raw nor'wester drove ragged clouds in tattered strands by the Napes, and howled wildly in the narrow gully below the Needle. What a Christmas Day!

The Needle was the symbol of our purpose. Probably little else was required of the whole outing to the Lake District. Chapter and verse of selected passages from *Nanga Parbat Pilgrimage* hummed through our brains as the rope came out and the first cracks were attempted. The holds seemed terrifyingly polished, lubricated by slime. The raw cold soon obscured whatever pleasure was to be found in progress, and at the windswept shoulder the pinch of wet-cold hands began to destroy my resolution; but Richard came up quickly and, with a characteristic edge and near-inflexible purpose, he attacked the final obelisk. The mantelshelf seemed impossibly polished and wet, but, after a try or two, he sat astride the summit, wrapping the rope around it as belay. In a few precarious seconds we occupied that famous block together. There are few pinnacles in British rock climbing, and none combine such a spectacular and testing move to reach a summit with such a grandiose setting. Wasdale was desolate, a far cry from summer evenings when it seemed impossible to breathe, even on the fell tops. We were too young to feel obliged to stand on our heads on the summit, in the Haskett-Smith tradition.

With help from the rope I was soon back to the shoulder, and Richard returned with the rope protecting him in an ingenious loop over the summit. An abseil led to the base of Needle Ridge.

The ridge appeared to offer few major problems, although the early polished slab proved difficult, with sleet in the holds melting down the rock below. As the ridge narrowed to a crest, holds increased in numbers and size, and it was possible to keep off the arête where the gale seemed likely to pluck us away. A couple of little cracks were very slippery but somehow secure, with lots of hitches on which to hang our thick spliced sling. The slack rope billowed into space and, as the last rocks merged into Gable, rain pelted in from the west and cloud curtains seemed to end the day. The summit attempt was abandoned as the main ridge was climbed, and we collected our belongings and scuttled to Wasdale Head and the traditional haven of Wilson Pharaoh's barn.

There lay the glittering prizes. Richard had long been scheduled to out-eat Paul Smoker in a meat-pie competition and, as the fells remained sodden, our remaining efforts were undistinguished. We were forced to settle for cream teas and black velvets made possible by the arrival of the club treasurer, who thereby set the invaluable precedent of the statutory single embezzlement, which was to be of such service in later impecunious years.

Engineers' Slabs (Gable Crag, Great Gable)

K. Wilson (Ed). Hard Rock. Hart-Davis, MacGibbon, 1974.

At the head of afforested Ennerdale, a few hundred yards from the point where an ancient track linking Langdale and West Cumberland leaves Aaron Slack, Great Gable plunges into a steep, craggy north face. Though large and of good rock, it is broken by numerous ledges and vegetated gullies, a disappointment after drinking in its forbidding aspect, characteristically gloomy, cold and often wet.

Yet, set in this chaos of detached buttresses and wandering gullies, there is a steep, compact, rectangular wall, a grey block of Lakeland granite almost 200ft high and quite unspoiled by ledges or vegetation. This wall is a 'slab' only in name, for it is slightly convex, providing steep sustained climbing in a remote and unfrequented mountain environment. At mid-height it is split by over-hangs; these, in turn, are vertically bisected by a steep chimney and crack line which suffers only one minor discontinuity. This fine line, from base to summit of the cliff, was ascended in a remarkable manner by F. G. Balcombe and his companions in 1934.

It was a feat of considerable boldness, lost in the obscurity of the twenty years which elapsed before a repetition. It compared favourably with the notable achievements of others on Scafell and in Wales. The climb, Engineers' Slabs, must have been sparsely protected, given the techniques of the time and the few stances, whatever the nature of the engineering involved. Yet it was neglected, left to its geographical isolation and persistent darkness, the challenge of its considerable technical difficulty ignored. Only in the 50s was the climb regenerated, to become a VS classic worthy of the fine dry day which is ideally required for its ascent.

Above a vegetated gully the 'slab' rears abruptly, with the lower cracks of the climb oozing a little slime in all but the finest conditions. Awkward moves lead up to a small stance below uncompromising-looking cracks which prove shallow, with a peculiar distribution of holds. A small stance is reached at about 80ft. Even with nuts a piton belay is probably advisable on this and the subsequent stance.

The long stride right to reach a continuing steep crack reveals the mounting exposure. The cracks above are steep and eventually demand a layback before a good ledge can be reached below the final groove. Traditionally, these moves must have been almost totally unprotected while the second remained virtually belay-less below.

There remains a steep V-groove, climbed by back and foot, and only dry in the best summer weather. During dry spells in early spring this groove can retain winter verglas, even when the rest of the climb is dry; at such times an escape up a steep arête on the left is necessary to complete the climb. Both escapes are quite difficult, even under modern conditions; on a hemp line, without protection, the lead of the groove was remarkable.

Extol, Dove Crag – Don Whillans' last great British rock route. *Photo by Bob Allen.*

Alan Austin exploring darkest Kentmere. *Photo by Ian Roper.*

Instead of retracing one's steps to the foot of the cliff, the finest way to complete the climb is to continue over the summit of Gable and descend by one of the ordinary paths (boots can be carried up in the second man's sack for this purpose).

Somehow this climb goes beyond normal rock climbing and is almost a mountaineering route, feeling much greater than its small size justifies. It is this special quality and particular atmosphere, together with an inescapable character, which creates the unique appeal of a remote, isolated and infrequently ascended climb.

Central Pillar (Esk Buttress, Eskdale)

K. Wilson (Ed). Hard Rock. Hart-Davis, MacGibbon, 1974.

At the core of the Lake District's finest mountain lies the roadless expanse of upper Eskdale. Unattainable without walking, it is one of England's most beautiful valleys. Esk Buttress complements the wilderness caught between Scafell and Bowfell, for while the valley is wide, open and treeless, the crag is towering, stark and steep, an archetypal precipice, unbroken by major gullies or obvious ledges.

This grandiose setting is not belied by its climbs, the finest of which is undoubtedly Central Pillar. Early explorations groped up its lower reaches towards the formidable upper brow of rock which caps the crag, blocking direct exit from it. Explorers like George Bower, Alf Bridge and R. J. Birkett were forceful assailants, but all were deflected by the upper bastions. A great hiatus appeared in the development of the cliff in the 50s. It was too steep and smooth for all but a few pioneers before 1959 and they did not come. All existing climbs avoided the upper wall at the crag's centre.

After this lull and a few exploratory peerings from all angles, Esk Buttress was subjected to the indecency of a mass assault on a fine June Sunday in 1962, the day of an appalling accident on nearby Scafell's East Buttress. Allen Austin, spidery Jack Soper and Eric ('Matey') Metcalfe were beaten to the crag by Peter Crew and Mike Owen, and were forced to compensate by producing Red Edge and Black Sunday. The 'first team' off from Langdale picked the plum while, less than a mile away, two Liverpool climbers of the 1959 generation died below the East Buttress*.

The climb has some great characteristics. Following Bridge's Route, it gains height easily at first, climbing pleasant slabs and little walls of solid grey rock between ledges for over 200ft. Then the rock steepens, the pillar proves intractable at pre-1945 standards and the old route is forced off into the protective recesses of Square Chimney.

*In a fall involving a very large rockfall, from high on Trinity.

Above the upper ledge of Bridge's Route, a slabby expanse eases a little where it abuts on to the deep V-cleft of Trespasser Groove, to the right of the main face of the Pillar. No obvious line suggests itself, but a few moves on squarish holds reveal a traverse out on to small holds in compact rock. Careful balance climbing leads out diagonally to a small stance in a V-groove. Though it has been used as a belay, this seems ill advised; piton scars mark the back of the groove. The grey-green rock above offers a few small holds leading to a bulge. The rock gives away little and after a series of difficult moves a long reach out right is probably irreversible. Beyond, a mossy slab is perched below another barrier of beetling walls, and a piton provides a belay at its upper edge.

The second man, belayed in this position, is excellently placed to apprehend his leader's fate. A slight traverse on to the wall, which tilts out above the groove below, leads to a piton. Despite the situation's unsuitability for such antics, a series of boulder problems ensues. A pull out on to a block is both insecure in itself and leaves doubts as to the block's stability. After standing on the block a long grope upward to holds in a quartzite band is the only escape. The band is seized, pulled on to and traversed to a cool haven in Bower's Route. Beyond there lies only a classic polished crack and the rocky dome of Esk Buttress's summit, with magnificent views down towards the lower valley.

The climb is certainly great, though it appears deflected, for one never climbs the upper wall direct; instead there are cunning sidesteps, which almost push one off the Pillar.* Yet this attenuation is not an overwhelming price to pay, and the validity of the route rests assured, despite or even because of the deviousness of the particular solution.

New Guides For Old

S. Clark (Ed). Borrowdale. *FRCC*.
S. Clegg, C. Read and R. Wilson. Lake District North. *Lakeland Climbers' Guide Books*.
D. Armstrong, P. Botterill, P. Whillance. Recent Developments in the Lake District. *FRCC*.

Mountain *64*. *(1978)*.

The simultaneous publication of three guides that overlap in area is symptomatic of the powerful resurgence of interest in rock climbing in recent years, and of the variety of styles, approaches and allegiances which have played a curious part in that. Indeed, a portly past guidewriter putting an alien hoof in the midst of the warring sects of chalkers, dusters, wall trainers and aid-choppers is asking to be savaged, as anyone old enough to recall the religious wars over The Cumbrian or even The Niche will certify.

*The direct became The Cumbrian (Valentine and Braithwaite, May 1974). Climbed without its two/three points of aid, 1977 (E4 6b, Berzins brothers). Rod Valentine repeated it free (12 June 1988).

Syd Clark's *Borrowdale* follows the traditional FRCC policy of providing a definitive guide of high quality aiming at maximum information, tasteful presentation and authority, while supplementing each *magnum opus* with more frequently revised, and therefore up-to-date, low-cost summaries of the best of recent climbing.

It is over a decade since the last Borrowdale guide, and the new one superficially retains much of the house style of the old series though closer inspection reveals smaller type and more climbs per page. Even more innovatory is the introduction of the 'E' grading system for the hardest climbs. This is obvious and necessary, and is also reflected in the other two books under review.

Borrowdale catches up with the 100 or so new climbs in the valley since 1967. The author has faced an uphill task and the guide has been long a-coming. That is no bad thing, as the guide includes much recent activity and is a monument to the 70s. The diggings of Great End Crag and the clawings of Goat are faithfully recorded, while in every direction the clean-up of this valley – once the pegger's playground and the bushman's Nirvana – has proceeded apace.

Great End Crag is now safe for those wishing to be photographed wearing only chalk and PAs. Decrepit age can only spare a moment of nostalgia for those slimy gropings up overhanging vegetation in the annual search for the mythological Styx before setting off (chalk bag and Chouinard nuts attached) to suffer the philistine delights of the nearest real or artificial climbing gymnasium.

Guides are more than the climbs they describe; they are equally about climbers. Myth-breaking and myth-making proceed apace as fellow travellers and guides play their part in this endless process. In my senility, am I right that a few old protection pitons become aid pitons on Falcon in order to ensure the modernity of the first free ascent, or is it lapse of memory? One wonders whether there are still more protection pitons in place on some climbs than the total at the first ascent, as was the case with The Niche a couple of years ago. But old peccadilloes are usually rightly erased, though one suspects the pace of some of the modern 'firsts' must be the slower for the puritanism. In all this the first ascent list remains invaluable, providing endless ammunition for the jousting when the climbing has to stop.

The thin *Recent Developments* book is the complement to the main series. It is the superlight guide for the superfit modernist who can afford to buy it – even though he climbs every day – to carry as he ranges the district in the search for adrenalin surge and E6. It is not intended to carry the authority of the authorized version, as many of the climbs have been little repeated. As such it works well. They are mostly there, the serried ranks of E1 to E5, filling the spaces which were eyed so closely even many years ago; the linkages of pocket and crack, green-bearded overhang and smooth wall.

For someone who divorced the Lakes after over-indulgence, it is chastening but inspiring. Can it be that there was more to the lady than met the eye? Birkness Eliminate, Deimos Horror free, the great spaces of Pavey filled, the cankers of the trivial peg routes removed and replaced by resplendent 6a. In this, *Recent Developments* is unique among the three guides, for at last it adopts the numerical grading of pitches and thus attempts to achieve parity with other areas. I have done too few of these new climbs to know if the grading works. I suspect that they will not wither as have the *Recent Developments* grades in the Peak District.

Lake District North emerges out of yet another formula. It reduces about a third of the Lake District's climbing to one slim volume by very brief description, much pruning of crags and climbs, a lack of frills and some advertising to keep the price down. It seems competent enough within its brief, but it comes into a crowded field.

Unlike the Constable selective guide, it does not offer illustration as an appeal, and comes closer to the FRCC guides in its basic market. It is a little old-maidish in its justification of its selections, difficult as that can be – there are antique echoes as it 'discourages climbing on Iron Crag', and I would have thought that these days one should not discourage it anywhere – while there is an excessive righteousness in its dismissal of poor crags, poor climbs and somehow, by implication, the poor saps who might be tempted to climb them and, worse still, admit it! There is an odd convention of giving date of ascent but no details of authorship, when really the latter often means more – as anyone who has to live in the same patch as a Livesey or a Proctor will have realized. There are a few inconsistencies like the description of Plastic Happiness and dismissal of the Girdle of Upper Falcon, when the best bits are the same – if they haven't fallen down.

But ultimately the problem with this enterprise is that its utility depends on the accuracy and range of description, as it is not at all interesting in itself. The niceties of E1 to E5 and the other grades, and the extent to which 'right' and 'left' are accurate, matter above all else. Certainly this leaves the joys of discovery to the beholder; the guide will have its uses for the initiate to the area. But one wonders whether it will withstand the rather telling competence, combined with a certain elegance, of the official series on the one hand, and the pictures of the Constable book on the other.

Illustration seems to be a problem in all these guides, and this is very likely the result of the peculiar nature of many of the crags. Indeed, as shapes, few of these cliffs are outstanding in their features. In many cases, they sprawl across and around woody hillsides and are a nightmare to draw. The *Lake District North* picture diagrams come out as either excessively simple or rather muddy, while I am not sure that the diagrams Heaton Cooper so carefully prepared years ago, in a whirlwind visit to Borrowdale with me, always fit the bill on crags which have so many routes because there is a good hold on every few feet of rock. Their very elegance sometimes obscures necessary detail, and it seems sad to admit that the next edition, some years on, may need to be reillustrated at least in part if the climbs are to be found. The omission of a Great End Crag diagram and of something which makes sense of the boulder heaps of Shepherd's and of Goat and Black Crag, is really serious in the official guide and detracts from its usefulness alongside *Lake District North*.

In some respects the effects of these guides were unexpected. They incited neither retreat into the frozen North nor, as the bad weather of the winter enforced on some climbers, a sinking into the depths of the limestone earth. The fine-tooth comb of the prophet McHaffie has continued to yield fruit and acts as a course of real inspiration, perhaps particularly when one is steeped in the area's varied climbing on rather a modest bunch of crags. One can anticipate the thuggery of the modern movement – it is everywhere – but even for the ancient one must continue to believe that good gritstoning will yield the Grail.

I only doubt if the peregrines swoop as ferociously as they once did on the remoter cliffs, and don't hasten to discover that their detritus has been totally replaced by the products of Boots.

There are now more peregrines than ever before and an even better Borrowdale guide (1986) with more cliffs included, a rebuttal to prophets of doom on all fronts.

Rock Climbing by Pete Livesey. EP Sport, 1978.

Crags 18. (April 1979).

Technical manuals, even on rock climbing, are generally a turn-off. Experienced climbers shouldn't need them – though there was a week when Malcolm Howell's rope fell off while he was leading Shibboleth, Jim Curran's fell off seconding Two Pitch Route on Curbar and mine fell off leading on Millstone!

But manuals are supposed to be for beginners, not for people who have known and forgotten again through old age. For the beginner, such books can be valuable. They can, for a week or two, seem like the Bible, though thereafter, if all goes well, such dependence upon the local library will be strenuously denied. So it is in that role that this book ought to be judged, rather as guides are better criticized for their treatment of the easy routes. Are neck-breaking errors advocated? Does the author know one end of a Sticht plate from another? Pete's credentials are, of course, faultless. One of the prime movers of the really hard rock climbing of the 70s – chugging by 2CV from end to end of England and Wales* and blasting out some of the finest new routes; hitting the Yosemite scene very hard for an alien; striking south to the magnificent limestone of France; and all that after doing a multitude of other difficult and strenuous things. He is also articulate, analytical, humorous.

He and his publisher are responsible for a very neat, coherent and balanced volume. It is illustrated in a way that should appeal to beginners, with a balance between what could be pictures of the readers themselves, and illustrations indicating just what amazing places climbing rock can get you to – dizzy sun-kissed California, rough Cornwall granite or even armpit-smelling gymnasia if you prefer (though they can be very boring after a while).

*This did not last for soon he opted for supercharged motors instead!

Angela Fuller (Soper) on Kipling Groove, Gimmer Crag. *Photo by Ian Roper.*   Ron Fawcett and Creation, Raven Crag, Thirlmere. *Photo by Brian Swales.*

Most refreshing is the straightforward and unencumbered way in which the approach to climbing is explained. This is neither equipment catalogue nor handjam instructor. Instead Pete goes for the experience of climbing. For beginners he advises thoughtful use of the help and greater knowledge of others, the advisability of trying to use the clubs (if they will let you into the clan), the limitations of instruction and, by implication, the 'instructor's mentality'. Climbing is about enjoyment. This book is about how to attain it, without too much obsession with technical excellence. The book moves quickly and lightly, much like its author in his best moments, into the idea of 'breaking out on your own!' For once a beginner's book goes some little way towards identifying the springs of climbing motivation.

Excess of self-confidence is, in a very English way, deflated by stabs of humour: 'The Belayer holds the rope. A very important person – as some leaders forget.' Equipment is both useful and a nuisance. The sport is about natural challenge, natural movement on rock. It is leading that it's about, the 'art of seeing, recognizing and anticipating what holds will be found ... holds are in fact for any part of the body, but they work better with some parts than others ... you must above all want to do it'. Although *Rock Climbing* rehearses most of the necessary technical information, it provides far more than that to the beginner and much of value to anyone with an interest in the sport. There is a perspective on the game, individualistic, imparted lightly, but vital. Environmental climbing and environmental awareness should go together. In rock climbing it is best (and safest) to be honest with yourself – 'Nuts placed above the head give a good deal of confidence, but do turn the lead into a sort of top roped ascent!' It has the right tenor, not too pious, in touch with what climbers are really like, and with their institutions – 'Much to the relief of climbers in general, the British Mountaineering Club (BMC) does not seek to govern them, but wisely realizes that they are ungovernable and so seeks only to help them.' It's a good point to make, and both Pete and Dennis Gray's foreword deserve BMC approval (though I thought Linnell, Kirkus and Co, not to say Menlove Edwards and even Puttrell, all climbed rocks 'for their own sake').

If there are criticisms, they are very slight. Double ropes make a leader's retreat safer by allowing one rope to be taken in while the other remains attached above. In 'Trouble – and how to get out of it' this is not mentioned. In falls into space there is a similar advantage: the belayer can take in on one while the victim prussiks on the other. It may be a quirk of my experience, but in two fatal accidents I have known with reasonably able but modestly experienced climbers, this could have made a difference. I felt a little weary of the same students and Ilkley pictures, but then I don't like Ilkley very much, whereas it's on Pete's patch.

Otherwise, it's great for the job and even has a few timely reminders for the old hands. If it works, as I am sure it will, its users will be abandoning it in a few weeks for greater things, and not long later will be baying behind Pete's heels on the great leaning walls.

'The Other Side of the Historical Coin'

Mountain 44. (1975).

The pre-war bit of Pete Livesey's 'Lakeland Commentary' (*Mountain* 39.), had already been raked over by Muriel Files in a letter (*Mountain* 41.), and Ed Grindley had also made his mark (*Mountain* 42.). I would like to add a little to the Grindley critique of what Pete Livesey regards as a powerful and useful ideology of free-climbing. The simplest way to establish the purity of a particular climbing practice, and the advance which it represents, is deliberately to misrepresent what has gone before. 'Lakeland Commentary' is a fine example of such misrepresentation, which is dubious at two levels.

The overall arguments about the difference between pre-1965 developments and those that came later are invalid. Important differences in equipment and attitude in the early period as compared to the later are studiously ignored. Prior to nuts, the conditions under which leaders operated were so different that they can hardly be imagined except by soloing the same climbs today. The increasingly technical climbs that have been made since seem to me to depend largely on more sophisticated protection, though I would be the last to deny that they involve very long sequences of hard moves, unlike the majority of earlier hard routes. Rather than stressing the differences, therefore, I would tend to interpret more recent climbing in the Lakes as being very much a development of what went before, particularly when allowances are made for the change in equipment performance horizons. Of course, this downplays individuals. Pete Livesey falls into the trap of personalizing the ideology of free-climbing – really these Yorkshiremen want to convert everything into their personal property. It is absurd to see any one figure as 'creating' the stress on free ascents of new routes or old artificial routes. In my own experience, early visits to Borrowdale (1961–4) seemed to be spent avoiding pitons previously used for aid, including those on The Niche. And this was not merely a Lakeland thing – people did the same on the Ben, in Derbyshire, in Wales, or in the Dolomites. However, no one claimed to be part of a totally new religion – rather we were part of an already long-established tradition. In my view, the same is the case with the recent spurt. It represents a hastening of a desirable trend in British (not Lakeland) climbing. It is only by virtue of extreme parochialism that it can be attributed to a few stalwart defenders, even when Allan Austin is one of them.

This leads to a further point: esoteric and tempting as these controversies may be, they seek to divide those who are actually closest in their attitudes to climbing. Is there really a significant difference between the climbing attitudes of the first and second ascensionists of The Cumbrian? Surely the only difference lies in the intolerance and bigotry displayed by the second, in attempting to exaggerate the difference between his and the former's ascent! I personally feel that I have seen enough to put these matters into a more rational perspective. If that means that I will not do a good number of climbs, so be it. But in sympathies and experience, the attitudes of most active climbers in the upper grades have hardly differed from those defended in the article. If some went too far away from the free-climbing ethic, they were criticized; if a new climb used too much aid, it was soon done with less. The invention of new ideological positions can affect such things, but in the 60s that did not happen.

Postulating a new ideology also requires some history, though that history may be used quite liberally to fit the position. It was at this level that the article was also weak. In the earlier parts, dealing with the post-war period, straight 'facts' were frequently wrong; on two occasions this served to boost the contributions of some big names at the expense of others. Thus, Mythril was led by Allan Wright, not Jack Soper; Daedalus, on the other hand, is attributed to Paul Ross. Well, he was on the first ascent of the first pitch, but I led it all, most of a decade after Post Mortem in a different phase of Borrowdale's development.

I suspect that these are not the sole inaccuracies, if only because it requires just a glance at the guides concerned to refute them. From my rather less involved position I see no reason to pursue *that* any further.

Steep Ghyll, Scafell

K. Wilson (Ed). Cold Climbs. Diadem, 1983.

There is a twisting slot between the upright tower of Scafell Pinnacle and the grey plaque of slabs where Central Buttress ends. In winter a tiny tongue of névé snow betrays the presence of something above, but bulging rocks from both sides come close to meeting in the lower reaches, where the Ghyll has more of the appearance of a chimney than a gully. Above, as the Pinnacle bellows out to the right, the Ghyll pods into a wide scoop-like depression before narrowing again in the upper section below the col of Jordan Gap.

It was rumoured that Robin Smith had done a winter ascent of the route in the late 50s. It is a route worthy of the man. But then it was rarely attempted, so that on our first try we knew precious little about it. Climbing on Scafell from the Salving House in Borrowdale was common enough at the time. It was a long, straggling line that traversed the Corridor Path from Stye Head on the particular Alpha/SUMC campaign. Often it was useful to have a change of leaders on the walk, for in heavy snow it drifted and was very time-consuming. But the first time to Steep Ghyll we were in luck, with hard, frozen conditions which boded well for the conditions on the mountain.

Mob-handed the team assailed the Gully, with the long, gaunt figure of Les Brown, not so long back from the first ascent of Nuptse (1960) in the lead. Jack Soper, Willis Ward, Oliver Woolcock and I were in the team, and there may have been others. Strong as the party was, after a couple of pitches we stuck, with Les's frame out in front, sprawling and scraping for hours in the nasty, red, brittle scoop of the third pitch. Eventually, with darkness pending, the bored and cold backmarkers abseiled off.

Steep Ghyll evidently needed more than a short, quick stab, so Clive and Steph Rowland and I returned some years later for a full Wasdale weekend. We had been convinced of the need for this a week or two earlier, in trying from Borrowdale. For hours we struggled up to our thighs in snow round the Corridor. The hour became too late to climb and rather than plod back we hit the Wasdale Head for food and beer. As we were penniless the rope was put in hock and Clive even managed cigars for the recrossing of Stye Head.

Brackenclose is the superior base. By 9am I was leading into the first scoop on a grey, steely day. The snow and ice were good with a smattering of worse stuff on top. Clive tackled the chimney by neat bridging, then spent an age getting a belay on the awkward ground of the scoop above. The slabs of the Pinnacle looked bare, but the steepening scoop was filled with a fragile névé which would just hold weight, the product of a recent north-westerly. Little rock showed.

It appeared likely that it would be one full run-out to Jordan Gap. In some sections the Gully was too flat-backed to allow a bridging technique. Straight ice axes sculpted narrow and fragile handholds which consolidated under mitten pressure, and the feet followed into these slots always wondering if the snow would hold. It was a delicate and balancey form of progress.

I've no idea how long it took; picking and chipping for little holds, teetering from one to another, holding some icy rock or ice-nubbin with one hand while poking around with the axe in the other. Front-points often broke through to the rock underneath, scraping and scratching. Once or twice dubious slings draped over even more dubious spikes created an illusion of protection. Clive shivered and juddered on his inhospitable shadowy shelf below, occasionally lighting up a fag. A black, close-fitting, woolly hat, like some leftover from Rebitsch and Vörg or the Death's Head Battalion, covered his ears. Cigarette smoke puffed upwards, alternating with a hacking cough.

Spreading the weight on the snow pockets became even more strenuous after 50ft. Spindrift from a wind sweeping across Scafell summit occasionally burst in a flurry down the scoop, filling face, anorak and holds. Progress grew even slower but it looked harder still to go down. Legs and nerves tired at the endless chipping and balancing and hanging on with one mitten. A final steep section of ice at least promised an easing beyond, but with maximum rope drag and no security beyond a good sense of balance it was the trickiest moment of all; that final move on to easier ground, the point of relaxation where so many leaders fall. There was really nothing to stop you for 100ft, which meant a fall of well over 200ft. The straight Charlet pick was carefully planted, and Grivel front-points placed safely out left before the other foot was recovered from below. Then it was a romp to the Jordan Gap.

Clive came quickly, very cold. It was never his way to hang about unnecessarily on ascent or descent. He was a concentration of mountain sense and agility and could be difficult to keep up with. On arrival he hardly paused. A savage wind blew through the Gap, flicking snow into nostrils and eyes. One glance from heavy-lidded eyes and, 'Insecure, youth – good lead,' was comment enough as he scampered off on the final few feet.

Ten years later, with Terrordactyls, it was much less awe-inspiring. Pat Fearnehough had never used them and as a step-cutter without parallel he remained scornful. The mentor of my earliest winter climbs in Scotland, he was testy as he planted the tools high in the scoop pitch. He used them, but carefully and without bravado, his legs still in the balanced bridging positions of old. The instinct was 'agin it'. Yet I suspect that by the summit he was a grudging convert, seeing generations of technique and mountaineering practice of considerable sophistication go out of the window, jettisoned like an old sock. Most convincing was the speed and the unjarred forearms. We descended Broad Stand with care, seeking the jughandles and slippery little steps amid the snow-cover in a place where we had romped so often on golden summer days. Later that night, as we sat in the pub, came as heavy a snowfall as you are likely to get in Britain. It was our last great climb together, February 1978, prior to the Latok Expedition on which Pat was killed in the Braldu Gorge, and the perfect conditions were obliterated.

Pat Fearnehough 1939–1978

Pat is gone and what gaps he leaves. No longer will he grin from his immaculate Ford as he arrives at the precise time agreed for a climb or a pint; nor will he frown at the unreliability and procrastinations of us lesser mortals. Pat was something of a grenadier at heart and had little truck with the generally sloppiness of the age.

He came from the tough east end of Sheffield and he took the traditional path west to the Peak. There he found an atmosphere more congenial than that of the narrow streets huddled in the lee of the black steelworks. Somewhere *en route* he left behind his drape suit and chain and National Service took him into the RAF Mountain Rescue Service. With them he gained much experience of the Scottish Highlands in winter and spent pleasant weeks in the Charles Inglis Clarke (CIC) hut on Ben Nevis. As a result his ice climbing capabilities were well developed by the late 50s, though based on a traditional step-cutting approach. He had the balance and precision of an alpine guide in minimizing the effort of cutting steps on ice, and an enthusiasm for action in all but the worst conditions. All this was combined with a thorough knowledge of many parts of the British hills, which made him a splendid climbing companion. Another legacy from the RAF were some firm and enduring friendships with his colleagues of that period, some of whom also became members of the FRCC.

After military service, Pat visited the Alps many times and climbed routes throughout the main chain. In the Peak he once took charge of young people joining the Peak Climbing Club, advising them on how and where to climb in an admirable manner and trying to ensure that they did not break their necks at a time when protection on rock was much more sparse than it is now. He produced one or two stiff new climbs on Stanage while helping to prepare the last Eric Byne guide to the area. Above all, he always enjoyed himself. He was one of the pillars of the Wednesday night climbing scene which operated for many years winter and summer without fail, ranging in its activities from ten to twenty hardish rock climbs on fine summer evenings to battles in the dark with Goliath's Groove, Byne's or Brook's Crack, the Flakes or High Tor Original Route. Occasionally due to blizzard, activity might be reduced to marching up Bretton Clough in knee deep snow before quaffing several pints in the Barrel Inn and hiking back late at night. There was an adventurousness and open endedness about such activities which was an inspiration to everyone involved.

In the mid-60s Pat visited the Lakes very frequently and came to repeat several of the harder climbs. He made an early ascent of Extol almost as an afterthought following a visit to Carlisle to mend his van, and made the third ascent of Ichabod the following day. In a very natural way Pat was drawn into Fell and Rock membership and he wrote the *Gable Guide**. The latter proved a long and onerous task. It was a lonely one at times, necessitating solo visits to remote little crags to which he would not normally have been attracted. Published in 1969 the *Gable Guide* was the epitome of the sober English guidebook, accurate to a tee and suppressing almost all vestiges of egotism. Characteristically, Pat was still able to revise it nearly a decade later.

Like most of his generation Pat married in the 60s; he and Sandra had a daughter, Sally. He also established himself in the Post Office Telephone Service, first of all on the lines and later under the pressures of the Control Centre. There he was a popular though individualistic member of the team,

---

**Great Gable, Wasdale and Eskdale*. Fell and Rock Climbing Club, 1969.

breathing angular good humour into what could be a wearing occupation. It was more secure than the application of his building skills which have their memorial in a host of natural stone fireplaces in South Yorkshire and, incidentally, in the new type locks which he and Al Maskery fitted to all the FRCC hut doors. His precision in such matters was matched by his driving – very fast, very smooth and, with one or two exceptions, undamaging to life and limb. In his early years he possessed an ancient Ford Prefect which had a propensity to turn upside down. But, as in all things, he learned quickly and well.

Pat loved the hills, winter and summer. He was a romantic at heart and he took time to come to terms with the shenanigans of the 'new' ice climbing. His temperament made him unsympathetic to the sectarianism of some younger climbers. His ideal on rock, ice and bigger mountains was that of unimpeded and relatively rapid movement. Ironically, this made him more in tune with modern alpine style climbing than many younger men. He believed in the minimization of dangers by avoiding prolonged exposure to them. This depended more on fitness, skill and verve than mounds of equipment and mere dogged persistence. Sometimes such a style won but on other occasions attempts at a 'spirited grab' did not come off. For example, he failed on the North Face of Ebnefluh in a storm, and in our attempt to climb the Bonatti Pillar in 1964 in what amounted to a one-day clearance in a series of stormy days. On occasion his reluctance to carry a heavy sack led to uncomfortable bivouacs as occurred

Escaping Moss Ghyll amphitheatre, in February 1978. *Photo by Bert Jenkins.*

Pat Fearnehough in the Karakorum.

after a wild winter ascent of Observatory ridge without crampons and in a storm. The idea had been to prepare for harder things!

Pat kept his scores with climbs and men. He did not easily let go. He still intended to climb the North Face of Monte Agner, on which he and Jack Hesmondhalgh were nearly drowned; he intended to ski powder with the best. On the way to his last Karakoram Expedition he finished the four-mile Islamabad Hot House Harriers paper chase with a 400yd Vladimir Kutz spurt which demolished almost all the opposition.

Pat had become ever more adventurous in his choice of expeditions of late. A few years ago he accompanied Peter Brown, Jack Soper and Rod Brown on a geological exploration in a remote region of East Greenland. He played his part in evacuating Peter who had sustained a dislocated shoulder. He led a group to East Turkey on a very smoothly executed trip in the mid-70s and the 1978 Latok Expedition was his third visit to the Karakoram. All this was achieved despite a demanding job and very much at his own expense. In 1975 an alpine-style push in the Tongo Peak area ended when Pat's companion was unable to continue. An attempt on the West Ridge of Latok in 1977 ended following the death of Don Morrison. After early illness Pat had led the last section to the Col and opened up much of the route leading to the final pyramid of the mountain, and even after Don was killed he moved up in support with more supplies. He was visibly shaken by the death of our friend but was still willing to try to scale the peak. Again in 1978 he could not resist the challenge of Latok II, could not bear the idea of not going. One of nature's Vikings, he was overwhelmed by an unholy alliance of earth and water, swept into the furious Braldu River by an insidious collapsing wall of mud and rock. Glaring deserts, warm rocks and icy fastnesses will never be the same.

A Hundred Years of Rock Climbing in the Lake District, Geoff Cram (Ed.) FRCC Journal, XXIV, 2 (1986).

Mountain 110. (1986).

Ever since its (Napes Needle) bold outlines began to stare at us on every railway platform and the newspapers realized that however poorly reproduced its form could never be mistaken for anything else, the British public has been open to listen to the little that can be said about it, and consequently that little has been said over and over again. (W. Haskett-Smith, FRCC *Journal* 1914.)

Here are shades of 'The Old Man of Hoy', in a former manifestation, readily packaged in its own striking image and unmistakable to a public perennially and healthily indifferent to climbing, yet fascinated by its occasional alarms and extremities.

Geoff Cram's swan song as editor is a bumper journal focused on climbing in the Lake District since the Napes Needle ascent of 1886. About a hundred pages divided into six sections tell of that ascent and short histories of significant periods of development. The first two are reprints. W. Haskett-Smith recorded the original ascent and its times, and a piece by H. M. Kelly and J. H. Doughty took the story to 1935. Authoritative pieces by John Wilkinson, like Kelly a long serving guidebook editor and past president, and by Pete Whillance, Ron Kenyon and Al Murray bring the story to the present day.

Kelly and Doughty (FRCC *Journal*, 1936–7) did a workmanlike job on new climbs and climbers between 1902 and 1934 paying attention to changing approaches down to the inter-war period. Nor are other key themes neglected, including the early recognition that women 'could not hope to develop fully their climbing potentialities under the conditions of the time unless they did some at least of their climbing quite independently of men.' (1921). It finishes perceptively with accurate speculations about the directions of future development, and an essential list of key ascents.

John Wilkinson makes a smooth and authoritative job of the complex period from 1935 to 1960. It is underpinned by knowledge of precise numbers of routes done, coloured by a real feel for the differences in circumstance and aspiration, peppered with speculations of a more ambitious nature. 'It may well have been the scent of victory in the air which stimulated the great burst of activity in 1944 and 1945.'

The individuals are paraded in significant numbers which supports impressions of levels of general competence as well as of the excellence and ability of a few household names like Birkett, Arthur Dolphin and Bill Peascod. Final pieces by Pete Whillance, Ron Kenyon and Al Murray approach the only definitive history of rock climbing in the Lakes in the period since 1960, despite disclaimers. They differ in character. Whillance points up the great importance of some key individuals, to an extent following Bill Birkett's technique in *Lakeland Pioneers* and the historically careless though visually attractive Border TV *Lakeland Rock* book of the films, and tries hard to pick out the key themes of the 60s. He makes too much of the north-south divide in Lakeland development, with its emphasis on Paul Ross versus Allan Austin. This reflects partly the essential inwardness of regional histories, as well as the distortion by Pete Livesey in his general reinterpretation of the past in the mid-70s. There is little hint of the most vital connections between key climbers, such as that between Les Brown, suitably emphasized as one of the most creative climbers of the era and Alan McHardy in his early Scafell explorations. Nor is there clear awareness that they with Soper, Crew, Ingle, Nunn, Woolcock, Boysen, Toole, Fearnehough and others active on occasion in the Lakes, were all part of the informal but immensely active SUMC Alpha Club axis of the 60s. Some had local Lake District connections too (Woolcock, Toole), but in general this group, including many others not notable for Lakeland new climbs, had perspectives of a national scope in rock climbing, and ambitious alpine interests. They first popularized numerical grading (Crew's translation of it from Helsby to his 'Cloggy' guide, followed after long delay by application to gritstone and limestone in the Peak in the late 60s), made early use of drilled machine nuts

(1961) and later wedge runners (1964–5) including micro-metal wedge chocks (Curtis, Webb, early 60s), did much free-climbing of routes considered over-aided, including for a time a willingness to avoid pitons even when there was no other belay (Astra). Their breadth of experience meant that they rock climbed everywhere in Britain and very extensively at the highest standards then known in Europe. While Oliver Woolcock and Paul Nunn were working on the FRCC *Borrowdale* guide, the former wrote what became the basis for the English guide to the Wetterstein, Karwendel and Kaisergebirge (although it was eventually published under another author's name) and Nunn translated about fifty route descriptions to climbs in the Vercors.

Ultimately almost all the group were Peak District gritstone climbers in origin, and despite lapses, especially on newly opened-up limestone or alpine and Dolomite routes, subscribed to the gritstone free-climbing ethic as enthusi-astically as Allan Austin. Rather than a 'Divided Kingdom' in those times, the Lakes was a peripheral colony overrun by a predatory gang of outside conquistadores. Paul Ross's persistence in a different perspective partly in-volved an unwillingness to accept po-faced 'purism' from outsiders when he knew that at his best he could climb with the best. In the end, while continuing to poke fun at the 'purists' for lack of humour, he gleefully collaborated with those visitors whom he found fun, even becoming an Alpha member before emigration and second wind pioneering on rock routes in New Hampshire. It should be remembered that his tastes and preferences placed him nearer to Al Harris than to righteousness, a trait shared by many who took to Borrowdale in the 60s.

From inside a narrow 'Lakes perspective', these continuities and personal connections might no longer appear obvious or important. Lack of it allows Hiraeth or Robin Smith to be forgotten despite considerable significance at the time, and makes McHardy's and Braithwaite's contributions in the late 60s seem isolated when they formed part of the same fabric. The former was one of the outstanding members of the Alpha group throughout the 60s and 70s and certainly its bravest soloist and, as so often then, this partnership was initially forged as much for alpine as for British purposes, and reverberated on to the 'Cumbrian' ascent and controversy which was similar in character to that over The Niche.

A reviewer's carpings and creakings are not intended to detract from the general excellence of the 60s piece. It leans over backwards to be fair to all participants and gets nearer to some kind of truth on the period than anything written before. It notes that some of the climbers had interests elsewhere, though giving an impression that this came later than Lakes pioneering rather than being simultaneous. Les Brown put aside Scafell and climbed Nuptse for the first time with Chris Bonington in 1961, just as he had done the second British ascent of the Walker Spur in 1959 with Whillans around the same time as Ross and Whillans climbed together with McInnes and Streetly (Red Slab) on the Bonatti Pillar. Place as such is not the critical strand of explanation in the complex climbing scene of 1960 any more than now. Climbers then were highly

71

mobile, arguably more so than today, and had wide horizons and ambitions.

The last piece tends towards a blow by blow story, detailed, essential, but less clear in theme than those before. Recent history is perhaps the hardest to write, and interpretation is least attempted amid the plethora of people and climbs. Key themes will be drawn out by others as the pieces fall into place. The atmosphere is repeatedly conjured up by reproduction of some of the key photos of the era, full-stopped by the urinal-like image of the Ambleside climbing wall.

The journal then reverts to its club functions, and reveals an astonishing range of 'usual' activities by members. The ascent of the North-East Spur of Les Droites by Geoff Oliver in the 1980s and 'Climbing in the Middle Ages' by Tony Greenbank speak of a vitality among climbers whom one might well have imagined long laid to rest from the rock history pages before. A 'better' history would probably be trying to do different things, and would be forced to transcend the regional boundaries. For now it's the best we've got.

ANOTHER DIMENSION – SCOTLAND

'Richard' (Alan) McHardy and I went in 1959, staying in Jacksonville, Glencoe home of the Creag Dhu. Big John McLean and John Cunningham demonstrated 'wee headies' and we were daft enough to try a summer Raven's Gully in the rain. After many falls we abseiled off an ex-army webbing belt.

Camping on Ben Nevis, the idea was (I think) to do Sassenach and Centurion. We climbed a slimy Douglas Boulder and went home to Llanberis, where sun was cracking the slates.

Nineteen sixty-two heralded the return match. Tower Ridge in February, the Cairn Dearg Buttress trilogy on three Whit days.

Observatory Ridge (Ben Nevis)

K. Wilson (Ed). Cold Climbs. *Diadem, 1983.*

Between the ice chutes of Point Five and Zero Gullies a narrow snow ridge plunges down from the summit cornices to a slight shoulder, hesitates, then bursts into a looming and steep-sided buttress above Observatory Gully. This is Observatory Ridge, harder than most and companion to North East Buttress, though not quite as long or as difficult. The buttress-like lower ridge is slabby at first, and then cut by a shelf which extends from the lower slopes of Zero Gully. Above this, short steep walls bar easy access to the medial snow ridge, beyond which the route becomes indefinite and in certain circumstances a traverse left into Zero Gully provides an easy way out.

The wind thumped around the outside of the Charles Inglis Clarke (CIC) hut. Most of the bunks were occupied and the pot-bellied stove was burning down in the morning gloom. In the shadows the greasy gas rings stood silent, their legs dipping into the squalid spillage on the cooking bench. Up to my nose in the sleeping bag I dreamed of stories of Antarctic expeditions, of good dinners, and of the 'birds' at the Rosthwaite Dance in Borrowdale. We were sick of Scots austerity.

A föhn-like thaw ruled. Observatory Gully had avalanched, but there might be more. A gale blew on the plateau. No one moved. One unlucky inmate groaned miserably with broken ribs incurred falling from top bunk to table in the early hours.

But if others were dormant, Pat Fearnehough never was. There had to be some action each day. In bad conditions we had climbed Tower Ridge again, Comb, Green and Gardyloo, and some longish bit of the Little Brenva Face. But

Rab Carrington tops out after the first winter ascent of Kellett's Left Hand on Gardyloo Buttress, 1976.

it was not enough. With an alpine season not too far away we practised holding falls on ice-axe belays, falling alternately from the base of the first pitch of Zero to the debris at the bottom. The red sweater went on and so did the kettle. Bacon and eggs were meticulously arranged in the pan. With a bite of bread and marmalade and a second mug of tea we were on our way.

Though conditions were repulsive we went light. It was to be a technical test, climbing with as little gear as possible. One 9mm rope, three slings and karabiners, one straight axe each, no crampons.

Blocks of snow filled the back of Observatory Gully. Crossing them, we took to the slopes leading up in the mist towards the Ridge, kicking steps in damp snow. It was a relief to be out of the gully lines in such conditions. Once on the rock it was a zig-zag progress up the front of the ridge, pleasant enough, with the occasional runner. Some short walls and icy ramps were more difficult, with little pulls up icy sections of rock. We moved steadily, always making steps for our vibrams, to the snow ridge above the lower rock difficulties. We sensed the day's shortness as the light faded behind thick, swirling clouds. Step-cutting led on and on to more rocks. The last few hundred feet were plastered and blasted by squally gusts, and in the storm it was hard to decide on any particular direction to follow, or even see where step-cutting might be possible on the complex, runnelled face. So we plumped for the apparent ease of the top of Zero, over to our left, hoping to escape the savage wind.

At first all went well; steep, neat, little ladders of steps on undisturbed névé. I hewed out a stance under some bulging ice, planting the axe as a dubious belay. Pat came up for the attack, but just as I expected him to launch out he stepped back in retreat. Spindrift poured over the bulge, coating our anoraks in ice and sliding through the holes in my elbows: 'The snow above is loose slops. It's going to be the one-axe pull.'

Pat's uncramponed feet scraped uneasily in the shallow ice-slots of the bulge. Using an ice-jug on the left, he thwacked the axe over the bulge, so hard that I thought he might break the second shaft of the week. Now the axe was in. The die was cast. Standing in two icy footholds, I leaned on the axe-belay, which met ice only a few inches below the surface, intoning the old rule of ice climbing – the leader must not fall. Below was the full length of Zero Gully.

His feet bridged up to former handholds, vibram edges braced on ice. After what seemed an age, those legs were levered up out of sight and the stiff rope followed, yard by yard through icy mittens up the ice-bulge into the grey mist and the dark. It tightened and I heaved out the axe-belay. Snow-glow just illuminated the edges of the steps. I shivered. A few optimistic bridging movements on thin crust led to the bulge. The pick went in above, but everything else gave way. Rope and axe pulled me into the gully above.

Pat was hulking. A shadow in the dark, rather spent, feet disappearing into a bucket step. We weren't out yet. It was a question of skimming the soft surface stuff away and hacking into the solid underlayer. Always a step or two ahead, with the odd handhold too. There was a sense of near-total isolation from the other man on the rope. Pat came up, missing all the holds in the dark, then led

Ben Nevis.

on, suddenly breaking on to the plateau. Almighty relief. It was 8pm in February.

In the mist and wind we groped from cairn to cairn, roped and keeping the cornices well away to the right. We turned away from the gale and aimed for the bivouac hut, at that time sited at ground level near the top of Tower Gully. A hole appeared and Pat went for it like a dog for a bone.

The bivouac hut of red corrugated tin was completely buried, but we knew it had been excavated recently. There we feasted on bread and cheese, and dried peas that we found on the floor. We serenaded the grey man howling outside with our complete repertoire of songs, a few hymns included. Of no great help was a Gideon Bible thoughtfully left for Lost Souls – we hadn't a match. Eleven hours later it still blew as dawn came and we hopped straight over the cornice into Tower Gully to escape the gale. It was still necessary to nick out steps for 1,000ft to make a safe descent.

Hours later, as we luxuriated in the hut, Dougal Haston's wild figure burst in with bad news. At 10pm Pat, Dougal and I set out to scour the whole of the base of the North-East Buttress from high in Observatory Gully to the bottom of Carn Mor Dearg Arête. For hours we probed and prodded for tangled bodies. Nothing came to light, and as we cramponed back to the very door of the hut we heard that they had turned up elsewhere. What a fraught black mound the Ben can be.

76

Filming The Bat and the Wicked

Jim Curran, Paul Nunn and Tony Riley, Illustrated London News
(1979). First Ascent Reconstructed

In August 1979 five climbers spent a week on Ben Nevis filming a reconstruction of the first ascent of the mountain's biggest buttress by Robin Smith and Dougal Haston in 1959. The film *The Bat and the Wicked* is based on the classic article of the same name by Robin Smith 'The Bat and the Wicked'.

Predictably the first drops of rain splattered the windscreen as we left the M6 and drove into Scotland. Not for the first time the whole idea seemed ludicrously improbable and likely to prove an expensive experiment. Rab Carrington and Brian Hall were to be the climbers. Paul Nunn was to organize locations and provide back-up camera work, and Jim Curran and Tony Riley were the film-makers. We could manage only one week of shooting on Ben Nevis and that in the first week of August, potentially the wettest month of the year.

We were attracted to filming a reconstruction of the first ascent by the sheer liveliness of Robin Smith's classic article. The Bat refers to one of many falls, a great backwards swoop by Dougal Haston out of an overhanging corner:

> Then his fingers went to butter. It began under control as the bit of news, 'I'm off', but it grew like a wailing siren to a bloodcurdling scream as a black and bat-like shape came hurtling over the roof with legs splayed like webbed wings and hands hooked like a vampire . . . I could have sworn that his teeth were fangs and his eyes were big red orbs.

Two great talents at the forefront of British climbing making repeated and stealthy attacks on this daunting rock climb, eventually succeeding in the middle of a moonlit night – it had obviously been a great adventure. Now a classic in climbing writing. Smith's account is as much about people as climbing, and it manages to combine several perspectives. Somehow he is intense about climbing. His use of language, particularly Scottish words, seems naturally suited to both the action and the atmosphere, yet communicates to a non-Scot. The writing evokes strong visual images and provided a challenge to us as film-makers. The narration had to be linked with suitable pictures which complemented rather than overpowered the words.

Somehow the limitations of the project turned to advantages. We were on a very low budget in film-making terms, although the Yorkshire Arts Association gave as generous a grant as they could. Low-budget filming was no novelty to Tony and Jim, whose first film, *A Great Effort*, won first prize in 1977 at the Trento Film Festival, Italy, for contributions to art and literature in cinema. It was shown on BBC2 in 1975. Three Himalayan films had followed, *Trango*, *Barnaj 77* and *K2 The Savage Mountain*, shown on BBC1 in 1979. Limited

Rab Carrington and Brian Hall, playing Robin Smith and Dougal Haston. *Photo by Tony Riley.*

The author, getting into position to film *The Bat*, falls. *Photo by Tony Riley.*

Tony Riley, North East Buttress, Ben Nevis.

finance meant that we could not afford extensive or sophisticated shooting techniques, or a large film crew. There would, therefore, be no helicopters or aerial shots; on the other hand there would be no time-wasting problems with co-ordinating such shots or a large team. The deliberate blurring of traditional film-making roles worked well in such a small group. Everyone involved had a stake in the project, all were familiar with the Ben and its moods, and all were rock climbers able to look after themselves and work as a team on a 1,000ft overhanging precipice. Paul had known both Smith and Haston and had also made an early repeat ascent of The Bat in 1962.

Jim had approached Rab Carrington at Easter and asked him if he would be prepared to act/climb the part of Robin Smith. His enthusiasm for the project was engendered by an immense respect for Smith and his climbs but tempered by the thoughts of having to fall off in front of a camera and of having his beard shaved. Such was the result of the latter process that everyone failed to recognize the friend of a decade – but he did look like Robin! Brian was taller than Dougal and did not resemble him except for a long head, wolfish grin and consummate boldness.

In Fort William it had stopped raining for the first time in weeks. The pile of equipment, said Rab, was more than had been taken to Nepal to climb Jannu. We were camping because the SMC feared the film might cause gross inconvenience to users of the Charles Ingles Clarke (CIC) hut – despite the fact that we were trying to honour two of the SMC's most distinguished members; and that hut remained empty for most of our stay. Such considerations hardly comforted the actors as they relayed two or three 60lb loads up 'the knee-deep black bog'. It rained that night and on Tuesday morning the great buttress on the north side of Cairn-mor-Dearg dripped and glistened. A shambles of climbing and film gear had to be reorganized while Rab and Brian donned late-50s period clothes and equipment. Much of the gear came from Paul's attic, though the hawser-laid ropes had been borrowed from friends. One of them had survived a 70ft fall on the Black Cleft of Clogwyn-d'ur-Arddu in Wales in 1959.

Past experience had shown the film-makers that early shooting is often disjointed and contrived, but that with steady effort a project tends to come together. We had just one week to do the shoot and were lucky with the weather: it was dry enough for the climbers to get up the route in their old-fashioned climbing gear and for us to use the film equipment, but there was also sufficient drifting mist and water-streaked rock to capture the brooding and gloomy atmosphere so typical of the mountain. Compressing the shooting into a few days also allowed good lighting continuity, while filming without live sound recording is much quicker and involves fewer repeats. It was possible to use Smith's narration virtually as a shooting script and to proceed more or less chronologically.

Despite lack of previous film experience, Rab and Brian needed surprisingly little guidance. They were so much into their roles that they called each other Robin and Dougal and the cameramen felt as if they were invisible witnesses to the first ascent. As they climbed, one camera operated from the ground and another from a position prepared by Paul on the climb. It was still wet and the first section was initially led by Paul and rigged with some furtive protection, while the cameraman was brought up to the first position on a freehanging rope before Rab and Brian began to climb. Paul supervised climbing sequences and allowed the cameramen to concentrate on filming without worrying unduly about stances, belays and other security. He had occasionally done such rigging on BBC outside broadcasts since Operation Overhang in 1965, and on a few film projects as well.

The first day went remarkably smoothly. After filming the first pitch the climbing became very serious as it was necessary to traverse a long slab of rock which ends abruptly in massive overhangs. A fall would have put its victim straight into space without enough rope to be lowered to the ground. Rab and Brian put on a virtuoso performance in climbing this section, for it oozed wet and slime and their equipment gave far less protection than is available to modern rock climbers. A chilling wind numbed the fingers but took up a little of the moisture as the day passed. Despite the climbing difficulties ahead that would form the climax of the film, the potential dangers of this day seemed in many respects the greatest. Like their predecessors, Rab and Brian came down a freehanging rappel in gathering gloom and Robin Smith wrote: 'Judging by the murky oaths floating up the rope he seemed to be down so I followed. Suddenly my feet shot away and I swung in under the great roof and spiralled down until I landed in a bog. Dougal was already away down to the hut for a brew and a bed.'

In poor conditions we had reached the Hoodie Groove and filmed the traverses which need not be repeated. A single nylon thread hung for 150ft in space – it was the route to supper and back to work next day. Paul used climbing clamps (jumars) to get back above the overhang next morning. The rope was already beginning to chafe badly at the lips of two of the overhangs and from then on a second protection rope was used. A further fixed rope led more easily to the Hoodie Groove which was to be the starting point for more filming: 'We stood looking into the little green Hoodie Groove. I was scheming to myself, now the groove will be terrible but nothing to the corner above, and I will surely have to lead the crux but Dougal shamed me with indifference.'

Now it was Brian's turn to lead, and as there was room for only one camera on the high-angled slab at its base Jim and Paul hung far down in a cocoon of ropes while Tony filmed from the ground. Brian had to fish with a sling for a small spike on the left wall, luckily he got it after only three or four attempts – Jim had visions of all the film being used up in attempting authenticity in this manoeuvre. Brian reached the big corner and Rab followed: '. . . I had to wake up and follow it myself. Half-way he told me about the sling on the spike and I made a strange can-can move to get my foot in the sling. I came out at the top of the groove in a row of convulsions . . .'

It had taken eight hours to film 40ft of climbing and ahead loomed greater problems. Paul, Rab and Brian were not optimistic about the great corner for it was running with moss and water as it usually does except on the few days of drought which Ben Nevis enjoys annually. Half the climb was filmed but it was taking longer and longer to reach our positions and the corner would be a very difficult proposition. That night decisions were taken. Rab and Brian would ascend the corner next day using every trick in the book to overcome its damp, slippery defences. Tony and Jim would concentrate on long-shots and Paul would ensure that there were enough supplies for several more days by visiting the fleshpots of Fort William.

Throughout the shoot we were fearful of normal Scottish weather. Rock climbers do The Bat in the very best conditions, which we did not have. Instead there was a compromise. After the first night it did not rain in the Allt-a-Mhuilinn, but rain occasionally came down past the bottom of the valley in great curtains, and it seemed to be falling everywhere else in Scotland. Each evening spectacular sunsets accompanied late camp meals.

Friday was crunch day. Brian and Rab had forced the corner and knew what was in store. Paul jumared up the ropes ahead and fixed a personal position far out on the left top edge of the great corner. From there all the action could be seen and it was possible to film and take still photographs downwards. He spent about six hours using one half-foothold. Tony was to film in the corner, right under the actions, while Jim shot from the ground. Brian and Rab were wearing full body harnesses under their tatty sweaters and worn anoraks, with the ancient hawser-laid ropes and nylon slings weighed down by steel snap links for protection. Helmets were rarely worn in Britain for climbing before the 60s but the steepness of the corner seemed to minimize the chances of head injury. Tony quietly asked Jim before starting the hair-raising ascent of the corner, 'Would you throw yourself off up there – just to be in a film?' Both thought not!

A lot of work went into arranging the falls, for there are three in the story. First it was Haston's turn. Brian calculated that he would fall about 10ft free and rigged a friction system to allow a gradual rather than a sudden stop. A combination of the system working farther than intended and Rab allowing him to slide a little at the end of the fall gave a 30ft slow-motion epic. Brian was stretched across the upper corner primarily attached to a modest right hand-hold. Tony and Jim checked out their cameras and Paul focused his Bolex. 'OK, Brian – action.'

As Dougal neared his ledge he was slowing down but flailing all the more, left fingers clawing in the crack and right leg scything moss on the wall. I pulled down the sleeves of my jersey and took a great grip of the ropes. Then there came a sort of squawk as Dougal found that his ledge was not. He got a hand on it but it all sloped. Rattling sounds came from his throat. In his last throes to bridge he threw his right foot away out at a straw on the wall, then his fingers went to butter . . .

Brian just fell out of sight of Paul's position, too fast to stay in the frame. For Tony he almost fell into it from about 40ft above. To Jim he fell all the way down the corner of the big open book. There were expletives and congratulations on the ledge.

Then its was Rab's turn, made worse by injury in a spring fall in Derbyshire and by the fact that Brian had already done his. He had to fall twice over the roof in the groove:

> At full stretch I could just reach two pebbles in a crack but as I reached up I felt a lurch in my stomach like flying through an air pocket . . . desperately I seized a baby nylon sling and tried to thread it around the pebbles, then I was gracefully plucked from the rock to stop 20ft under the roof hanging from the piton . . . with the traitor wedge hanging from me and the threaded sling sticking out of the corner far above.

Then there was an immense sense of relief and anticlimax. A little film of Rab leading, the eventual success, Tony's climber's eye view of the fall contrived by dropping a protected camera spinning down the corner. It remained only to withdraw slowly and carefully, clearing the equipment from the great buttress. Saturday was spent on cutaway filming and ferrying down loads to the road. The film was in the can and we were tired. 'At last I emerged still fighting on to ledges and bewildering easy angles and great good holds . . . by this means we put an end to this unscrupulous first ascent.'

Unusually for this film team, there was too much climbing footage. The climbing action had to be broken by expanding part of Smith's narration where he and Dougal spent time in the valley between attempts on the climb: characterization could be developed by such scenes as buying fish and chips and waiting for the pub to open. Much of that came later.

Far Far Away Land

While writing the *Borrowdale* climbing guide and collecting material which eventually became *Northern Limestone* and *Southern Limestone*, and doing bits of guide stuff on Kinder and Derwent Edge with Oliver Woolcock we did a lot of climbing, but the places became over-familiar. Even favourites paled, as is their wont.

Thus I snatched at a lift north with Brian Henderson, a pipe-smoking Geordie activist in Borrowdale who fancied an outing. We picked up Brian Robertson in Edinburgh. He was an ambitious, tough climber very intent on his own plans with a life agenda seemingly inspired by 'Triumph of the Will'. I have climbed with all manner of folk, thought him basically safe and interesting, and thought Whit 1966 as good a time as any to break the mould.

After an entertaining traverse across the Etive Slabs with much good climbing but a mysterious relationship with existing routes (The Thin Red Line) a long pilgrimage north began which has never ended. Following roads of painful slowness we visited Gairloch and points north, staying a few days with Tom Patey in Ullapool and making the first ascent of The Old Man of Stoer. Our cohesion broke down when Brian R tried to get Brian H to drive him to Wick to

Smith's Gully, Creag Meaghaidh.

take his driving test. This proved too much even for the latter's legendary tolerance, and with a puff or two of his pipe he spirited us back to Borrowdale.

In 1967 Clive and Steph Rowland, my wife Hilary and our fifteen-month-old baby Louise went to Creag an Dubh Loch near Balmoral. The runes were set against us and it streamed with water. Gairloch provided a fine weather alternative, and Beinn a' Mhuinidh a new route. Clive became ill, possibly with a virus caught from our infant. The local doctor diagnosed polio, so we went home, where he recovered. The north-west remained under our skin, and next Whit we went there rather than Lundy.

Emerald Gully (Beinn Dearg, Northern Highlands)

K. Wilson (Ed). Cold Climbs. *Diadem, 1983.*

> Bad weather, bad conditions and aberrations from the right way will provide a guideless party with as many exciting and trying situations as they ought to wish for. R. L. G. Irvine, *Alpine Club Address, 1908.*

With a big grin Tom Patey had promised, 'An easy couloir, grand in scale, ignored only because of its remote situation; no one ever climbs in winter that far north in Scotland.' After an hour's moor-bashing the first névé came into sight around 11pm. It was perfect for a fast solo front-point to an impasse. Black in the shadows of Quinag's Barrel Buttress a bergschrund loomed, separating the névé and ourselves from the rock of an unwanted barrier in the gully bed. It was of daunting height and steepness and it looked near impossible. We all milled about the edge of the black hole. Tom even prodded his axe across at the sandstone doubtfully, but without the benefit of a rope and daylight it looked like a defeat. Even Tom's inexhaustible optimism was dented. It was 1am and the pit by our feet seemed bottomless in the moonshadow. Tom suggested that a human pyramid might do it; some of us worried about how the tail of the party would make the crossing. Eventually we demurred, unanimously.

At least the long slog back remained moonlit. Quinag sank back into a hump behind, quartz pavements speeded progress, and as usual Tom scurried ahead, ever-anxious to be first to the road. Eventually four oversized men crammed into a battered Skoda, the hero of Tom's extensive medical practice. The car rattled off south on endless single-track roads towards Ullapool. Too near dawn we three bunked down in Tom's garden shed.

That shed was a legend. It was fitted with bunks and cooking space and was used to seduce southern sceptics to the North. Climbers of all descriptions could find a welcome there, a few yards from the sea. Tom always entertained, for he hated dead time. Most of all he advertised the merits of the northern winter and summer. He had done dozens of climbs alone or with visiting friends. In the shed a campaign map showed the whole of the North, star-rated for quality. It will keep people happy for generations. Over late-night drams the doctor talked of objectives and prodded us towards those unfitted to his designs. Ideas and suggestions ranged the whole region with occasional excursions to the Alps and Himalaya and every manner of wild anecdote. Unfortunately we had not quite the numbers or the voice to sing with Tom's squeezebox.

The next morning was dark and we woke late. Tom was off on his rounds. We were armed with verbal details which got us to the base of the cliffs in an hour or so. Spring blizzards blew thick cloud in from the west. Most of the Inverlael Gullies had been climbed by Tom on lone afternoon jaunts. There was little to be seen through the cloud, though we knew that the big mixed face of Beinn Dearg lay to the east. The route to do was unmistakable, an ice-tube dropping out of the murk with at least two biggish pitches and quite a lot of easier ground. It was already 2pm.

Snow fell steadily on the plod into the gully. I set off up the first ice-tube, which was not as difficult as it had looked. The snow-ice was good and easily hewed into fine pigeon-hole steps and mittenholds. Occasionally a draught of spindrift cooled our work. Like Green Gully I thought, as time passed and progress continued in slow but steady arm-aching effort. A rock-piton on the left improved the view until at last the angle eased back into a gully of fine solid snow. It took the rest of the rope to climb up it to a belay below a beard of icicles, dangling across a steeper part above.

Brian Fuller followed easily and quickly up the step-ladder. After a momentary halt to hand over Tony Riley's rope, he hacked away upwards towards the icicles while I anchored them both – one above, the other below. By the time Tony came into sight Brian was just a pair of crampon heels high on the right wall. Watching was anxious work as time evaporated and darkness crept in. It would be a long, long fall if he slipped, 50ft away without protection. But he kept moving up and we were comforted by the knowledge that he rarely parted company with the rock. On a trying bit he swung and poked with the pick for a few moments to no avail. Then his pick found a firm sod – a pull, a scrape, a flash of Fuller's famous fangs, and he disappeared into the grey-black mystery above. Two ropes trailed up behind, one attached to each of our waists. He was our anchor.

When all the rope had gone Tony and I shouted but there was no reply, so we followed in close file. It was a groping, awkward process in the conditions, especially at the bulge, and we were worried about dislodging one another. Torches stayed off most of the time, in anticipation of terrible times ahead. After the wall a traverse left led back to steep snow and a characteristic long flog for the top. Crampon-bashing up completed the trip to the plateau, where the wind howled.

Then the anxious question was, which way from here? To the east the crossing to Beinn Dearg looked too long. Nor did the Pass of the Fools, a feature on that route, sound encouraging. So it was west, aiming for the sea, playing our last card. At least it led homewards. The leader poked along, too near the cornice, peering out and down into mists below with the thin torch beam.

There are gambles and gambles. This one paid off and we were saved a wander by torchlight around the wildernesses to the south. We picked a way round the long Glensquaib escarpment until open slopes led down to the deep heather. Torches flickered and faded for the last leg, then there were a few footprints beyond a stream. We were back on course. One near-extinct torch led on down, looking for the old red van. It eventually found a matching tiny light, the living red end of a cigarette, last of several that night. Tom was somewhere behind, lolling on the Skoda: 'You're a wee bit late. It is gone one and the blizzards are closing the Braemore road. We'd best be off.'

Foinaven Saga – The Cnoc and the Maiden

Mountain 62. (1978).

You may reach The Cnoc with the resolve of a medieval pilgrim. Sutherland remains too far, whatever one's relativities, when it takes nearly as long to get there as to Yosemite and costs about as much even if you don't crash on the single tracks. Even the sober SMC *Journal* laconically refers to whatever unnatural activities might occur in this region as if they were the merest eccentricities of the Far Far North, unrelated to the serious business of keeping the Sassenach hordes from the sacred portals of the CIC hut.

For very old climbers Foinaven and Arkle are best remembered from the names of famous racehorses, long since rendered to the public as glue. The thousand-plus miles from central England are an initial irritant, squeezing past the Bank Holiday lemmings as they head for the sea. Surely the conquest of 5c on bone-dry 'Cloggy', or in the recesses of the East Buttress of Scafell, is preferable to exhaust fumes in the Tyne Tunnel and so many miles to go?

A few hours later the A9 weariness combines with the attractions, real and imaginary, of Yo-Yo, The Giant, or The Pin in dry weather, or at least a few beers with Big Ian in the 'Coe. Further on the oasis of Inverness nestling by the sea is little compensation, as it is superficially too like returning to England. The burning oil and rattles of a battered Ford motor combine with the peculiar burnings of the long distance driver's stomach to force a halt.

It is the bright arrow of Loch Shin, projecting the single track road into the midnight sun, which marks the real beginning. The rural idiocies of arable and green grass fall behind, the trees falter, gnarl and stoop, and by Rhiconich gneiss moonscape conquers the narrow margins between quartz heights and the sea. It is another country, a land of unseasonal sun and sudden gusts, of drifting North Atlantic fogs, seeping grey and lulling stupefying sunsets, narrow fiords and twisting roads. Almost all the inhabitants live at sea level, while the interior is vast; it was always endless wastes, but became more so in the Sutherland clearances of 150 years ago, as James Loch, political economy and rationality combined to flush people from the inland glens to the sea's edge. From the black down-tilting syenite of Ben Loyal to Cape Wrath and Handa, a thin layer of habitations facing the ocean is nearly all that remains. Only the odd keeper, birdwatcher, fisherman or deerstalker trespasses inland.

The Cnoc a' Mhadaidh is a mongrel cliff of quartz and gneiss, not far from a point in the great bog of Strath Dionard where the quartz grabs the dominant role in the major cliff formations of Urbhard and Creag Dionard. It sprawls round a glaciated outlier of the Foinaven massif, dominating the lower strath – four miles from the road, across bog churned by the tracks of the Sno-Cats which carry well-heeled paying fishermen to the Loch 7 miles in. They do not take their litter home.*

Thus with Creag Shomhairle, a popular cliff at the head of Loch Eriboll, the Cnoc a' Mhadaidh is the last of the great gneiss cliffs in the North West, on the final far-flung spurs of Britain before the sea. The scourian gneiss shores up the old red sandstones which still face the sea's onslaught, providing a rock landscape of low altitude and unrivalled splendour from Torridon and Carnmore, with Loch Maree as the apparent geological break. A John Gill could spend a lifetime by Maree side and in ten generations might reach the final rearings of red gneiss at Sheigra – 'If I had a thousand homes and lived in each a while, I'd build them all along the coast from Sandwood down to Kyle.'†

Four miles to the cliff seemed a relief in 1970 after the customary 7 or 8 miles to the main Dionard crags. The springy fishermen's path allowed the steady placing of one foot before another to the 3-mile marker, a few yards short of the tiny hut inhabited in the summer months by the formidable and enigmatic ornithologist. There he stands guard over the rare greenshank, one of the treasures of Dionard, and has carried out that same loving chore for every summer in a decade and more. To reach the cliff is flat, across a bog which trembled for yards around on our wet first encounter. Below the crag a combination of deep heather and huge fallen boulders provides a final defence to its base.

Superficially the cliff is not particularly attractive. A monster roof blocks out almost all sensible lines, except to the far east of the cliff and in a rather vegetated area of gullies to the west. With extreme optimism Dave Goodwin (Spud) and I plumped for a try up the middle, as a first groping exploration, climbing first up streaming wet slabs of fine rock for two or three pitches towards the left extremity of the great roof. Climbing such good rock in such conditions has its rewards, but eventually I stalled below a smooth overlap still more than 100ft below the roofs. A piton remains from the highpoint, where we left our rope in position in the hope of a resurgence of weather or bravery.

On the next day Tom Patey appeared, and a large party of both sexes took to a lobster boat to attempt the first ascent of the Maiden stack in the fierce sea north of Whiten Head. Ferried by a veteran boatman of Durness, we crossed the three-mile channel at the mouth of the deep waters of Loch Eriboll. The stack

---

*Lately they have proposed to rape the valley with a road, a sacrilege in one of the last few wilderness areas (1987).

†Song by Dave Goulder.

was breaking the waves of the open sea and the boat heaved close in to the plinth at its base. The engine sputtered as the bows rose and fell in the swell, while the day had about it a relentlessly grey and raw cold unusual in June, ever threatening strong wind and a squall.

Already as Tom uncoiled the rope and Clive Rowland, Spud and 'Fred' Fuller established themselves on the plinth, small boats were running for shelter on the horizon. As Tom rushed the leader's position in his usual way, I perused the great quartz crumbling masses of Whiten Head – too far to walk, and perhaps not worth the effort.

Tom swarmed up the greasy quartz, following a steep groove which was littered with sharp medium-sized holds of dubious stability, and traversed a horizontal shelf to belay. There followed a steep boldish wall with little protection which I led without thought, ever conscious of the strengthening wind on the small holds. The others came up below from a fine little balcony, while Tom smartly evaded the very steep final wall to reach a crumbling arête and the summit.

In a very little time we all stood on top, and the boat with Steph Rowland, Di Cundy and the redoubtable ferrymaster hid under the lee of the stack. Tom elected me to fix the abseil – 'You're an expert on this engineering.' The ropes spread near-horizontally in the wind as we cast the abseil line, and it was only after a little untangling and adjustment that its extremities were freed from numerous sharp flakes, which ensnared them despite the weight of surplus iron tied to the rope end.

As engineer, I entrusted myself first to the abseil, which was free throughout most of the 130ft or so to the plinth. One by one the others followed – with a sense of urgency, as the waves grew ominously on the seaward side of the stack and rushed through the channel between the twin spires. The anxious boat party were already starting manoeuvring to within jumping distance of the plinth.

Last of all Tom set off and lowered himself into space. Only 20ft down, he stopped in mid-air, tugging at the old wire figure-of-eight. After a moment of tussle in an attempt to free his woollen jumper from the device, he fell clear from the rope, near 100ft to the pavement of the plinth. Massively injured, he lay on his back still and unbreathing, with little sign of the cruel damage of the hard rock. We ran from our retreats on the plinth, where we had stood to avoid the possibility of falling rock. Within very few minutes of trying to find a sign of life, we were forced to conclude that he was dead.

There were hard decisions to make as the waves grew from the west in an ever-strengthening wind and a steelier greyness howled in from the west. The body was lashed high on the plinth; the boat steered perilously close as we jumped one by one into the heaving bows. An overloaded boat turned its nose into the north-westerly as we headed out in an arc towards the tiny bay west of Loch Eriboll.

Whether truly serious or not, that journey frightened a crew of landlubbers into wet shivering numbness. With impassive features, our great old pilot urged

Spud on in his efforts to pump out the water, which slopped into the boat as we mounted each high wave. The water threatened to silence the motor, and on occasion made impossible the steering needed to prevent us meeting the cold walls of water almost broadside-on. After hours of calculating swimming ability in cold spring sea against the long distance to land, we stuttered into the tiny hidden bay, weary from the lashing wet and stress.

There were still duties to perform, the police and Tom's family to inform. But most of all there remained a climbers' problem, our problem: Fred, Clive and I resolved that we must wait to return if possible and rescue the body. In a few hours, as the grey, evil day ground on, a team of strong policemen arrived with the inspector from Dingwall, and we took ship for the Maiden in a powerful little fishing vessel.

The sea was rougher than ever, and the ship ploughed through the waves which had so dwarfed the lobster boat. In less than an hour the Maiden Stacks were at hand. Once again, with many helping hands and adroit tuning of the engine, we jumped on to the plinth, fearful of a fall between the bucking boat and the wall of barnacled rock. We wrapped Tom in a sea rescue corset, and it required all our strength and that of five or six brawny police to get him on the boat. Once we were aboard again, it crashed back across Eriboll at a high rate of knots, drowning those unfortunates who could not cram into the tiny wheel-house. It was a bad business, and the fishermen wanted it over. When asked over his dram why he had doused his passengers, the skipper could only utter into the night: 'I dinna like policemen and revenue men.'

From a climbing point of view it was the end of an era. Tom had exercised an unchallenged hegemony over the North-West, and his going left a void in his fief which could never be so adroitly filled.

In the grey aftermath, our retrieval of gear from The Cnoc's streaming wall took only a few hours. There seemed every reason to leave the whole vale of tears to the legendary beast of Wrath, the dragging and dreadful Clo Sang.

It was not to be! Within a year the Sheffield tribes were again huddling in their encampment by the sea at Sheigra. The early sweet success of 1969 still overcame the superstition and the risks of a grim *déjà vu*. In that year a great spurt of good climbs of about VS or harder had been found in the main Dionard crags, and the wealth of possibilities remaining forced a return there. Meanwhile, Bob Toogood and I aimed at The Cnoc.

It was dry, and the slabs to the roof were climbed direct up an obvious and straightforward line; rough red rock and fine small holds. Then came the problem, for above loomed a 60ft roof crack which we judged climbable only with the aid of bongs. For me, I wanted a cunning, classical, relatively free route, and the left corner of the roof offered more of a possibility than was apparent from below, for a great flake squeezed into the roof and formed a high-angle crack for about 40 or 50ft. With some jiggery-pokery it was climbed, while the slabs below were showered with loose flakes and the tenuous vegetation which so often fills vital cracks on igneous cliffs.

At last, after what was probably a very long time, I grasped a big handhold, pulled up and found myself perched atop a 10ft jet-black block on the edge of an equally black wet-streaked slab, which disappeared into space below. After belaying to it, I realized that the block was totally detached except for a base on a high slab angle. Fortunately Bob Toogood is very cool and very light, and when he arrived we fixed a piton in the bedrock under the roof before the next stage.

Above, the roofs continued to prevent us aiming direct for the top and the Garbet Hotel, and Bob traversed the black slab before groping and bridging into a vast nest whose owner, perhaps fortunately, declined to put in an appearance. Above this belay one short swing up an overhanging groove led to another overhung slab. Still escape direct looked remote, while retreat looked increasingly complex.

Bob launched out on a long slippery slab traverse, got well committed and thus climbed excellently. Eventually he peered round a little steep rib and the grim set of his face cracked into a grin – it was a rerun of The Dialectic on Dionard in 1969, and after hours on the crags and some qualms we were in the clear. It was somehow reminiscent of gripping times on German and Austrian walls in the 60s, so 'Quergang' seemed appropriate. That year no one else came that way, nor probably in the next.*

Two years later Martin Boysen and I climbed together a few times – which we had not done, except in winter ramblings, for a decade or more. Fresh from the idyll of Dionard, we struck at The Cnoc for a last climb on the way out.

Holding up the left centre of the crag is a huge pillar beginning out of the slabs and doing something, one hopes, to support the massive roof superstructure. Again the June weather was good, the midges had been quiescent, and after a leisurely amble down the valley and a long engagement in conversation with the birdman we idled at the crag base in the sun, taking a gaze down the raw glaciated expanses of the lower valley. Once Bob Downes, Mike O'Hara, George Fraser and other less well-known names had their Carnmore. Now, in 1973, we had ours.

The pillar looked formidable – but leading through, it all went so smoothly as to be hardly worth a knee tremble. Magnificent climbing, alternating slabs and steepness with bogglingly good and convenient holds. In only a hour or so, after a particularly fine pitch perched on the edge of the pillar, we emerged at the end of the slabby gropings of Quergang. Pilastre was its complete antithesis: direct in line without the slightest deviousness; VS or a little more; totally uncomplicated and brilliant rock needing only the minimum of cleaning; free from its inception.

Again two years elapsed before Bob Dearman, Phil Burke and Simon Wells took the 60ft Great Roof direct with the aid of bongs, followed by two fine pitches to the top of Hard VS. This is a formidable and serious undertaking, and might

---

*Nor maybe for more than a decade, or at least the state of belay, grown into the crag, suggested that in 1983, ascending a parallel line (Familiar).

require a few Friends if it eventually goes free. Bob attacked the right centre of the roof in 1976, and with some aid climbed a great red groove-overhang leading to another fine exit. Some would say that with Denny Moorhouse – king of Clog – as his second, Dearman could hardly fail! Meanwhile, pleasant but less spectacular routes were done on the left-hand slabs of the crag, in 1975 by Tim Lewis and Bob Toogood and in the following year by Brian Griffiths, Bob and myself. The cliff is beginning in its development to belie its initial appearance of near-total impregnability, though a good proportion of the climbs done require a degree of sophistication in climbing ability, combined with readiness to effect self-rescue should you fall into space. No routes have been repeated – while remarkably, with the cliff approaching its tenth anniversary as a climbing ground, this June it allowed us to slip through the right centre of the Great Roof with minimal aid, on a route not unlike Armageddon on the East Buttress of Scafell (Wrath, 700ft, HVS: Boulton, Lewis and Nunn; one aid piton left in place).

That our ascent was orchestrally accompanied by thunder and torrential rain after weeks of drought should come as no surprise, and we could only thank our lucky stars for 'green caterpillars' and modern front-pointing techniques, by which we made our escape. Too recent for full digestion, it still had all that epic quality which renders the long journey to this land of extremes worth while.

Tom Patey is Dead

Mountain 10. (1970).

> Though frost be fierce and pain be dire My oath shall be my burning fire
> > Hartmann, *Nanga Parbat* (1937).

> The mountaineer it seems . . . is impelled through life by the old jostle of romance.
> > James Morris

Tom Patey's death comes as a grievous shock to us all. He was killed instantly in a fall from The Maiden, a fierce little quartzite pillar off Whiten Head in Sutherland. To his wife, his family, his friends in mountaineering and elsewhere, and to his patients in his rambling medical practice, the loss is immeasurable.

This many-faceted man was the son of the rector of Ellen near Aberdeen. He attended Gordon's College, Aberdeen, where he developed a musical talent much appreciated more recently by mountaineers. The stark Cairngorms intruded on his adolescent years. With other schoolboys of a group known as the 'Horrible Highlanders', he tramped the 'Munros' in the late 40s. By 1949 he had a rope.

In 1950, 'Goggs' Leslie and I emerged shaken but triumphant from a hole in Douglas-Gibson Gully cornice, thereby ushering in a new era of winter expeditions on routes which had hitherto been regarded as solely within the provinces of rock specialists. It was also our first première.

Thus began a series of dramatic climbing successes which made Tom the 'Grand Master of the 50s' in Scotland. In this period, he did over seventy climbs in the Cairngorms. Outstanding among these were the first winter ascents of Tough-Brown Traverse, Eagle Ridge and Parallel Buttress at Lochnagar, and Route Major on Carn Etchachan, together with early winter climbs in the northern corries of Cairngorm. Despite his image in England, Patey was never solely a winter climber, and many of his numerous summer routes were formidable – Parallel Gully B and Vertigo Wall, for instance. The first ascent of Vertigo Wall was made in damp conditions in October 1954, and was a major epic. It was as important to the development of Creag an Dubh Loch as was Great Eastern to Scafell.

In the early 50s, his activities extended to Applecross and Skye, while forays to the Alps also became possible. Here, his boldness and ice experience paid off on the first British ascents of the Sans Nom Arête of the Verte and the North Face of the Plan. In 1957, he was a member of the highly successful Mustagh Tower expedition and, in 1958, as a surgeon-lieutenant in the Royal Navy, he returned to the Himalaya with Mike Banks to make the first ascent of Rakaposhi. Service with the Marines took Patey to Devon, where he attacked the local outcrops with customary vigour, making a number of new climbs and starting the exploration of Chudleigh Rocks. Nevertheless, his activities remained widespread. Central Pillar, on Creag Meaghaidh, initiated the development of open-face climbing in winter. Zero Gully (with MacInnes and Nicol) was the first big Nevis gully to fall. New climbs in the Cairngorms, on Ben Nevis, and in Devon, followed, Finally, a winter trip to Romsdal brought him into contact with the local guru, Arne Randers Heen, with whom he made an early winter ascent of the Romsdalhorn.

Patey's move to a practice in Ullapool took him into the centre of the least-developed area in Scotland. In the ensuing feast of new climbs, he did hundreds of routes, some of them solo. The most notable include The Nose Direct (VS, solo) on Fuar Tholl, the Cioch Nose in Applecross, the Gnome Wall (solo) on Ben Eighe, and many routes in the Fannichs and on the Tollie Crags. Numerous winter climbs on Ben Dearg and in Corriemulzie, and a scatter of climbs on most major crags between Ullapool and Cape Wrath – of which those on Sgurr an Fhidhleir are among the more formidable – also fell to his restless energy. Many of these crags, like Alladale Slabs (Whigmaleerie: 800ft, solo), had no previous routes. Despite his ineptitude as a swimmer, it was Patey who initiated and dominated the stack climbing mania, thus earning himself the title of 'Dr Stack'. The Old May of Hoy (with Baillie and Bonington in 1966) was followed by ascents of the most prominent smaller brethren, including The Old Man of Stoer and The Herdsman.

Clive Rowland and Tom Patey, June 1970.

The Maiden Stacks, Whiten Head, Sutherland.

Tom leading the last pitch on the first ascent.

Forays outside this northern kingdom continued to be fruitful, especially in winter. Creag Meaghaidh remained a favourite, producing a stream of routes of which Diadem and The Last Post were the most impressive. Occasional climbs were also made on the Ben. Most notable of all, however, was the winter traverse of the Cuillin Ridge with MacInnes, Robertson and Crabbe.

In the Alps, partnership with other leading mountaineers led to first ascents like the West Face of the Plan, the North West Face of the Aiguille Sans Nom, the North Face of the Point Migot and the West Face of the Cardinal. Tom's secret weapon was his great catalogue of alpine possibilities. He did his homework as meticulously as he wrote his articles. In 1969 his alpine prowess received full recognition when he was elected President of the Alpine Climbing Club (ACC).

Patey was an extreme individualist and often admitted that he had a 'healthy disregard for the rope'. 'Once in a while it is very refreshing to climb alone . . . By tradition the climber who habitually climbs alone is regarded as reckless. Nothing is further from the truth because if he were other than safe he would be dead.'

On ice, Tom's easy grace could be alarming. He would often impatiently throw away the rope and churn off with two axes and crampons, as on his phenomenal solo first ascent of the Winter Gridle of Creag Meaghaidh.

He was a gregarious man, and he carried his own indefinable atmosphere with him. He was also a great entertainer – in conversation, in lectures, and in his songs and articles. In the television spectacular game, Tom naturally became a key personality. His overall success in entertainment resulted from his ability to make satirical and penetrating analyses of all that was going on around him. His enormous vitality and enthusiasm, coupled with his warm personality, brought him many friends.

There was something youthful about Tom, a wild, devil-may-care gaiety within the discerning humour. He always showed his pleasure in climbing. Fate has intruded, prematurely cruel, on a man ever 'a little older in wisdom, a little younger in spirit'.

One Man's Mountains by Tom Patey. Gollancz, 1971.

Mountain 19. (1972).

This posthumously published volume consists of a collection of articles, songs and verses written by Patey during a period of almost twenty years of climbing. British climbing literature extends to a number of anthologies; but few post-war British writers justify personal treatment. That is a first measure of this book's importance. Some pieces specifically set out to show the main strands of development in Scottish winter climbing since the war; but, quite apart from these, Patey's insights into the personalities involved come nearer to giving an overall picture of the varied strains of development in British climbing than do many volumes which set out with that sole task. More than any other facet of British climbing, he illuminates the best elements in the interplay between friendship and competition, individualism and the social world of climbing – together with some of the least desirable. The author plays a dual role: he is both major protagonist and critic, extreme individualist and gleeful socialite, grinning from behind his squeezebox.

The man's enthusiasm radiates throughout, reflecting his love of action, his restless energy and his distaste for apathy or half-heartedness. This fire amounted sometimes to impetuosity, but it was his ability to turn mere events into happenings that endeared him to many of his friends. His enthusiasm or even haste reflected the real need to strike when the iron is hot, his consciousness of the importance of employing time to the best advantage to miss no opportunity.

The articles cover some major events in British climbing, like the ascents of Zero Gully, the Cuillin Ridge in winter, the traverse of Creag Meaghaidh, and a number of redoubtable adventures abroad and in good company. Another vaster volume could have been as adequately filled with more great climbs by the author, but perhaps that is hardly the point; for Patey was not just a climber of climbs, he was a shaper of events. To this end he had an ever-expanding file of ambitions awaiting the right day, and, if necessary, the right companions. He was a creator and a fulfiller of dreams for himself and others. Humour is ever present in the articles, but only gradually did he come to build articles round it. His early writings are about climbs. By the 60s, more of them, if not all of them, are about climbers while only the most outstanding rock features, like The Old Man of Hoy, are personalized and thereby given a greater part in the proceedings. It is the competition and friendship between climbers which is savoured, encouraged and engineered, while it remains at defensible levels. The hypocritical posturings of traditional elements in the British Climbing Society (BCS) and the multi-faceted manoeuvres of the new professionals in doubting collusion with commercialism are both lampooned, while the morbid predilections of Eiger fanaticism at its worst have appeal as a subject, and yet are decried in their inevitable outcome. 'Amid this seething anthill, one must not overlook the importance of Staying Alive.'

Egos fall like flies, though a few near-heroes survive the blast. Even those pricked and prodded are allowed a little sanctuary from the author's gibes. ('Caricature is the highest form of compliment'), but they are deprived of grounds for retort above all in that Patey was not self-righteous: he pilloried himself just as much as his contemporaries and his enduring friends.

As a climber he had little time for technology – the most avid practitioners of modern arts are subjected to singular scorn – but great respect for technique. To him, aids were the merest of means, an evil necessity at times, heavy to carry and slow to use if one had not lost them on the way. Conversely, what was all-important was morale. An avowed enemy of diffidence, he wrote jokes, stories, songs and verses that were wider ranging, more acrid, and less printable than the articles which form the bulk of the book. The songs and verses are thus less representative than the latter: they only hint at the keenness of his wit, tolerated by his subjects only because he presented them with such grace and charm, accompanied by the squeezebox music, in circles wide and friendly. If they seem less vivid on paper, their life and function should be recalled.

Naturally the volume leaves a great deal unsaid; yet it does say more than a thousand technical manuals. It especially underlines the absurdity of asking for the rationale behind the lunatic occupation of mountaineering.

Millennium (Foinaven, 1982)

Familiar tilting quartz, the slab of Dionard's biggest buttress dropped from sight, drawing the eye into a non-existent down-plunging girdle traverse. The tantalizing weakness beyond the big roof was already climbed, bruted down in 1969. The ice-smoothed walls of the left flanks have been ground out by past ice ages, sliced off 200ft from the ground. From the last trickle of slab it had then taken all day to climb two steep and precarious pitches into easier slabs above, and aids and tricks as well, with a pathetic stance between and no good belay.* Four years on and wanting no more of that, I stopped before on the traverse, belaying in comfort in a niche, and brought up Martin.† As he came, loping easily on the slab, I recalled the twelve years since our ill-fated attempt to make the first ascent of the Medlar on Raven Crag Thirlmere. The Medlar tree had been very small and waved around unnervingly when you stood on it. The gas pockets were positive but small, the rock very steep, but climbable; it ought to go free, but did not, either to us then or to the subsequent first ascent which Martin mooted and Chris forced.‡ But Martin had glandular fever, and I had only repeated the route last year. Now here was another problem.

There was an alternative to traversing or going back down. The overhang is really double and very big, but after Vector it became best always to expect that God had put holds there in anticipation of the coming of Joe Brown, especially in the steepest and most frightening places. Doubtless too he would have taken away all the holds on the slabbier bits in between, but we ought to be able to do those anyway. The rule was to get what runners you could, have a general idea where to go, but think only of the next few feet and of the contortions needed to climb them.

Martin picked up some extra gear, scowled and ambled off round a little rib. After delay and a few grunts he came back muttering. 'It was very steep,' which I knew, '. . . but worse, it was sodden, with water draining down the big crack and black hanging groove.' Everything had seemed pretty dry in the whole of Foinaven, lichen crunching to dust on two new routes yesterday on Creag Alasdair, but this was a kick in the teeth – it would be hard enough when it was dry, if that day ever came. There was a tiny tree in the hanging black groove.

*The Dialectic, Paul Nunn, C. Rowland, R. Toogood (1969).
†Martin Boysen.
‡Chris Bonington (1964).

The wan sun on distant Creag Shomhairle won, and we fled the blackness with hardly a twinge of regret. After all there were other more amenable crags and climbs nearby, and two more good new routes came in the next twenty-four hours.

Years passed, with only a visit or two to the Far Far North, and none which touched the big crag. Once or twice I walked past under the Castell Cidwm-like lower walls. Three routes seemed few on such a monster, and only Clive's and Ted's route ever repeated in a decade or more, but so what!* Always the big overhangs looked wet even at the driest times of the year. Whit passed Whit, and the Karakoram intervened. Sometime or other we climbed on The Cnoc a Mhadaidh, nearer in that long valley, fell flat on our faces as the British airborne reaction to war did its coast to coast run near ground level. But like Clo Mhor we never went back. Instead there were unclassifiable horrors on Creag Riabach, adventures with the sea.

So it was a question of keeping the idea alive, and as always in cold northern climes, choosing the time, but the 70s passed. Nor in May 1982 did the weather seem promising. In England and Wales some things dried, but it was nothing out of the ordinary. The only good reason for going that far was that the others wanted to go too, to break the mould.

There is increasing discipline south of the border, and it is bad. Rain spat at the windscreen on the A9, and we failed to find Clive, elevated of late to Laird of Cawdor. As lairds do, he had left for Gangotri in Northern India the day we drove up, but reckoning on the uncertainty of the times we ignored misleading telephone communication until we were well north of Perth. Then it was too late, and we slept in a mossy wood somewhere east of Culloden Moor. Still speckles of water fell on the endless single track road by Loch Shin. A pale grey sky promised nothing. Sheagra beach can be a romantic spot, white sand on an azure sea. A cold westerly echoed only the dread of the Norsemen, with sand in the eyes and harsh memory, Tom's squeezebox playing from deep inside a crowded tent and Glenmorangie, more than a decade ago. Four people stiff from the journey stalked the cliff tops as the surf rolled into detergent foamed zawns. There were no basking sharks to distract, thin memories only of children of all ages happily playing in the sea at midnight and carry-outs lost in the Oldshore cattle grid. The gneiss turns soon to Torridonian sandstone, the cliffs grow in stature, with fine lines from a mile, but the reality is a perverse alchemy, gold to dust, and birdshit.†

We walked back to the wispy green of the camping ground, and Christine rebuked the inaction by wandering south, flower-watching. Ted and Sheila Howard, Al Wright, Pete, George and his girlfriend has big tents, so we put our little ones in the sheltered lee.

---

*Cengalo – a nickname attached to Ted Howard for an obsessive desire to climb that mountain's NW ridge in the Bregaglia.

†Though in May 1987 Martin Boysen led an impressive crack (E4 6a) and wall (E3 5c) in this area, with Rab Carrington.

There was no more drizzle, and Bob thought there might be something to be done in the last zawn. So we went, and he led a little ramp from the low-water mark, chucking off superfluities. One rope length reached the top, but like all sea cliffs seriousness grabbed us straight away. Below was a capped slab, undercut in its turn by the sea. I thought I would do it, but it came almost out of the lowest water. Oh, dry, it would be nothing, but with irrational skating feet only the assurance on a wired nut made the drive up the crack seem feasible. Then the slab led on, very good rock with a roof above, one obvious way to go with only the slightest choice, diagonally, to the grey skyline. Ooze seeped here and there, and there was the usual sea stink of well-salted rotting decay. A short excursion on to the slab, and a very few brittle holds, were seductive in the general gneiss solidity. Sliding jams in the wet crack did not seem to matter once new fangled Friends stood close by, and it was not too long before Alec's fine tea at camp over the hump, and the pub.

In that short span from Sheagra to Cape Wrath it has not rained hard for weeks. There were any number of baked local noses to prove it. As so often the climatic barrier was very few miles south. So Whit Sunday had to be Foinaven for the whole beach party.

Strath Dionard is too long, in heat a shimmering bog beyond the midway becks. All greyness dissipated as we plodded three or four hours with the big sacks. Even the undersurface water gurgled below rather than sucking in half a leg. With food and fuel for a day or two the luxury of reaching Loch Dionard with the temperature in the upper 80s was too sensuous to be admitted in the land of the kirk. Alec, Bob, Christine and I put up the purple pyramid in the heat, conscious of the daze of incipient sunstroke. Ted's team came later, brewed and like us lay down. It was only later in the afternoon that action became possible.

The big buttress looked dry, even through the telephoto. But was it? Some time in the afternoon Alec traipsed towards it in red underpants, festooned with gear and body still smiling an Easter Verdon tan. Chris and Bob headed for a big white wall in the left sector of Urbhard's vast extent, an area usually streaming but now snuff dry. There was hope in the air.

I knew where to start. A little quartz wall led to a 50ft diagonal handhold, anyone could see that. There were old grass sods on moves, loose stones jammed in the tiny overhung ledge to be liberated. It looked easy, for a very short distance, but as soon as the first few moves were done, the atmosphere was there, with shiny smooth quartz bulges rearing up above in all directions. Fortunately it was dry here, and the long handhold turned into a standing place under a roof. A clutch of small wire belays took some fiddling before Alec came up.

Above it looked complicated, with a weeping scoop up and left across steep walls. Lines of seepage touched most holds. Alec stood about, probing and fingering at the sharp little fingerholds, throwing down some loose edges. Then suddenly he set off, sprawled wide in a bridge across a wet groove. A good handhold took him round a little arête into the scoop, which was wet but better protected. Above again, the wall steepened and the ooze covered all the critical holds. After quite a long time he came back, complaining all the while about my antique rack of gear.

This had not been anticipated. I had a conviction that he was going to sort this nasty piece of work and leave something less evil for me. In any case there was so much steep rock above that I could hardly contemplate the idea of either of us not getting up pitches once we had embarked. Fortunately the weather looked like holding, and we had all week.

Swapping rope ends took time. You could always abseil to the ground from here, I thought. With chill fingers, a creaking body and a mind even less well geared, the initial traverse seemed unnerving and the standing ledge in the scoop a haven. So I stayed a while, hanging nuts in little flakes to beef up the protection. Going on higher, a hex slipped into a wet scummy notch right next to the committing move. That felt better.

The move was horrible, a semi-layback with wet feet on slimy little holds, in a place where they ought to slide off under the leverage. There was no elasticity in muscles tight from an hour standing under the weeping roof, so that an inordinate amount of energy burned to almost no effect as the feet pedalled upwards. The reward was blissful, the comfort of a deep soggy handjam, at which point concentration on the hopeless footslithering miraculously evaporated. Protection above was bombproof, so that I launched straight on up to another overhang, but such confidence paled at the smoothness beyond its lip, and some back-pedalling became desirable. The coward's way led round a steep rib to a stance. It mirrored that below, including the relentless weep. An antiquarian at heart, I eventually put in a piton when the wires seemed too poor for the job in hand.

If Alec was annoyed at not doing the pitch below, he didn't show it. Instead he hardly stopped before moving up and folding his long body into a little niche under the next roof. His left foot kept stretching out and out, pawing around for a hold to balance, then he seemed to lurch out alarmingly, grasping a rickety spike on the lip. His legs went even wider apart, and a toe shifted up to the spike's point. Then he stood up on it, and was gone on to white walls above. Every inch of rope went out before he called me on. At the roof the moves turned awkward, though I should have been able to repeat his one-leg stand, but the fright at the idea of the spike parting from the rock seemed to prevent the essential muscle power from materializing. It was only with a great gut grunt that I went over. Beyond was easier and led into the anteroom of midway slabs.

Above, the great roofs loomed. It was time for tea and the first problems were solved, so we sidled off down the slabs, and through waist-deep heather to the tent where the others weren't back yet. They were tiny dots, high in the upper cliffs of Creag Urbhard, after climbing six or seven pitches of a route up wonderful smooth dry quartz walls. Ted's team meanwhile had done three long pitches into a hanging groove to their right, and left ropes hanging to return tomorrow. I remembered looking up it half a decade or more before, when water poured from every cranny. Ted had decided then.

Avoiding the drink – Am Beauchaille. *Photo by Tony Riley.*

Am Beauchaille – the route. *Photo by Tony Riley.*

Christine Crawshaw leading the second ascent of Dark Angel, Sheagra.

When Christine and Bob got back we ate in the semi-dark near midnight, accompanied by few midges and a still warm breeze. In the night the purple pyramid became so hot that everybody had to escape outside just after dawn, and by 6.30am it was sunbathing temperature. Loch Dionard hardly stirred.

There was brew after brew, a full works breakfast. Eventually Ted and co. set off for the crag, while Sheila embarked on an extended sunbathing programme. Meanwhile Pete Phipps sorted his flies in anticipation of trout for tea. I sauntered to see Chris and Bob start climbing, and back to strong black coffee. Then it was time to go.

The heat was back and we sweltered in underpants to the cliff. With a bandolier of Friends and nuts we crossed the slabs, seeing an old red rusted belay piton, a relic from earlier forays, *en route*. The little midway stance looked much the same, and above there was no view but overhangs. Perched there we tossed a coin. It was mine.

I was apprehensive upon entering the first groove. Still water bled from the corner crack and etched out blacker spidery lines down the dark rock. The tiny tree remained, and green moss in each notch or cranny. The right black wall is near vertical, and sliced off at base in a roof. The left pushes ever out, Skull-like.

The whole is but the first hung groove, the *hors d'oeuvre* before the even bigger swelling of the buttress above. A natural reaction was to hang runners round most things in sight, which once done, justified pushing off up the groove. After a slippery bridge round the initial overhang, it was a question of faith in the dwarf tree, to which I hung unashamed while rooting moss and loose small stones from the thin crack in the diagonal corner above. The slick foot on the wet wall gave no grounds for confidence, and dutch courage only came with a supersolid nut in the crack to justify real climbing. Still it was an insecure process, with left fingers stuck into the slippery crack and feet planted on little edges, as the left wall pushed the groove ever out. A point came when a leanaway jug was just in reach, but it meant leaving the crack and corner and launching up, scuttling up the feet behind in a high step prior to reaching a left finger lock from some higher flat holds. Rather frantically I hurtled loose blocks off on the right, and they trundled in uproar as I heaved my 13 stones up on to the shelf, fearing all the while a sudden slip on still slimy shoes, or a sudden seizure of the claws. Amazingly there was not just a slab between the roofs, but a square and fine ledge for a belay.

An excited brain forced the biggest Friend I had into a crack above, out of an irrational fear of losing invaluable gains in a sudden geriatric totter off the ledge. Other excellent belays, based rather on the principle 'Enough is not sufficient' followed. Above, the biggest roofs of all loomed, and I began to develop a severe case of belayer's neck through trying to observe the inexorable line to which we were committed while bringing Alec up. Cold at first, he warmed to it, and grinning evilly at its excellence.

Both of us then stared at the prize. Reverse Vectorish, a steep thin ramp ran up through the big overhang, cut through by space at one point. In 80ft, with roofs opening up below, it eventually broke through to the large expanse of grey slabs above. There were imponderables, like whether there were holds on critical sections, and how much protection there would be. But what a pitch!

Alec grinned still, but with a frown, as he went up for first inspection. There was a slight easing of tension as one or two small wires lipped in under the first big roof. A traverse right followed across a slippery weep. There, things stood still for a while, and with difficulty he dried at least one PA toe. After much thought, and with me concentrating very hard on the rope, he straddled up, bridged on 'nowt' except wet vertical ribs. A hold appeared, so he just kept going to yet another roof, and protection god-given, as it so often is in the worst of places. The time-honoured head lock under the overlap helped while he contemplated the last traverse out right. After a bonus frequently comes the pain, and the footholds ran out as the angle of the slab eased, while the rock above bulged. A big groping hand on the end of a very stretched right arm reached a hold, he went for it, with feet jiggling about across the slab out of his sight below, then there was a pinch and a pull, and he slid a shoulder into a little groove to take off the weight and was there, but for the rope-drag and the shouting. The drag proved very real, and took a lot of heaving, but 20ft above he pronounced himself secured.

Why is it that, once the tension of the lead is dissipated, seconding can seem so frightening? This was one of those pitches where a second's error can lead to a plunge into space, but that is unlikely to be so fearsome as a leader's fall. Yet it always feels infinitely worse, and the wet section especially involved absurd, insecure contortions. Beyond the lip though, it eased, and Alec laid back at the belay. The grey walls above were obviously climbable, though they forced a few detours on us, but in an hour it was in the bag.

Ted had completed his route, and Bob and Christine repeated it in the last light. We packed in the morning to try to do another on The Cnoc a Mhadaidh the next day, while the latter pair decided to repeat our route. Both parties left early, going in their different directions. Alec and I simultaneously let in exhilaration and fatigue before The Cnoc, and made only the tiniest unsuccessful feint on a new line. Then we walked out, along the stalkers' path by the peaty stream and back to the high road.

We had been far away, discovering red-headed female bombshells in the unlikely bar of Riconich, and more predictable pints of heavy, and slept like babes, before voices raised us from the dead at two or three in the morning. 'Yes, we did it, brilliant, it took over eleven hours, what a pitch . . . !' and so on. Then the midges broke the moratorium and bit hard, driving us inside before the mud from their midnight ramblings in the great swamp of Dionard could be washed away. It was late next morning before we woke, even later after washing, eating, brewing, sunbathing, sorting . . . then, first ascent and first female lead complete, it was choc ices and a swim.

102

Scottish Guides

Scottish Climbs *by H. MacInnes. Constable, 1971.*

For climbers who like a crag, or even a mountain, to themselves, and who still appreciate large scale, remoteness and seriousness, and are prepared to dig out their boots and walk, the MacInnes books should provide an inexpensive vision of Paradise Regained. Like all visions, it will have defects in detail, but by the time the climber reaches the point where he can criticize the margins between IV and V–, he will have gone beyond the introductory stages for which the book caters. Personally, I find the vision a timely one, when there is such a risk of sinking into a potage of minutiae in the open air bedlams* south of the border.

Polyphemus Gully (Lochnagar)

K. Wilson (Ed). Cold Climbs. *Diadem, 1983*

In the Alps 6am jars the senses, but if it is bright and clear the pleasure soon takes over. Crouching in a Scottish bothy as the wind wails and the snow sifts in through the door is quite another sensation.

Somehow a pan gets to the Primus, bacon sizzles, more bodies stir and groan. Long before the real awakening (there is the secret) it is a long plod by the snow-drifted path towards Lochnagar. Mound on mound of boring heather. Mile on mile it seems, always with clouds holding back the dawn. How can it be barely freezing when the wind buffets so hard? There is a temptation to go back, but what has Ballater, or even Royal Braemar to offer the likes of us, still half-city-slickers from Manchester, Britain's counter-capital?

Wet-warm at the col, the wind comes from the south-west, a hot winter gale from somewhere in the Canaries. Still it seems better to press, for any other approach achieves nothing in the North. A little frost from a mid-week freeze remains as incentive. Will it be enough?

The great chute of Raeburn's Gully is barely visible in a driving mist. Not knowing the cliff well we use it to locate Polyphemus. A swathe of ice droops in from the left out of some unseen recess behind. That must be it. Despite forgotten complex descriptions the way looks obvious, as far as we can see, which is not beyond a first 100ft or so of steepish ice. More worrying is a trickle of water emerging from under the ice. The south-westerly is at work already. Companions go different ways. Some go back.

I sort out a belay below the ice and Bob Toogood sets off up an ice chute and then by a delicately-carved traverse right to an upper fall. An overlap steepens it all. A solitary ice piton gives a hint of security but Bob prefers to trust his workshop-made hammer, a ferocious tomahawk-like object which bites firmly

*Now supplemented by indoor ones (1988) – known as climbing walls.

Lochnagar. *Photo by Tony Riley.*

despite the melt. Leader and rope disappear in murk. The waiting game leads to cold feet, hands and a shiver or two. A duvet would have been nice. 'Have we anything to eat?' 'Not much.' Melt water soaks through a porous old anorak. He stops, obviously taking his time to engineer a thorough belay. Then the slack rope goes out quickly and without a call. It is my time to go.

The melting ice crunches a little under the crampons. The new slightly curved implements seem to work, but lack security. They have too few teeth or is it the lack of angle? After all, they are ten years old already – it's hard to tell. The pitch is not too steep, but there are awkward steps and some traversing. At the stance Bob is well satisfied, grinning in elfish pleasure.

Some easier stuff follows, nice but unremarkable. Then the gully rears and Bob takes a stance out on the right wall. A wind howls above but only sends the occasional whumph of spindrift upon us. No problem on easy ground. But Bob does not like this belay. It's solid but I weigh 13 stones to his 9. The prospect ahead concentrates the mind wonderfully as the upper gully tilts into sight 25ft above; a hanging gutter. Some rocks between us are steep and almost devoid of snow or ice. Black and naked, short but mean. Out investigations reveal no outflanking move, so up it is. Grade 4/5, like any other, can mask a multitude of sins, especially of omission.

A very long Lost Arrow piton materializes in my left hand, brought for just such circumstances. I beat it into a crack at face-level. It sinks in as far as the very finely engineered little eye. In goes Bob's rope for a belay and mine on an extra karabiner as a runner. Things look better. I move up stiffly into a corner. I'm icing up with the wet and cold, building up for a rheumy old age. A few little rock ledges take crampons and 5 or 6ft are won. There's nothing much for the implements. Scraping up carefully in a bridged position allows a long left-hand reach with the axe. The pick swings upwards and lodges in God knows what, but it holds, though the spindrift makes it hard to see what is going on. Bob huddles into his hood. It is a familiar scene. It is now a question of using the axe and bridging to gain a little more height. Then the hammer should go in too and all should be well. With luck.

Carefully feet are worked up on precious little, front-points splayed wide on rock. Then the right hand freed to make a longish swing with the hammer, the target safely a foot or two above the axe. The right wall is in the way and it is awkward. The hammer fails to lodge. Feet are braced harder, axe grip tightens and another hammer blow at a different target area. As the hammer swings something shifts. The axe! Whoops! It's too late. The axe parts company from a bit of ice to which it had feigned attachment. Straddled legs remain momentarily frozen in position and my body tips over backwards before crampons skate off the rock walls and the gully below approaches at speed. One unfortunate foot catches the wall and is yanked round, splaying crampon points in all directions.

'Anything broken?' enquires Bob as I hang there. 'Maybe,' is all I can manage in reply.

Fortunately Toogood is a cool customer, and for him climbing only gets interesting when he is totally committed. This was not yet the case. It was evident that the top was near and as light was short, up might yet be the quickest way. I struggled back one-footedly to the belay, feeling painfully sick and dependent, and remembering a broken leg on Monte Civetta. We had got out of that, so why not this? 'Good thing about the peg,' we agreed. It winks, unmoved, as Bob prepares to lead. Darkness looms and I am glad he is a potholer.

After swapping ropes he moves up into the corner a little rustily, working up his concentration and brandishing the great black Sheffield tomahawk. His wiry legs stick out precariously in much the same position that I had achieved. Shivering with shock I grip the rope. There is no messing. The tomahawk whips backwards and slams into the ice, then Bob follows as if attached to it by a string. I sigh with relief despite the pain and the dark. There is little to see above, but the ropes keep going out until Bob camps under a biggish cornice to belay. With a tight rope I wobble, mostly on one foot, up the steep section, leaving my beloved piton behind, half hoping that some future sufferer might also find it useful.

The cornice takes no time. Bob digs and shovels and ferrets a way into the arm-deep slops before moving out into the maelstrom above. It is a cold thaw and a white-out, and about 6pm, late in January. A compass helps the way down, but a bent ankle does little to aid judgement, and for hours we seem to plod trackless wind-blown snow. Just as we are convinced that we have lost the route we hit the path to Glen Muick. Long after midnight, on the motorable path below the Loch, I go to sleep until Bob gets back with the red van. At the bothy Ted Howard adds insult to injury, regaling us with tales of booze and dance in Ballater: 'One of the best Saturday nights the lads have ever had.'

THE ALPS – DOLOMITE DREAMS

In early imaginings, the Dolomites and the Bavarian limestone mountains played a key part. Stimulated by Hermann Buhl's book and subsequent reading, and by the accounts of the possibilities given by Les Brown and others, I had to go. It was my first destination – to the Tre Cima di Lavaredo in 1961 – as a (small) fee paying passenger in Bev Clarke's old van from Ambleside. Though I was scarcely aware of it at the time, Richard and I were being pointed in the right direction by older climbers, in this case Ackers Atkinson, Bev and 'Handsome' Harry, a merchant seaman whose primary talent was to reduce women to drooling condition within minutes in any situation. Via a seedy night club in Munich, of which I have only the vaguest of memories, we careered to Cortina, the first of annual visits for seven years.

Tofana – Pilastro de Rozes

SUMC Journal *(1964)*.

Purple bellied clouds wallowed around the Tre Cima. A chance to climb had arrived at last, after the weeks of impatience and the long drive. Margaret filled us with bread rolls and sweet strong coffee and retired back to bed as we set off.

'Pilastro'. The name rolls off the tongue and is full of associations. Buhl perched on the lip of roof after roof 'the abyss ever deepening below'. The tale of Trevor Jones's sack, which penduled beyond the pimples of the Cinque Torre and the ribbon of road, only to return to a position suspended 'sixty feet out in space'.

It was a pleasant amble to the start, ideal on the first route of the season. Nor was there any introductory rubbish. From the outset the rock was steep, mixed grey and yellow with a comforting piton every now and again. On the stances one wondered whether the distant clouds meant bad weather.

After a few pitches of manificent rock climbing we came upon an enormous hole, green and dark. Though we tried to calculate its depth it proved beyond our puny mathematical resources. It was really just an excuse to fester, so after a while Martin ambled off onto the yellow stuff above. There were two lines of overhangs, with a frightening-looking steep wall between.

The first of these would have been hard had my guardian angel not pointed out a crafty piton in a little hole. As it was, one just swung out and pulled up on big jugs. Martin led the long steep wall, where holds and one's feet always threatened to swing out. He belayed in etriers below the upper roof. Seconding carefully I was at last able to clip into a few pegs below him. He then leapt over the top roof, even using aid at one point. It was a bit steep, as he said.

So this was the famous chimney, a horrible green and yellow niche blocked by overhangs and exuding unpleasant moisture. A little stone wall on the ledge showed that some indefatigable multi-day party had passed by. They had left us the biggest wedge I had seen in my life. As we hadn't a block and tackle we left it with the naked women in the litter of German magazines.

The chimney was mine, or it was going to have me; it depends how you look at it. So I stepped into its maw and wiggled up the back until there was no alternative but to traverse out above the horrible void. At the end, perched on one wall a rather strange motion from a squatting position seemed necessary to reach a peg stuck into a bit of firewood. However after standing on that a mighty ring peg came into sight. After a lurch up, it went on a little further but nothing much stuck in my mind.

There was a ramble for a few pitches up easier cracks and chimneys, and a traverse, and then the top. The pace was beginning to tell by now. The wine in the refuge at the col between the two Tofanas helped us along.

Margaret made lunch and we lazed away the afternoon in the sun. By evening she had conveyed us to the Civetta which was to pose quite different problems.

Civetta (1987)

There came route on route, magic names. Livanos on the Sualto, a missed descent and cold, gearless bivouac. Andrich-Fae on the Punta Civetta, more smoothly done and back for tea. Adders scattered from the baking slabs of the Civetta's south-east flank. A 'call-out' to carry a casualty for several hours along the path to the Coldai Hut.

Then came the Philip-Flamm; Martin and I solo for a 1,000ft, overtaking the authors of the Saxonweg on the Cima-Grande before they were out of bed, up the critical middle section without a pause, though Martin had broken his glasses and had to follow my verbal directions, climbing, as ever, near faultlessly. Then the falling rock, blood spurting, broken leg, little memory except good tight ropes from above and shifting the awkward weight upwards in a rope sling, using every trick in the book to second the pitches. On top still by 5pm we hobbled three-legged round terraces to God knows where, bivouacked, climbed a band next morning, hobbled more, until the Torrani Hut came in sight. At least we had done the climb inside a day, and had friends at the Coldai to heed the call of the Torrani Hut custodian.

'One of these old classics . . .' – The Bonatti Pillar, 1964.

SUMC Journal *(1965).*

'All the rope'; the usual shout as the drag stopped me dead, eyes already searching for a piton. Above the small ledge an enormous convex slab swept out of the dark couloir to the golden square cut rib, only to be chopped away into the overhanging voids of the West Face. Below its merging into vast red-brown walls, a few piton dribbling cracks indicated the way.

Purple shadows surged upwards from the valley, pushing the last sunlight towards the apex of the pillar. My friends below were in twilight, and in the west thin vanguard black streaks aligned themselves across a light blue sky, their lower edges livid above the limestone hills. Mont Blanc retained its usual nightcap of fluffy cloud. Quitting the valley in the inky blackness of early morning, at this furthest probe it was as if we had been flung on to the mountain. The long, gasping flog from the Chamonix camp via Montenvers and the Mer de Glace in the night, then six hours in the ominous shadow of the ice-plastered couloir, the last hours of fine rock climbing, all seemed to have passed in a matter of moments. The Bonatti Pillar in its magnificent reality was transfigured from an idea into a succession of strenuous cracks, precarious traverses and snow ledges. On the pillar it felt safe and seemed to matter little that we were a few pitches short of our admittedly ambitious objective, the

Holding the rope for Les Brown. West Face of the Dru, 1962. *Photo R. Evans.*

Petit Dru in November.

bivouac place below the big roof, though I recalled photographs of a blood-spattered Hamish MacInnes, a pensive Paul Ross.

Pat, Mick and Brian had the pulpit below prepared while I abseiled. The deep powder snow was flattened, awkward stones removed and positions chosen. Gleefully the sacks were upended, emitting duvets, 'long johns', some the worse for wear, stoves, food and a bivvy sheet – all that equipment cursed silently when calves cramped or biceps ached. Beyond the flickering light of the brew stoves, evil weather gobbled up the world in darkness and wind. Inside the old, warm, familiar bivvy sheet I soon slept.

A violent smack in the earhole amid a salvo of buffetings, shocked me awake, inside a balloon swinging out over space. Lying awkwardly away from the opening below Pat, claustrophobia forced me to poke a cagouled head into the raw outer atmosphere. Mick and Brian were huddled, two-tone humps in the snow and hail. It was not yet midnight. I retreated.

Eventually it was as light as it ever would be. The Flammes des Pierres shredded swirling clouds; fearful rumblings came once or twice from below; it snowed spasmodically. Inside the sheet life was tolerable but outside the wind drove freezing particles through every weakness of the clothing, powder snow lay thick on every projection, while the rope left in place up the slabs above beat relentlessly on the rock.

Above, at least twelve pitches to the summit and an unknown descent in a white-out; below, 800ft of rock and a 1,000ft of treacherous ice gully; little hope of a lull once the storms had begun. The debate was short and to the point. Abandoning two karabiners and a sling, we pulled down my abseil rope and dug out another sound block to start the steep descent.

The rock descent went with surprising smoothness. Once or twice the ropes seemed likely to jam and gave anxious moments. Seven abseils or so and we were donning crampons at the base of the pillar.

The upper couloir ice is steep, but had been well frozen with only a thin powder layer on the previous day. Now, wet snow lay on top of ice everywhere except where small avalanches had occurred. The old steps had to be much deepened, when they were recognizable, on the 400ft traverse of the upper basin of ice. A few rock outcrops have some security. Once, a wedge of ice containing Pat's steps slid away towards the rognon, and only the rope checked a long toboggan.

A spike, encumbered with weathered relics of rope, provides the first abseil point in the true left bank of the couloir. Things went well enough for several abseils to the narrows above the West Face exit. At a point where an ice axe belay had been used in ascent, the melting snow had revealed a stout rock peg. However, as the morning progressed, the peaks resolved to lighten themselves of all they could jettison. Water poured between snow and ice and occasional stones began to thump down. Once, unable to reach the abseil point below, I stood in an ice step in the couloir, while Pat descended to another peg somewhat above me. A huge stone clattered quite suddenly from the Flammes des Pierres and disappeared momentarily into the upper basin. It reappeared, trundling over the rock steps above us, plummeting down the gully centre, its crashing echoing between the containing walls. Feeling exceedingly vulnerable, I stood in my rickety ice step, gripping my axe ready for an avoiding dash on the unstable surface snow, the bulk of which was continually increased by the great swirls from the grey clouds around us. The rock bounded down just above us and, as if by a miracle, disappeared through the crust of snow. The snowy blanket saved us from bombardment later that day.

After a limbo of wet abseils, with wet hands, on streaming rocks and ice, Pat and I reached the last steep wall. In the couloir we abseiled in two parties, to avoid being too bunched together. Pat swung down the last wall and over the bergschrund and I hurried after him, accompanied by a salvo of small stones. Grasping the rope between our four hands, we fled down the snow cone below, into the mists. The rognon was safe, and there we awaited our companions.

After some anxious, uncomfortable waiting, we heard a distant shout from beyond the streaming boulders, which were the limit of vision. 'A rope stuck.' Now, the first sensation was relief. A little later, among soaking junipers and crumbling moraine, came disillusionment; beyond, fatigue.

The Capucin

SUMC Journal *(1963–4).*

> A squat ugly yellow face
> It leers in its over verticality
> Epstein crude, a narrow pyramid
> Grotesque challenge to the creeping men
> Progressing on evaporating snow,
> Gazing far away, growing to it all
> Deigning to judge Mont Blanc's cold snows
> The Aiguille Moine's shiny rotten tooth
> The expanse of Switzerland's glittering blanket.
> Perversity of the insect,
> To cling to this eroded spear
> And feign enjoyment between the shivers.
> To descend glad while the giant stays
> His heavy browed overhang and cowl
> Balanced to the roots in creaking snow
> Surrounded by the lifeless world
> The cold contempt of the altitudinous eroding wind.

Some concerns of two decades have lost little immediacy . . .

The Grand Capucin, East Face. *Photo Mountain.*

The Alps and Alpinism, Karl Lukan (Ed), introduction by Christian Bonington and translated by Hugh Merrick. Thames and Hudson, 1968.

Mountain 2. *(1968)*.

Have the European Alps lost their 'soul'? Their valleys are patched with a rash of extortionate suburbia, their mountains overrun. They are encrusted with hotels, huts, paths, ladders and latrines, and festooned with cables, crosses, 'one-up' record books, pitons and commemorative plaques. Men blast through Mont Blanc itself and fly far above it. At the same time the tone of alpinism is set by climbers who may be as much motivated by a newspaper contract as by aestheticism; men who will make a great climb fit the logistics of camera placement, or who will make a lesser climb great on behalf of the press barons. With such a situation, is it not reasonable to suppose that both the Alps and alpinism have suffered mutual debasement?

The authors of *The Alps and Alpinism* argue, sometimes greatly, sometimes passionately, but always with conviction, that the Alps have lost neither their meaning nor soul, and that both survive into the atomic age. This handsomely produced volume compares the present with the past, and finds that each has its advantages and charms. Yet the prophets of doom are fully quoted – nowhere more succinctly than in the cartoon in which that great climber of the late nineteenth century, Hermann van Barth, gazes down scornfully from heaven on a ladder of pitons (cartoon – Ernst Platz, 1911). A vein of optimism nevertheless overcomes the doubts. Death-fixation climbing, which is probably confined to relatively few, is relegated to the backroom. Emperor Maximilian and the subject of mountain accidents are dealt with in a few telling photographs and illustrations. Generally, the Alps are seen to have a beneficial, almost sublime, influence which is likely to continue for long into the future. Chris Bonington's foreword fits the theme well, although his comparison between mountain thirst and drug addiction may only be valid for the minority of those who enjoy mountains.

The theme of this book is indeed ambitious. It seeks, predominantly in pictures, but also in words, to portray the development of the European alpine world: from Neanderthal man, crouching in mountain caves, to today's specialists in climbing, skiing, canoeing, photography and art. Although this is ambitious enough in itself, the authors have also endeavoured to follow up a multiplicity of subordinate subjects. As it stands, the book is thus an imperfect attempt at the impossible! Adequate coverage of some aspects of the project, particularly in the sections on climbing and skiing, has led inevitably to the skimping of others. So unusual are many of the prints, and so excellent many of the photographs, that the remaining literature seems redundant. From the cover onwards the pictures tell the story – protecting the alpine image, stressing the continuities of alpinism, and justifying the sport in an age when there is such antithesis between its need for remoteness and its popularization.

Too wide to jump, too far to fall.

Those who seek a survey of the latest extremes of the Alps will be disappointed. The setting of much of the book is pre-1939. It attempts to depict the wide background to alpine development. Visiting climbers have a habit of forgetting that people live in those deep valleys. The book, characteristically, begins at that point, and with telling realism quotes Guido Rey, writing of the mountain dwellers: 'Perhaps the troubles and the worries that appertain to town life are not apparent in the mountains, but there is instead a sort of stupor, a dull continuous suffering . . . hopeless resignation to fate . . .'

It is thus that the authors achieve so much in short space, by adept quotation and masterly illustration. The words fall aside and one follows the pictures through a multitude of subjects including superstition; alpine dangers; war in the Alps; hunting; the Alps as a health resort; the face of the climber; women in the Alps; night on the mountain; storms; mountain railways and refuges, and so on. This is a book to dip into again and again, a fine compendium with a breadth of view that is itself compelling. It is somewhat emotional, and occasionally the overall logic is obscure, but the project was a bold one and a narrow view would have killed it. That the Alps seem alive at the end is a tribute to the book's success.

> So take heed bergkameraden
> Do not venture on the Face
> For the spectre of John Harlin
> Waits for you to take his place
> Another soul sent to Valhalla
> Another murder for the wall
> For the Eigerwand in winter
> Is the hardest climb of all.
> Song by Tom Patey

A New Direction – The Alps in Winter

Illustrated London News (*September 1979*).

In recent years a new wave of successful British winter alpinists has emerged.

British alpinism has boomed in the last two decades. In 1961 the Eigerwand had not been climbed by a British party when a German group climbed it in winter. Most British alpinists boggled. Five years later Dougal Haston joined four Germans who completed the Eiger Direct, a new route in winter. This was a multi-day effort, using a great deal of manpower and equipment; but it was a major feat. Slowly a new dimension in British mountaineering was emerging.

More than twelve years have passed since the Eiger Direct, and from a British perspective much has changed. Though the élite of British climbing has suffered sad losses – including Ian Clough on Annapurna, Mick Burke on Everest and Haston in 1977 in a skiing accident – the British are now outstandingly successful in the Alps and uniquely active throughout the world in seeking and solving new mountaineering problems. The fund of proven

Dougal Haston attempting the winter ascent of the Central Couloir, Grandes Jorasses. *Photo by Chris Bonington.*

experience in Britain is greater than at any other time and there is a core of active climbers who live in the limbo between total commitment to climbing and the need to eat. Ironically, the few household heroes who are fully professional are usually past their prime. Thus the great success stories, particularly in the Himalaya, ultimately rest on a considerable number of people with great technical ability and mountain experience. Many have concentrated their energies on winter alpinism and alpine-style ascent in areas other than the Himalaya.

In the past the British alpinist could be easily parodied for his dependence on guides and money. By the late 50s he had been replaced by '*das* blue-jeans', the young, keen and impecunious denizens of the illegal fringe camp sites in the major alpine resorts. Such climbers were usually capable in technical rock climbing, learned in Britain, but lacked mountain sense and panache on the snow and ice. Though many major ascents were completed in the 60s a few weeks in the summer could not always overcome the insular practices of British climbers.

Recently there have been signs that this era is over. Increasingly the best British mountaineers are active in the Alps summer and winter. The siege tactics used on the Eiger Direct are no longer deemed necessary or desirable. Developments in ice-climbing equipment and technique, speed ascent, and clothing have improved to extend survival time in harsh environments. Some years ago Joe Tasker and Dick Renshaw ascended the north face of the Eiger in winter in a manner as apparently controlled as the German ascent in 1961. Since then small parties have attempted and sometimes completed winter climbs on the most difficult faces ranging from the Dolomites to Mont Blanc. There is more patience in learning new skills, including skiing, and more readiness to assess weather and conditions and to make use of expert local knowledge. Perhaps most important of all, though, many rock and ice skills can be learnt in Britain.

The best climbers are coming to know the great alpine faces extremely well and their judgements in all conditions are more reliable than previously. Nevertheless, alpine winter ascent involves several days with the mountain in conditions of isolation much greater than can be found in the summer months. Indeed this emptiness re-creates the mountain experience for many who have learned to loathe the summer hordes. Both climbing and bivouacs are in sub-zero temperatures. Progress is slow and risk of frostbite serious, and though there are long, stable periods of weather the conditions are such that it is essential to hit on one of these in order to reach the climbs, complete them and descend. Winter is attractive because it extends climbing beyond the limits of technical rationality – more advanced techniques merely allow the risks taken to be widened. One must enjoy the adversity, extreme as it is, to keep pushing on when success seems remote.

Many of the biggest North face climbs have now been conquered at least once in winter but that scarcely detracts from their ferocity. The Grandes Jorasses and the North face of Les Droites are two of the most serious alpine climbs in the Mont Blanc area and in the Alps. In the last week of February 1978 Rab Carrington and Al Rouse set out to climb the 4,000ft of the North-East spur of Les Droites. They have climbed together for many years and are among the most experienced British alpinists. They had made at least one serious attempt or successful climb in the Alps each winter since 1974–5. They succeeded on this and a number of other important winter ascents, and their efforts were imitated and surpassed by a small group of other British climbers. Notable were Dave Wilkinson, Bill Barker, Andy Parkin who made the second solo winter ascent of the Walker Spur, and Roger Baxter-Jones who soloed the Charmoz North Face. Others have followed, never great in number or as spectacular in their ascents as some much publicized French solo climbs, but worth while and pioneering nevertheless.

Roger Baxter-Jones (1950–85)

Alpine Journal (*1987*).

Born in London, Roger came north to Leeds in 1968 to study English at the University. It did not catch his enthusiasm, and he shifted into rock climbing with the talented Leeds group of the day, living it up, working at Centresport

Roger Baxter-Jones not enjoying monsoon and leeches *en route* to Jannu, alpine style, 1977. *Photo by B. Hall.*

Takaoh Hoshini after the third winter ascent of the Walker Spur, Grandes Jorasses.

and teaching dry skiing. A solid rock climber, he knew from the talent of some of his friends that he was unlikely to be tops. So he chose different ground.

After doing the major alpine routes in summer early in the 70s, he soon turned to winter, trying the Super couloir on Mont Blanc de Tacul with Paul Braithwaite in 1972. His skiing was ever more developed, with a drive, enthusiasm and calculated risk well beyond the norm even among mountaineers. He had a practical side to his nature, securing his accommodation for three years of rather enforced mature studenthood in Sheffield by refurbishing the old house in which he lived for its owner. He got his degree but the frustrations of study probably required such a release for volcanic energies. When he could not reach the Alps he made intense forays on to British mountains, especially in winter, where he was a formidable exponent of 'mixed' climbing. Perhaps most notable was his ascent of Red Slab on 'Cloggy' with Paul Braithwaite in the winter of 1979, but whatever he did, he enjoyed.

He could hardly wait to escape from the claustrophobia of English existence, a trait which he perhaps shared with his sister, who worked for the EEC. He made the second ascent of the Whymper Spur Direct on the Grandes Jorasses with Nick Colton in the mid-70s and in 1977 skied down the Vallée Blanche and across from the Dent du Requin to below the North Face of the Aiguille des Grands Charmoz, made the first winter solo ascent of it, returned to Chamonix and skied down, again, for his skis. RBJ's hard work and talents were beginning

117

to pay off in a field that suited his massive energies, stamina and calculated optimism.

An obvious candidate for the Himalaya, he joined Rab Carrington, Al Rouse and Brian Hall in their bold alpine-style ascent of Jannu in 1978. In 1980, after trying the South-East Ridge of Makalu with Doug Scott and Georges Bettembourg, he almost succeeded in a solo ascent. In 1982 he played a notable part in the new route on Shisha Pangma with Scott and Alex McIntyre, again climbing in alpine style. In the following year came Broad Peak, with Jean Afanassieff as partner, climbing in two pairs with Andy Parkin and Al Rouse. He then made two attempts on K2. The first was foiled when Jean became unwell at high altitude. It was a mark of RBJ's determination that he then recruited a Spanish companion and again climbed alpine style beyond 8,000m to be foiled by bad weather on the uppermost part of the route. It would have been the first alpine-style ascent.

Meanwhile Roger picked off an impressive number of first winter ascents in the Mont Blanc Range and worked as an off-piste ski guide there. He picked up on inner game theories of sports performance and tried their application to skiing. One of Britain's leading mountaineers, a member of the Alpine Climbing Group (ACG) Committee for years, and certainly one of the strongest ever, he was a top off-piste skier, and a mountaineer of impeccable judgement, able to guide on routes of the highest standards with a considerable margin. He avoided the trap of expedition mania, which can prevent mountaineers from keeping up their 'bread and butter' climbing and enjoyment. In recent years he was a pillar of the Chamonix Franglaise. The place's cosmopolitanism and endless changes delighted him and fitted his temperament; he was a major performer in its raucous modern circus. At the same time his sympathies were ever more French, in language, tastes and attitudes and in autumn 1983 he married Christine Devassoux. They moved into a house in rue des Sauberands, with her daughter Melanie; he took French nationality and membership of the Guides Bureau. RBJ became a part of Chamonix and could stand back from the crowds.

It seemed natural that, when Andy Parkin was badly injured in Switzerland in 1984, it was Roger and Christine who were at the centre of organizing help and relaying messages in Chamonix, co-ordinating the concern of French and British friends, while feeding, accommodating and entertaining them.

Of late he avoided the Himalaya, though for how long one always wondered. He died with a friend client on 8 July 1985, when a serac fell on the North Face of the Triolet, in a classic *mort d'un guide*.

Albigna Interlude (1987)

Sunday morning we moved. After the alpine starts for film work 6.15am was luxury. The Volkswagen van juddered down the St Moritz cobbled hills, then more smoothly on to the Milan highroad.

No wind ruffled the lakes. As yet no sailboard gaudied their expanse. The Nietzsche memorial plaque, on a discreet bend, slipped past, as it had with Al as we roared by on the Gold Flash twenty years before, aiming for the North-East Face of the Piz Badile. Soon the high valley rim dropped away into the Maloja Pass, and we descended to the Albigna cableway.

A few brown-faced boys and girls up from Milan clustered by the kiosk to pay. It would be the second *cabina* for us. Below the sun level as yet, the Romansch valley spread towards Vicosoprano and Bondo. Granite boulders littered the fields. The river ran fast, blue and white, between hay barns and conifers. The road was unmistakably Italian, all Roman round arches along its edges. Fourteen years ago, with a one-year-old child, Hilary and I had camped down there. One night we were interrogated. 'Wo ist mein Bustenhalter?' This caused a moment's deliberation. How were we to explain that a cow had eaten it?

Comparatively the buttress of Piz Cengalo had been a doddle.

The *téléphérique* is ancient, but still somehow relaxing after multiple helicopter flights. It had been a workers' *cabina* for dam building. The dam wall came near and we alighted. A short walk right took us above its too pervasive presence, with wide views into the interior of the range. One path led left, to a place where we had seemed to spend weeks abseiling from tiny spikes, before repairing to the Albigna hut. Today there were to be neither film crew supplies nor filmic tedium.

Abseil in Albigna.

Martin Boysen and Ian Nicolson on the Col Roseg.

Martin and Rab headed off towards a tilted shield of rock overlooking the valley, with little information but much enthusiasm as usual. Paul ('Tut') Braithwaite and I had other preconceived notions, dreamed up on a previous Sunday ascent of the ridge of the Pizzo Frachiccio. A wall of perfect granite swept from the ridge 1,000ft to the screes. In its highest reaches a bottomless dièdre plunged into space glistening in evening light. That was to be the way.

Like much else in a glorious but over-sensational summer, the day proved dreamlike. The slabs, ramps and then steepening walls provided an intricate entry to the dièdre, with rock so good that each move tended to be an engrossing study of intricate holds, blind arêtes and beetling bulges. Each time an impasse threatened, a new solution emerged as if by magic. Then came the groove, wide splayed, ledge free. Tut spread himself across its fine features. Once or twice we had to winkle out loose stones to place nuts for protection, but fine climbing came move after move. At last the familiar features of the existing ridge route came in view (Cajori-Kasper route), and we ambled up to a known abseil descent, then made haste for the workers' *cabina's* final plunge.

Another Sunday Tut, Rab and myself made a trio. Above the abseil gully was a beetling East Buttress of Scafell-like cliff. Slabs led up into a bomb bay, above which all looked fierce.

Rab pointed his resolute chin towards a slab to our left, launched onto it, then made an impressive little descent. From there he was able to gain a slab enticing us up into the grooves above. Tut and I followed, not without excitement, and Tut led the grooves above in a long pitch to an awkward-looking roof. After that Rab entered a Mickledore Groove above. On the ridge again it was the usual haste, for the *cabina*, a beer or two, evening banquet hanging over the river in Chiavenna, and back for make up at the Hotel Krönenhof Prontresina at 5.30am, for work on Monday.

Via Maiden Maiden VI July 1981; Via Mafia della Glencoe VI August 1981.

A GLOBAL SCALE

The opening up of the Himalaya and other distant ranges by cheaper transport and state policy offered boggling opportunities for new mountaineering experiences post 1970. In my case not all planned ventures succeeded in leaving Britain, with an abort of a trip planned to the Cassin Ridge of Mount McKinley in 1969 and another (to the Trango Tower) in 1971 caused by renewed hostilities in the region. Abetting the pressures in this direction were vast improvements in equipment, as spectacular in their impact as the sophistication of rock climbing equipment in the same era. In 1970 ice axes tilted downwards, ice screws improved, but boots remained leather, heavy and primitive, gaiters were poor and shell clothing defective. Subsequently massive improvements continued – ice axes and hammers, crampons, outer and under clothing, boot manufacture, ice pitons, harnesses, rucksacks, gaiters, karabiners, tents, stoves, down and other warm wear, and in rock equipment also. Overwhelmingly, equipment became lighter, allowing survival in conditions unthinkable a decade earlier.

Vitaly Abalakov and the Russian élite, Caucasus, 1970. *Photo by Hamish MacInnes.*

Norge. Troldtindene. Romsdal   26 7 1965

Dear Paul.
Made it!! Really great – as good as anything in the Alps. 4580 feet. VI Sup.
Almost all grade 6 with five pitches of A2 & A3, rest 5 & 4. 5½ days on the
final ascent. 78 hours climbing. Norwegian party did our alternative choice
(N Face and N Arete.) Easier route but 11 days. All celebrated last night at
Grand Hotel's invite. Also tonight on Norwegian Travel invite. Having
plaques presented! Regards to Dearman & tell him to stop farting about on
little things like Prow and Central Cheddar.
Cheers,

Tony (Howard).

A Dream of Ushba

Mountain 16. (1971).

The 'Jewel of the Caucasus' they called it, and Dennis Gray hooked us all. His
enthusiasm was infectious. Alan and Barbara McHardy worked like mad on
gear and Chris Woodall acquired a mountain of food, but somehow no money
appeared. At Easter it all reached a nadir. Dennis had to drop out to work in the
Lakes. Then, when it looked a dead duck, chance played an ace. Pete Seeds, a
journalist, wanted to climb, so we went to the Lakes. He was enthusiastic and
several long gambles paid off. By courtesy of the *Sunday Mirror* and Fiat we
found ourselves in the Central Caucasus, complete with a specially drafted
leader, Hamish MacInnes.

The Elbrus-Ushba region is the Mont Blanc of the range, unmatched for
altitude and for quality and variety of climbing. Here are the Soviet Trades
Union Camps to which climbers come in the summer. Before long the area will
become a major European ski resort. I was glad to be there before it all
happened.

We were pushed too hard for time by a month-long visa which covered a
1,500-mile drive in each direction. The testing journey left us understandably
lethargic, and negotiations with regard to objectives, together with some bad
weather, strained our luck in the first couple of weeks. Frustratingly, our first
objective, the North Face of Nakra Tau by the Abalakov route, never came into
tolerable condition. This rather ambitious first objective (about one and a half
times the length of the Matterhorn North Face and of similar seriousness and
overall altitude) was subject to bad weather, soft and dangerous snow conditions, and potentially lethal serac avalanches. A near miss in bad conditions and
continuing bad weather forced us to abandon the project.

Our attention shifted to the Ushba region. But new snow fell at 11,000ft on
20 July. The inexorable scissors of time now made us give up our plans on a

new climb on Ushba,* which seemed unlikely to come into condition quickly enough. Instead, we grabbed at an objective which suggested itself overwhelmingly from the German or Skelda bivouac – a new climb on the North Face of Pic Schurovski. With some head shaking but much sympathy, Paul Rotatiev, Vice-President of the Soviet Mountaineering Federation, agreed to our plans.

We aimed to storm it, without tents, sleeping bags, or large sacks full of food. We worked off our frustration in a brutally simple plan which placed a massive premium on a small quantity of high quality gear, the use of Terrordactyl axes to eliminate step cutting and, above all, on experience and speed.

On 24 July the dawn was frosty. Moving solo, Hamish, Chris and I crossed the glacier and ascended the runnelled ice above the bergschrund. In the gloom a party of friendly Russian instructors paused, lights twinkling, to observe our eccentric individualistic progress.

A steep couloir necessitated the rope. Hamish led, Chris followed and I prussiked, taking pictures. After a few rope lengths we escaped on to rock as ice particles and small stones began to bespatter the lower cliffs. Rocks (4/5) and perfect snow followed to the base of the first rock barrier. A beautiful traverse on perfect ice led out right to a granite rib and a patch of sun.

The rib was steep and a little loose, and gave way to typical Nevis mixed ground (5+ rock). The lower barrier passed with remarkably little incident, and we emerged at the foot of the Central Icefield. Luckily the sun passed away again behind the mountain, leaving the ice firm. We did not see it on the wall again that day.

At 12, after several rope lengths on ice, we reached a small exposed shoulder (a possible bivouac site). Probably we were nearly half-way up the face. Confidence overtook us as we scrunched through our staple diet of Mapleton bar. Hamish, with his Lawrence of Arabia neck-shield flopping, led up the short and very steep ice field below the Central Rock Barrier. He had to cut a few steps in the approach to the only feasible-looking weakness, a gully-like depression between the icicle-festooned walls. It became apparent that Rotatiev had been right in stressing the steepness of the face and of the Central Barrier in particular. On close inspection the rock went a little beyond the vertical everywhere but in our depression. Even there it was extremely steep and required devious route finding.

Hamish led the pitches in about three hours. The first was extremely difficult mixed climbing on steep insecure ice and loose rock for about 80ft, while the second was an easier groove (Scottish 3/4) to a horizontal rocky traverse and a good small ledge. The climbing, typical of harder winter routes, was an admirable lead in any conditions. Half-way up a Caucasian face it was remarkable.

To reach the upper ice field was the next pressing problem. Above were ice-decorated walls for several hundred feet. Binocular study had revealed an ice

---

*A version of this route was done by Mick Fowler and Tony Saunders in July 1986. ('Ushba from Russia with Love', *Mountain* 114.)

chimney and possible traverse to the lower lip of the plunging upper slopes. Chris grated round the arête in crampons, carrying the large sack which he preferred. The chimney, again far steeper than we had anticipated, involved an athletic spurt of dynamic bridging. A gloomy traverse in the gathering storm and failing light led to the edge of the ice. A small buttress of rock seemed the only feasible bivouac site.

Thunder crashed round the summit and sheets of hail swept down the ice fields as Chris and I excavated for an hour. Hamish engineered a brew in his slot. Pitons and a tiny wire sling secured our position, while my antique bivouac sheet hung down as a curtain. It seemed that we would probably be able to manage the ascent but, with four or five pitons left, we would certainly not be able to retreat.

5am. Hamish sets out in rapid moves across the encrusted ice to the lower outlet of the steep upper ice field. The storm has given way to a fierce frost, but white wind-torn streaks threaten its return. The upper ice field is steep but not too difficult, and the gradual fading of the sun prevents the development of avalanche danger. It is very long.

12. At the base of the summit pyramid there is perhaps 700ft to go. On my lead the clouds mass and the wind rises. The rock is much worse than we expected. The snow had seen too much of the morning sun. Chris takes the lead from a horrible stance on steep mush, just in time for the full blast of the snow to begin. As he ploughs up the deep snow, avalanches of powder drown his yellow cagoule. Seconding involves swimming up a trough of horrible insecure snow. At one point Hamish and I inhabit a small ledge while Chris is totally lost in the maelstrom above. Eventually we follow tightening ropes up.

4pm. The Traverse of the Screws avoids the final impossibly steep 100ft of avalanche snow by an escape to the last few feet of the North-West Ridge. A great mass of soft snow is removed; screws protect the leader and second alike. On the ridge in a brief clearance Hamish swarms up the last rocks and flails up the final insecure mound to a stormy summit.

8pm. The second bivouac is a collapsible snow cave on the Ushba plateau, after a plodding descent through deep snow which is threatened by avalanches and punctuated by apocalyptic visions of the huge ice walls of Bezingi to the east. Mist cheats us of respite at a food dump at the head of the Ushba ice-fall. The limitations of alpine tactics in the Caucasus become apparent as we shudder through to morning in a pile of powder snow on a steep slope, with a cold wind blowing.

26 July. The mist clears briefly to reveal Ushba towering over us. Hamish's camera is frozen as we descend to the food dump. After twenty-four hours without drink, eating is difficult. Hycal renders one completely speechless. The Ushba ice-fall provides the sting in the tail – a nasty 80ft abseil from ice screws into a yawning green hole, followed by a run in balled-up crampons below a monster serac in the mist. Something falls, but it is too thick to see. After a moment peering up into the gloom of yet another storm, the crashing noises

descend to our left. Towards mid-morning we skirt the last large crevasses and slide down soaking snow on to the upper Skelda Glacier. Schurovski is plastered, and streams of snow run down the lower slabs out of the mist. Ushba is hidden in mist and snow above the crumbling ice-fall. Richard waits to help us down at the German bivouac, while Tut assists in the rescue of an unfortunate Bulgar in a deep crevasse. Our toes are uncomfortable: Ushba will have to wait.

Asgard Outing

Mountain 26. (1973).

One spring evening in 1966 at Tom Patey's house in Ullapool, the Revd Frank Wilkinson, chaplain of Peterhead Prison, ran quickly through slides gathered during long years as a missionary on Baffin Island. It was fairy-tale country, remote, ice-bound in half-light for much of the year. The long fjords sliced into granite mountains of unrelenting compactness, while they in turn were half enveloped in great ice mushrooms, ice caps which dominate the geography of the area, make its weather, and spill over the top of many a Yosemite-style wall. I wanted to go.

A phone call in May 1972 settled it, for Doug Scott, Dennis Hennek from California, Tut Braithwaite, and myself. It seemed an excellent scheme, for I had always thought Eric Shipton must be right in that little expeditions are more likely to be good expeditions, even at their most extended; and I could think of few places more suitable than Baffin for such an approach. Anyway, the battle of Everest seemed to me to have undermined the very term 'expedition, which now implies multiple forms of exploitation and rigid organization for which the only compensation for many individual climbers is pretentiousness. The alienation of heart, combined with the extreme graft involved, seems to me to be the complete antithesis of what mountaineering is all about. A small group, friendly, intimate, motivated but not utterly achievement-orientated, promised to get away from all that.

I was a late arrival. Doug had got some money from the Mount Everest Foundation and Dennis had meticulously ordered food, both in the USA and from the Bay Trading Co. in Baffin; he had also organized most of the equipment. There were no strings: the plane left in a couple of weeks.

We assembled in Hudson Heights near Montreal, where Mrs P. Baird entertained us royally. Dennis proved to be anything but the lean, rock-drilling technocrat that I had half expected. Instead he was a muscular, blond, fun and pleasure-loving character who seemed to enjoy the occasional discipline of climbing, and who was prepared to take great pains to do it well. Within a few hours we seemed like a team.

On 3 July, we flew to Pangnirtung, a dusty Eskimo settlement across the Cumberland Sound. Blue skies, after a murky journey, boded well.

From the beginning there was a sense of unreality in this land of myth and magic enjoying its brief summer. On 4 July, Jok Polliollik and another Eskimo took us by sledge and skiddoo 20 miles down the fjord ice towards the mountains. There was a gala atmosphere, even when a sledge broke under the weight of five people and a boat. The Eskimos played at shooting imaginary seals and we consumed food and brews together when we arrived under the great face of Mount Overlord. It was a light-hearted and fortunate start, for the sea-ice was late, and we were saved at least two days.

Then we conned one another. None of us had ever carried such monstrous loads as we assembled. Food for nearly three weeks, tents, big-wall gear, fuel: the pack frames bent and creaked under the load, and so did we. Somehow, tottering upright, we trekked off from the dump at the fjord head into the Weasel Valley's pebble flats. After two days of wandering through moraines which disappeared into soaring granite walls and a grey snow-laden sky, we camped to rest for a day by the frozen waste of Summit Lake.

Again the ice was useful. On consecutive days we tramped on snowshoes 6 miles over the lake-ice, taking half-loads to the Turner Glacier and a camp below Asgard. On 9 July, we stamped out tent sites by a glacier lagoon. It was snowing heavily, but we were all pleased – the carry was over.

Mount Thor and the Fork Beard Glacier from Summit Lake, Baffin Island.

126

Snowshoes were essential to get far on glaciers in 1972. Crevasses were deeply covered, making unroped wanderings hazardous, though we sometimes indulged ourselves. It froze for only a short time at night, leaving a weak crust. The camp was idyllic, on the snow at the junction of two glaciers, by the blue lake, with the plumb-vertical walls of Freyr Peak opposite and Asgard behind. Rocks trundled from an outlying minor summit, but we were adequately distant from their path. Moreover, we were well fed and well equipped, and on 10 July the weather began a lasting good spell.

Out first objective, the main cause of our weight crucifixion, was the West Dihedral of Asgard. Doug and I broke a track on the 10th, and dug a trench up deep insecure snow on the lower slopes. The dihedral is a real siren, drawing the eye up its clean-cut features for over 1,500ft. On a sparkling morning, we snowshoed over the light crust to the base of the face again. Cloud rolled in dazzling furls over the ice cap to the north. Doug and I carried gear, while Tut led up the initial 1,500ft of snow and mixed ground. It was unsafe and avalanche-prone, with little security. A last lead of over 400ft led to the dihedral base.

Doug set off up an iced chimney with Dennis seconding, while we cut a large platform. It seemed that the donkey-work was over. For today, tomorrow, maybe the day after, we would swing and dangle, hammer away, and sleep in our hammocks in the relative safety of the vertical. This opinion seemed confirmed when the 400ft slope avalanched in a sea of slops, although it was modified by ice lumps falling from far above and blowing in a keen wind into the dihedral.

But our confidence was premature, however well equipped physically and mentally we might have been. Apart from the cold on this side of the mountain, which could have been a problem in a really prolonged attack, the dièdre was not a pegging fault but a closed granite joint with aberrant, unlinked cracks. Dennis found himself faced with a painful choice at 200ft – the first of several long bolt ladders or nothing. The bolting seemed premature, and perhaps ultimately undesirable. In the early hours of 12 July we reached camp after about twenty hours' absence.*

Snoozing reappraisal led to a quick decision. Late on the 12th, Tut and Doug broke tracks to the North-East Ridge of Asgard North Peak. Next day, lightly equipped, we all set off in relentless sun. For me the route had immense appeal; it was a smooth pillar of slabby and near-perfect granite, about 3,500ft high from the glacier. It was to be an alpine-style push with no provision for stopping.

Doug and Dennis led up the magnificent lower slabs, while for a time Tut and I suffered the divorcing experience of prussiking. Then, about midday, we led on. It was a flood of pleasure to me, with corners, jamming cracks, delicate slabs, and a gradual steepening of angle as the upper pillar came nearer. We stopped once for food, and then followed a crack system of escalating difficulty, deeply reminiscent of all the best alpine granite climbs I have experienced. We used few pegs, nut protection being usual. In the late evening, a cold mist flung

*The route was climbed by Charlie Parker, 10 September 1975, in a remarkable solo.

a grey cloak over us. At midnight, after about ten hours of leading, Tut and I relegated ourselves to the rear for the headwall.

The red granite, compact but split by a crack system, reared up towards the summit. There were four hard pitches for Doug and Dennis, and airy swinging prussiks on lightly frozen ropes for us. Dennis did the all-star lead on a Curbar-style 140ft crack. It took at least two hours of real struggle and was extremely difficult, especially coming as the penultimate pitch of a hard climb. Doug finished it off up a gritstone jamming crack at Hard VS, straight to the summit. During the sojourns we dozed in our duvets, waiting for the sun to reappear. At 6am on the 14th we were on the table-top summit in brilliant sun.

The aftermath was deflating. The glacier lagoon had flooded and the tents were threatened if not awash, 55 miles out from Pang. Good weather has its costs. Attempts at a quick descent of the original route were defeated by obnoxious deep wet snow, which reduced us to a commando crawl, ludicrous and deadly serious as we sank into crevasses. It was easy to see how people fail to make it under such circumstances. Fortunately the lower glacier was better, and we reached the snowshoes and the camp thirty-three hours after departure.

The blue tents were dry but afloat on the packed snow under them. With joyous, tired sploshings they were rescued, and re-erected uphill. Six more hours and they would have been drowned. Two-ton eyelids slumped to sleep, despite the relentless arctic light.

Two days later we began the tramp out. There was more to do, but we were tired and a little self-satisfied. We crossed a col below our route with 70lb sacks, and descended dreadful deep powder on the Caribou Glacier at less than a mile an hour, tripping occasionally as the snowshoe tips crept under the crust, and finding difficulty in swimming out with the sacks pushing our faces into the morass. After a snooze at Summit Lake, we continued down to camp in a fine spot below the 4,500ft face of Thor.

With battered feet and still heavy loads, our retreat became a ramble. Time was taken up with peering at flowers and wildlife, snoozing and eating food remnants.

We took the best part of a week to cover the 50 miles or so to Pang. By then the mosquitoes were coming to life, the pack-ice was breaking rapidly, the arctic summer was weakening enough to allow a little night, the food was eaten, and it was time to go.

We had no commitments, except to ourselves, and they were satisfied. Success was aided by fortuitous good weather and a late winter. Dennis's meticulous organization, and especially the freeze-dried food, made the carry possible. Without air-drops or great expense, we got ourselves from Pang fjord head to Asgard, and back to Pang. We did a dream of a climb, and each led his quota. Almost all the climbing was VS, or harder, so all our egos were satisfied. As an exercise in logistics, and as an intensely personal experience, the expedition was gratifyingly complete. Amazingly, it was a product of motivation which was less 'achievement-' or 'summit-orientated' than most such excursions. Perhaps therein lies its validation.

Pamir Postscript (1981)

A hardback edition of *Storm and Sorrow in the High Pamirs** is welcome not only because the Soviet camp in Central Asia in 1974 was attended by a dozen British climbers but because this epic story ought to reach a wider audience in Britain. Bob Craig unfolds the complex web of events with sensitivity and an eye for poignant detail which can scarcely be faulted.

The 160 climbers who assembled in the Hotel Sputnik in Moscow in early July 1974 had little inkling of the enormity of the tragedy in which they were to be prime actors. Disparate groups rambled the corridors and lifts of the hotel, exchanging greetings and resting prior to the shuttle flight south to Soviet Asia. Most had jetted in from Paris, Tokyo, the USA or Vienna, but the British travelled at a more leisurely pace. Six Scots came overland in a Ford transit which rolled incongruously through the Moscow boulevards. With an atmosphere of even greater anachronism the English group had come from Derby by train, rattling through London to Harwich and the Hook of Holland, where our coach, with grey uniformed 'Boris' in charge, was a tiny Western outpost of Eastern Europe. Europe was traversed in a daze of passport waving, collection of equipment from helpful German manufacturers who arranged for it to be presented to us in our sleeper at midnight, and hourly infusions of tea from the samovar at the end of the coach.

Among the groups assembled in Moscow the Americans were prominent. Nineteen climbers, golden suntans and a hint of training, orange duvets and custom-made caps all suggested team spirit, organization and financial backing. The mix of age, experience and sex seemed to indicate a degree of modernity and a taste of the Massachusetts Institute of Technology personality inventory in team choice. The leaders, Pete Schoening and Bob Craig, were well known for their near miraculous survival of disaster during the K2 Expedition of 1953, when Schoening stopped a fall involving six other men. To us the former seemed strong, stern, a little dour, while Craig was more open and approachable, quick to talk, humorous and more ready to bridge the generation gap in their own party and between its leaders and all the British climbers, none of whom were close to forty with the possible exception of Graham Tiso from Edinburgh. Schoening and Craig almost seemed to represent two political faces of the USA, and their party likewise.

Social contact soon came, particularly with this group, and with it the realization that there could be races at this Olympiad. It was also soon evident that our main competitors might prove to be some of the Americans. During the three days in Moscow, with its whirl of meals, circuses, sightseeing and adjusting, we realized that one group of Americans came close to sharing objectives with us. We and they wished to do a route on the East Face of Peak Lenin, and they believed in some priority achieved through earlier formal approaches to the Soviet Mountaineering Federation (SMF). Perhaps character-

---

**Storm and Sorrow in the High Pamirs*. Gollancz, 1981.

istically, while our plans remained, our group seem to have worried more about exchange rates or where to buy the wine. This contrasted with the slight unease sometimes apparent among our new neighbours.

The British contingent had reason for a degree of equanimity. The planning of both the Scots and English ventures had been low key. The English group of six involved a series of interlocking, longstanding friendships, with a record of past success and deep experience. Even Speedy Smith, at twenty-four the baby of our party, was a well-known rock climber. I had been on the same climb with him on the steep limestone of the Vercors only weeks before the Pamir Expedition. Guy Lee and Doug Scott had known each other for at least fifteen years as had Clive Rowland and I, while Tut Braithwaite, Doug and I had shared expedition experience in the Caucasus and Baffin Island, the latter of which had been a very successful light expedition to Mount Asgard in 1972. Our trip to the Pamirs materialized from a few meetings in Derbyshire pubs, and had been suitably sponsored by the Whitbread Trust.

There seemed every justification for entertaining great hopes. Doug had recently exceeded 27,000ft on the South-West Face of Everest, Tut Braithwaite was going great guns at altitude, Clive Rowland has a long record of competent and controlled success, while Guy and I had likewise climbed widely and at a high standard. The British had another advantage in not being troubled by great power status. While this was the first American venture to Soviet peaks for many years, there was a history of British contact with the SMF. This had not always been easy, but British alpinists have generally impressed their hosts in the USSR by their technical competence and spirited companionship. Lord Hunt led a successful expedition to the Caucasus in 1958 and another to the Mount Communism area of the Pamirs in 1963. Joe Brown, Ian Macnaught Davis and several Russian masters of sport climbed that mountain, but the brilliant young Scot Robin Smith and his companion Wilfred Noyce, one of the greatest climbers of an earlier generation, were killed on a nearby peak; the venture took on a blighted air unhelped by a subsequent, rather slighting, book by Malcolm Slesser which served to make relations more difficult with the Soviet climbers for some years.

Eventually, not without complications, Hamish MacInnes, Alan McHardy, Tut Braithwaite, Chris Woodall, Pete Seeds and myself climbed the North Face of Pic Shurovski in the Caucasus in 1970. Hamish had the advantage of specialist contacts with Anatoly Abalakov, Eugene Gippenreuter and other key figures in the Federation after a successful two-man visit in the early 60s, and thereafter there had been frequent contact on mountain rescue matters. In 1974 two of us had visited the USSR before and we were confident that the pleasant welcome extended in 1970 would remain now that we were invited visitors. There was less uncertainty about the formidable trappings of Soviet society and the formalities of Soviet mountaineering practice than might have afflicted newcomers.

After the journey to the Achik Tash valley and the early acclimatization there was a rush into action in which the English group were very forward. Doug and

Tut were particularly quick in ploughing a way up the dangerous slopes of the Krylenko Pass (19,200ft) and Americans, Japanese and some Soviet climbers followed our footsteps towards the East Face of Peak Lenin. The crossing of this pass was a shadow race for the foot of the East Face, which dominates the Saukdhara Glacier across the range from the Achik Tash valley. But it was never more than a phantom competition, for after we had established a camp on the Saukdhara and started a path to the face itself the Americans were a day behind, and such games of petty rivalry were granted short shrift by that misleading whaleback of a mountain. Storm and earthquakes, which hurled ice and snow avalanches from the flanks of most of the peaks, foreclosed upon us all, killing Estonians on Peak Lenin and Jon Gary Ullin from the American group on the attempt on Peak Nineteen – Craig survived despite sharing the same tent and being buried, to write this book. Thereafter national barriers began to crumble in the face of ever greater odds. We grew closer to Vincent, Benoit and Bernard from one of the French parties, to Geoff Lowe, Bruce Carson, Fred Stanley, Molly Higgins, Allen Steck and Bob Craig and other Americans, and to the Dutch, some of the Ladies' Party and the Soviet climbers. Despite death the meet had to go on.

Eventually there was better weather and some achievements. Lenin was climbed by a variety of traditional routes, the French climbed a new spur and skied the North Face, which was to lead them on to ski down Annapurna in 1979, with the loss of one of their strongest, Yves Morin, near the summit. The English allied with three Scots and did their new ridge, elegant-looking, long-winded, curiously parallel to the French route. John Roskelley and Geoff Lowe revenged themselves on the North Face of Peak Nineteen. But eventually, when most climbers had been channelled on to the easier routes of Peak Lenin, the mountains moved again and dealt a blow to the solar plexus of the whole meet, which doubtless remains painful for all who were there.

Among the groups on Peak Lenin were two teams of women. One attempted the Razdelny route, a long ridge leading from the col (19,685ft) south of the summit. This international group of women were finally able to push four of their members onto the ridge. There they were caught in a severe storm and after a night out Eva Eissenschmidt died of exposure before they were able to get back to the Razdelny Pass. But the storm caught others also. Nine Soviet women had worked their way systematically up the Lipkin Spur with the intention of traversing the mountain. They were caught close to the summit by the storm, and, despite belated attempts to rescue them, all died within two days of high winds and bitter temperatures. British, American, Soviet and French climbers were all mobilized in an attempt to reach them, but we knew it was too late even as we began to plod up the Lenin Glacier during the last day of storm. They had been out too long in too exposed a position, a view borne out by the brave and plaintive radio calls which the last survivors struggled to transmit through the maelstrom. Rescuers could only open up the descent for the various groups trapped in less hazardous places, as they crept from their tents and snow holes on the first day's clearance.

131

Peak Lenin is not a very difficult peak for all its 7,000m, but it shrugged off this particular assault with harsh disdain. Its broad slopes gave little shelter from the storm and created difficulties in route-finding in the wild weather. Added to that, unseasonably heavy snowfall greatly increased the avalanche dangers. Eventually the bodies of the Soviet women were located and the scattered parties streamed down from the Razdelny Pass and the Lipkin Spur, crossed the Pass of the Travellers for the last time and wandered down the flowery plains of the Achik Tash to Base Camp to spend a day or two before departure haunted by the deaths of so many of their former companions.

Many participants left the USSR mesmerized and shocked. Death should never be taken lightly, particularly in mountaineering, which Bob Craig himself has defined as a form of organized quixotism. Probably most of the climbers needed time to let memory fade, not least our Soviet hosts who lost most of all, the cream of women climbers, wives, mothers, friends. The burden of the tragedy will probably never lighten much for Vitaly Abalakov, the grand old man of the camp, for it was his from the beginning and he continued to assume it as bad news was followed by worse. Relatively little has been written in English about the affair, but it ought to strike a chord in the memories of British readers, not only because of the immediacy and humanity of the writing, but because we too suffer our disasters, in mountains and elsewhere. Always, as with our Cairngorm accident of 1972, in which there are some curious parallels, there is a need to allocate responsibility. In *Storm and Sorrow* such issues are carefully skirted with a necessary humility in the face of natural forces of massive power and unpredictability. There are lessons there to be learned by us all. If trauma produces scars which cannot be forgotten and therefore must be well preserved, Bob Craig offers us an ikon for our times.

Recently Vladimir Shatayev's book Degrees of Difficulty *(The Mountaineers, Seattle, 1987) has been translated into English, and deals sensitively with the worst accident in Soviet climbing history. He was married to the leader of the women, Elvira Shatayeva, who took me to task for going down alone from our ridge of ascent as they went up, and died as we toiled back up the Lipkin Spur.*

Latok – Karakoram

Illustrated London News (*October 1977*).

In 1977 among the steepest and most savage mountains in the world, four remained unclimbed deep in the Karakoram Himalaya. Baintha Brakk, or the Ogre as the explorer Sir Martin Conway called it, is at 23,900ft* marginally the

*Now thought to be over 24,000ft.

132

highest, but the three Latok peaks appear technically as difficult and dangerous. All are rock mountains, with problems quite different from the endless snow plodding of most Himalayan peaks.

In 1975, thirty Japanese mountaineers divided into two large expeditions to attempt these peaks. They were following in the footsteps of British explorers Conway, Eric Shipton and more recently Don Morrison, who in 1971 was the first to lead an expedition into the Biafo region after a long period when the area was closed by the Kashmir dispute. After exploring the topography of the area, powerful and heavily equipped Japanese teams tried to scale Latok 1, Latok 2 and Baintha Brakk. None was successful and one climber died in an ice-fall on Latok 1. If strong parties like the fifteen-man team which attacked Latok 2 could be defeated, these were obviously formidable peaks. As a result the region, previously known only to a few devotees, became famous in world mountaineering. In 1977 Don Morrison mounted another Yorkshire Karakoram expedition to the 23,320ft Latok 2.

The Latok 2 expedition was small, with a five-man team, and meticulous in the details of its organization. Equipment and food supplies were carefully chosen to be both cheap to transport and effective on the mountain. The members were all Sheffield climbers of considerable experience. Though Don Morrison, the leader, was forty-eight and considered this likely to be his last Himalayan venture, he was a fit and experienced man with first ascents west of the Biafo and in Canada. Pat Fearnehough, thirty-nine, a veteran from previous expeditions in Greenland and the Himalaya, was primarily responsible for the choice and dispatch of equipment. The other members of the expedition were Patrick Green, who trains chefs and was invaluable in that most crucial role of arranging the food supplies; Tony Riley, who was the film maker, and who was making his second Karakoram expedition; and myself.

Latok 2 first revealed itself from Mango, a green oasis sandwiched between the Biafo Glacier and the great mountain hulk of Mango Brakk (21,000ft). For two seemingly endless grey days we had tramped the loose stones and dirty ice of the snout and terminal moraines of this 30-mile river of ice. We were the first expedition to enter the Karakoram Range from Skardu in 1977, and progress had been rapid. By 23 May the spectacular flight past Nanga Parbat (26,000ft) was accomplished. After one night on beds kindly freed for us by Nazir Sabir and Ashraf Aman and some rapid purchases of paraffin and supplies to be carried by the porters, two jeeps were loaded in the morning cool at Skardu. By lunchtime a bone-shattering 50-mile drive was over and we were deposited under a forlorn tree in Bahar amid the desert sands of the lower Braldu valley. By evening the porters had appeared, and we were on our way; after five days we neared our objective.

The Biafo yielded up its secrets with reluctance. The twenty-five hillmen from Askole, the last village, 10,000ft up, disliked the ice and took every opportunity to escape on to the grassy slopes at its edge. Going uphill with their 56lb loads they moved relatively slowly with frequent halts, and our progress was punctuated by heavy showers of cold rain and sleet. It was not surprising after six hours' march that the porters veered from the mid-glacial ice into a series of satanic seracs of ice-blocks and moraines to reach Mango. This entailed an extra two-hour walk to get off the glacier, but led to fresh water, grass and small junipers for firewood.

We idled in the grass while tok cakes and transport drivers' tea were prepared over the smoky fires. Grey wraiths of low cloud blanked out the great peaks and prepared us for the next dousing, creating a Glencoe-like atmosphere. The porters were naturally reluctant to take up their loads again but eventually they set off in close file, hardly pausing as we passed telltale bear droppings. As the porter column stopped before taking to the ice again, rain fell in sheets and they were unwilling to continue. Don, the headman, and Captain Javed Ahmed, our liaison officer, conferred and we agreed to pause for the night. It was barely afternoon but we, too, preferred to camp rather than push on in vile conditions over the hostile wastes of ice. The porters scuttled into nearby caves and we quickly erected the tents. After five days the altitude of almost 13,000ft was beginning to tell.

In the evening the cloud parted to reveal the long line of mountains 5 miles away on the other bank of the glacier. Dongbar exceeds 21,000ft and there were others scarcely less high. To the north-east a great sunlit cone of ice and snow towered higher than any other mountain in sight. Persistent dark clouds clung to its foothills but the sun glinted from the ice cliffs of the South Face and illuminated the perfect little spike of the final summit. We peered and rationalized. The plunging 5,000ft of the West Face, sun-lit red granite, left little doubt. This apparition was Latok 2.

Base camp was established on 1 June. There was heavy overnight snow, and Don and Javed had to work hard at 6am to induce the porters to go beyond Baintha (13,800ft). Once persuaded they pushed off ahead in the deep snow despite their ignorance of the precise direction. Stumbling through the endless mounds of loose stones covered in knee-deep snow between 14,000 and 16,000ft, most of us suffered the headaches of acclimatization but the sun shone and the view was astounding.

On the Latok Glacier the porters finally halted and Pat Fearnehough's enterprise in finding a tiny grass patch protected from falling stones by jutting crags saved us from a bleak base camp. The porters took their rupees and with one exception rushed off towards Baintha. Hussein Shah was engaged as the liaison officer's cook and occasional porter.

Within a few days, advanced base was established 3 miles up the Latok Glacier in a bowl of snow. Pat Fearnehough became ill with bronchitis that had persisted since we left Rawalpindi and had to retreat to the Horn's Hotel, a well appointed boulder at Baintha, 2,000ft below base. Pat Green went with him when his illness was most serious. This slowed the movement of supplies but, on 10 June, Don and I set out on a glittering moonlit night from advanced base to open a route up the 2,500ft gully leading to the col of the West Ridge.

The possibility of climbing the enormous West Face couloir had also been considered but in practice it seemed too dangerous. As high as the Eiger North

Kamikaze pilot? Dave Wilkinson in the
Latoks.

Towards Sinkiang from the Latoks.

Face, it was threatened by a serac wall in its lower reaches and the exit cracks
could not be seen. In contrast the West Ridge appeared relatively safe.★

Underestimating the length of the gully on the first attempt, we tried to carry
too much. A long slope of debris led from Clapham Junction, an avalanche-
raked basin, to the gully itself. Green ice towers threatened from the right while
a steep rock wall cut off the gully to the left. We traversed to the right on brittle
green ice, roped as the slope became steep. From an old Japanese piton Don led
upward on the front points of his crampons, axe and hammer picks biting little
into the ice. He fell from 50ft as one crampon detached itself, slipping off his
neoprene gaiter. The rope stretched and my steps broke away, but from an
upside-down position I found that the fall was arrested. There were few words.
Don recovered my dark glasses, attached his crampon and led his pitch again.

Time, energy and nerve had been expended. The sun caught us half-way up
the couloir, the snow began to collapse and we were forced to deposit our loads
on a rock pillar and retreat before the avalanches began. By mid-morning we
were plodding back across the plateau to advanced base. It had been the first day
of an extended campaign to reach the col and to carry to it the supplies and
equipment for an extended push above 20,000ft. Tony had filmed our progress
from advanced base with a massive telephoto lens.

Each day avalanches destroyed yesterday's track and the night shift had to
make the route anew. Over 2,000ft of rope were fixed in the gully. A blizzard

★It is frequently swept by serac fall (1987).

wiped out much of our progress but the big avalanches which followed left our cache of gear intact, though as I fixed rope in the upper couloir three avalanches in succession swept over Tony as he painstakingly carried gear up the ropes below. Don and Tony eventually pushed through to a little rock neb which sheltered a tent, and on 20 June the two Pats and I followed in their tracks with enormous loads. Led by a renovated Fearnehough, despite doubts as to whether he should be up there at all, we made the col on the morning of 21 June. It was a great morning: we had reached the first milestone *en route* to the summit at about 20,000ft. Moreover there was an idyllic camp site behind a solitary rock tower, sheltered and safe, with views from the Choktoi Glacier and distant Sinkiang to Nanga Parbat.

The col was nearly ¾ mile long, with massive cream-whorl cornices, a 4,000ft drop to the east and wind-slabs on the easier slopes. Some pinnacles required a full morning's attention and fixed ropes to safeguard a retreat, especially by laden climbers. Beyond them the ridge reared in a ferocious step. Despite this we retreated in jubilant mood after enjoying climbing without large sacks. Pat Green, meanwhile, painstakingly clamped with more necessary supplies up the last rope on the gully.

All three of us tackled the knife edge next day. As the sun touched it conditions softened and progress slowed. After 500ft I fixed a rope on to solid rock pitons and descended from some very steep ice.

Numerous consecutive days of hard activity were sapping our strength. Pat Fearnehough decided to bring up more supplies. Pat Green and I watched him go in the early evening and were relieved to see in the gloom a tiny figure emerge on to the lower glacier. The avalanches occasionally swept away the gully fixed ropes.

For most of 24 June Pat and I rested, brewing tea as often as dwindling resources allowed. Late in the afternoon we set out and I filmed Pat as he crossed the fixed ropes of the ridge. We took almost all the remnants of food and enough gear to camp directly under the steep step; unless supplies came soon this would have to be the last throw of the dice. This camp was more exiguous than the last, with a manufactured spyhole through the cornice a few feet from the tent door. We suffered a cold and windy night; thick, frozen rime formed inside the tent.

Streaks of cloud in the morning seemed to presage some change of weather and at 2pm we agreed that in the soft snow conditions we should stop.
For reasons unknown, support from below was fading away. The step was climbed and 700ft of rope fixed, with a final struggle to get on the sun-softened snow slopes from steep rock. Our sacks were too heavy for this type of climbing and a 2pm we agreed that in the soft snow conditions we should stop.

We went back to a cold and thirsty night in which Pat brewed tea to ease the passage of time. The wind continued cold and the sense of isolation heightened. Evidently a storm had drowned the powerful Japanese attempt which foundered around this point. Higher on the mountain, without support, two climbers would stand little chance of safe retreat.

At dawn, loaded like donkeys, we began the long descent, stripping the route of gear as we went. As we came down the upper gully a heavy load attached to Pat slipped into a newly opened crevasse and it took all our strength to retrieve it. Then two figures came into sight, clamping up the ropes in the lower gully. Pat and Tony were on their way to help and took a good proportion of our enormous loads as we shinned down the fixed ropes.

It was Tony who explained. Don Morrison had been killed, snatched from life by a crevasse fall on the lower Latok Glacier almost a week before, on his way up with supplies. The lack of support, the contrary movements of people, all now was clear.

In a few days everyone was off the mountain and we prepared for departure. At base camp a stark cairn and memorial stone commemorated our lost friend high on the moraines. A few miles west is the peak he climbed with Ted Howard in 1975. Already a new resolve began to crystallize. After so much effort, with one or two more men, perhaps also more supplies, there seemed little reason not to push the west ridge of this mighty mountain to its finale and to complete our filming activities. Despite the tragedy, it remained remarkably hard to leave.

There followed the remarkable epic on Baintha Brakk, when Chris Bonington and Doug Scott reached the summit and were able to retreat with companions Mo Anthoine and Clive Rowlands only after an accident, in which Scott broke his legs, and a prolonged storm.

Latok 2 Again, 1978

Illustrated London News *(October 1978)*.

The Braldu river was in furious condition this summer when two expeditions traversed it on their way to the Karakoram. The notorious Braldu Gorge links the landing strip of Skardu with the last village (Askole) *en route* to the climbing. On 16 July the eight climbers, two Pakistan liaison officers and fifty porters of the Latok 2 and Women's Expedition to Bakkar Das seemed fully exposed to its hazards. After 3 or 4 miles walking from Chokpoing the gorge narrowed. The path was forced to the river's edge and the climbers and porters teetered along wave-washed boulders below a vast earth and rock slope. On occasions the porters had to be pushed and pulled over obstacles, no mean task when so many are involved.

Intermittent stonefalls, earth slides and rising water made the next two hours a whirl of activity. Two hours and baking dust led to the only spring in the 12-mile trek from Chokpoing to Chongo 'the village of the rotting man'. With the temperature at about 100°F we slid into the shade for an hour's snooze before trekking to Chongo.

Monday was a short day, a 6-mile stroll to Askole, a rest after the Braldu for climbers and porters alike. But for the women it still had its excitements. With their twenty men they crossed the Braldu by a *jula* (rope bridge). It had a span of about 400ft and the whole village turned out to observe the spectacle. The birch twig ropes are held apart by a man who spans the middle of the bridge. The four women led by Jackie Anthoine, had the task of finding an approach to their unclimbed mountain – Bakkar Das (19,900ft)* dominates the Askole valley but presents a huge rock face which is manifestly unclimbable. To ascend the peak they had first to find a way of approaching it, for a series of deep valleys separated their objective from the nearest paths.

For us there remained only three or four days of fairly straightforward glacier travel, gaining height steadily to Base Camp at 15,600ft. I could see that Fida Hussein, our Sirdar, shared my relief. At that point Pat Green came sprinting across the fields from Askole village.

The news could not have been worse. Pat Fearnehough and Dr Peter Thexton had been following one day behind us from Skardu and two runners had just come up with the shock message that a rock and earth fall had swept Pat into the river. The Braldu had extracted its price after all.

We spent two days in Askole absorbing the shock and making the necessary arrangements after Pat's death. A search for the body by local police proved fruitless as persistent landslides buried the spot in tons of rock and earth. Pat Green went post-haste over the Skara La pass to Skardu with the news. We discussed our options and decided to continue, as little could be achieved by retreat.

Three damp days took us to Base Camp on the tiny grass patch below the Ogre's Thumb. The porters struck once, fearing that a rapid push up the Biafo would mean lower pay, but Saeed, our liaison officer, and Fida Hussein agreed terms and they continued. After most were paid off late on a wet night three remained to help carry supplies to advanced base, and in two cloudy days they helped establish this camp beyond the yawning crevasses of the Latok Glacier were Don Morrison died. We were pleased to see that the cairn built by Pat Fearnehough remained intact and impressive high on the moraines above the Uzzun Blakk Glacier.

After the last three porters left, the weather cleared, and a pattern was established of three or four good days and five or six bad which persisted throughout the expedition. Dave Wilkinson and Pete Thexton then investigated the base of the Great West Face Couloir as an alternative to the West Ridge, but the entry was a death alley of stonefall. We reverted to the ridge with its advantages of old anchors and fixed ropes low down. By 1 August Dave had led through the narrows and much equipment had been moved part way up the 2,500ft slope to the col, while a chain of old and new fixed rope led almost to the safe camp site of a rock island. With all four of us about to establish that camp the weather broke and forced us back to base and a routine of eating and reading.

*The peak remains unclimbed.

Latoks II and III from the Baintha Lukpar Glacier.

In the next clearance Pete and I set up camp one and the following day opened the route to the col (20,000ft). In two weeks with three fully active climbers we had done three weeks' work by last year's standards. I plodded the couple of hundred yards to the site of camp two with a heavy heart, for last year Pat Fearnehough had led all this section in a remarkable recovery from illness. Both of us took photographs and films before sliding down the new fixed rope to camp one. There Dave and John had come up and we cowered out of the heat of the afternoon, four to a tent, while snowslides raked both sides of the rognon. In the evening Dave and Pete moved back up and camped at the col while I remained and descended next morning with John. He now had to leave to fulfil professional commitments, but was able to join in the Japanese Ogre victory celebration at Baintha before the descent to Askole.* Another push by Dave and Peter reached the col on 11 August, while I was incapacitated for a day at advanced base from the exaggerated effects of a sleeping pill. They placed more gear and food at camp two, but were driven down by a blizzard which lasted for three days.

After 15 August cold clear weather brought the best break of the expedition. On a very cold night we climbed quickly to camp two and Pete crossed most of the col ridge alone that day. Dave and I completed this section to the final

*They climbed a new route on the Ogre South Face, just failing to reach the summit and recovering a rucksack and summit film belonging to Bonington and Scott. A year later, Tetsuji Furutu heralded a UK visit thus: '26 April I get married; 27 April I arrive Sheffield for honeymoon. I wish to meet many fit and proper persons!'

pyramid of the mountain early next morning with heavy loads and established camp three. Evidently we were now well acclimatized and on 18 August Pete and Dave climbed the first knife-edged ridge of the final pyramid. Climbing morning and evening I carried the necessary remaining equipment from camp two to camp three. Now terrifying clouds were streaming between the Latoks at high altitude and a ferocious gale on the highest summits was the harbinger of the next storm. It had still not reached us at dawn, so all three of us ascended the knife edge *en route* for camp four.

Our fixed rope now ended just by the point from which Pat Green and I retreated last year. Above, the ridge proved technically easier but hard work as for hundreds of feet one sank in snow to the calves. At a steepening, Dave came through and, stalwart ice climber that he is, soloed 500ft of highly exposed ice with a heavy load. Pete and I did likewise before fixing a line on this section. This lightened Dave's load and he plodded out a fine ladder of steps up through the swirling clouds enveloping us.

The storm was on us as the site of camp four opened out, a snowy shoulder seemingly almost level with the massive towers and ridges of Peak 6,960m to the west. We dumped our loads, slid into 'windlord' protectives and had little time to gaze as visibility faded. Lightly laden, the solo descent was as fast as we dared make it, as new snow blew on to the hard ice of the slope and we crammed into the tunnel tent at camp three. The storm was unabated overnight and another week without progress threatened; but as we retreated next morning in a foot of snow, with the storm still persisting, we knew we were climbing well and that in the next good weather there were few obstacles to an all-out effort.

In the next days of bad weather Saeed joined us in rock climbing on boulders near base and on 25 August Dave and I visited the Latok 3 Japanese Expedition on the Baintha Lukpar Glacier. They had problems as their liaison officer was homesick. Makato Hara regaled us with sake and dry fish. Good weather came as we feasted with the Japanese. Much enthused by the company he hailed us: 'You, British are kama-kazi pilots'.

On 26 August all three of us were back in advanced base, where our two tents perched by now on plinths 3ft above the glacier surface.

Yet again we climbed the dangerous and boring slope to the col in early morning frost. Hardly lingering at camp two, by midday, after about ten hours' climbing, we were digging out the tent at camp three. Food and gas were still plentiful on the mountain while we had ample rope and other equipment in our upper camps. At dawn next day there were again signs of bad weather but we moved with all the gear we required to camp four by midday.

As we were a little ahead Dave and I carried on to investigate the rock barrier which appeared to be the most serious obstacle between us and the summit. Dave led a long slope and probed one route, but we retreated from a wall of steep rock equivalent to a major British rock climb which, at 22,000ft, was too great a barrier. We led through on a 400ft rope to a likely point of weakness about 150ft from the easing of the ridge. Above, some steep technical climbing was required, but we were confident of success next morning. As a high cold wind blew in we deposited several hundred feet of rope and the climbing ironmongery and slid down the ropes 500 or 600ft to camp four.

High wind and heavy snow came before midnight and for over ninety hours there was little point in putting more than a hand outside. On 1 September the weather had not cleared. We were physically stale and underfed in order to preserve supplies for a last push. Icy rime reduced our insulation and we were irked by morning dehydration headaches. In need of rest and food, our chances of success now dwindled. Suspending belief and disappointment in the trouble of striking the tent and fastening crampons in the icy wind and in the dangers of teetering with loads down the arête with its covering of feet of new snow, we went down. That night we reached camp two and next day in slightly improved conditions we left the mountain.

Ironically at Skardu the monsoon had passed. I stayed a night with Jack Turner at the Rest House as he received the radio message that at least the Americans had settled some of their scores with K2, with two ascents – several without oxygen.* Only the Japanese on Latok 3 remained in action despite expiry of permission, while Skardu was an abandoned Wild West film-set devoid of expeditions and porters.

Baleful Barnaj – Jammu Kashmir (1979)

Kashmir Roadsign: 'Death lays his icy hand upon the speedking.'

At dawn the train crept across the flats of Jammu, gateway to Kashmir and the western section of the Greater Himalayan Chain. At the station packed humanity rushed to taxis, but there is a pile of baggage to manhandle through the crowds. This is a journey without much respite. Thirteen hours in a crowded train and then twelve by an overloaded bus, climbing through monsoon rain for several hours on the Srinagar highroad, then teetering along the Chenab Gorge. A road has been chiselled and blasted from the massive slopes, seamed as they are by side valleys and landslips. A battalion of labourers maintains its ephemeral existence.

Exhausted by early evening after days of travel, we emerged at the hill station of Kishtwar, at 6 or 7,000ft, an oasis of fine arable high above the Chenab river. The air was cooler, a light breeze swept across the great *maidan* (open space). Rose gardens surrounded the *dak* bungalow which became our temporary base and only the narrowest of lanes continued north and east. We were nearing the limit of mechanical transport. Soon everything had to travel on men's backs or on mules. The pace of the expedition slowed. There were arrangements to be made, bags to be repacked, last minute supplies to be bought, but the scramble was over and we reverted to the pace of the Raj.

*See R. Ridgeway *The Last Step* (The Mountaineers' Seattle, 1979).
This route was attempted again by a Japanese expedition in 1985, and by a British party including the author in 1987. It has still repulsed all comers!

The caretaker of the bungalow, Ghulam Mohmed, showed me his photos of Nikki Clough. He has seen many expeditions come and go and had his own views on our venture. 'Barnaj, no people, very bad, very cold place.' From our previous attempt to climb in the area we knew it well, for we had been beset by almost daily snow and storms in 1977. Now in a hopeful frame of mind as good weather persisted, donkeys were arranged to meet us 20 miles away at the road head at Galhar, loads of 156lb were measured out for them. Ghulam Mohmed's fine curries and scrambled eggs represented a last few days of civilization. Here, too, were some Polish climbers and vodka, reminding us of the great winter Himalayan climber, Tadeuz Pietrowski, whom we met here in 1977. From here, only 100 yards from the bungalow, our expeditions went their different ways: Mo Anthoine, Joe and Valerie Brown, Pete Minks and Bill Barker travelled due north for two days before striking up to Brammah 2, while we turned east after a few miles to follow the Chenab.

At least this time the little bus was available to carry us the last 20 miles up the road to Galhar mule station. Full to capacity, it lurched along the forestry track with the white waters of the Chenab over 1,000ft below. The incense of the driver's tiny altar signified a hope and a prayer for us all.

After 10 miles the devastation from last winter's severity is revealed. Trees lie in their hundreds, overturned like skittles by a vast avalanche. In late August the snow still lies awaiting another winter and a narrow rut carries the road onward. Woodcutters transformed the massacred forest into railway sleepers. It was a scene frequently repeated thereafter. The destruction was so great that an official emergency had been declared, with helicopters carrying in extra food to isolated villages. Houses had collapsed on their human and animal occupants, many cattle had been slaughtered and some avalanches swept down with such ferocity that they blocked rivers and exploded up the opposite sides of valleys.

We needed seven mules to carry our gear and for five days travelled with the three muleteers. We meandered through the forests of the Chenab for two days, following a path which picks out a tenuous and tough route through a massive gorge. It is a major highroad, laboriously constructed and maintained; duck-board platforms cling to vast, mossy granite cliffs and along them clatter mules and humans. It is busy with Sikh grain traders, trains of sheep carrying their tiny loads on buckled backs! 'Hotels' supply tea and rice and a bed for a pittance, if one dare brave the insect life of the rope beds and the exotica of the food. Meat means lizard as an aphrodisiac, visibly green and scaly through the yellow dripping curry. We left a lot of scraps.

Beyond the pleasant vale of Athole Bob Toogood became ill with stomach trouble, and reluctantly turned back. We climbed towards Machail, 2,000ft in perhaps 22 miles. At 10,000ft and the end of familiar ground the mule men would have preferred to stop. After long bureaucratic delays in Delhi, we were in a hurry and unwilling to break loads to fit our gear to porter loads, even if such men were available. Hanuman Suthar, our liaison officer, used guile and persuasion to get them to continue to Base Camp. Eventually they succumbed to cajoling, high pay and intervention from the local police. It was a coup, as they had never visited the Barnaj valley, feared the height and its cold as well as being frightened of evil spirits. I persuaded them that I knew it contained some of the region's best grazing and that they would probably be glad to return once these initial objections were overcome.

It took a day and a half to reach the flowery fields of the upper Barnaj Nullah. It was more extraordinary than I remembered, like a transfigured Lakeland valley. Below the snout of the glacier our base nestled under small warm cliffs by a stream of perfect clarity springing from the rocks. Edelweiss carpeted the valley with a host of other tiny flowers of exquisite colours. Much of the green foliage was seared a dark autumnal red by the sun of a weak monsoon. Half-wild horses roamed a mile away and further down the valley summer graziers kept a few cattle and goats. Framing such scenes in every direction are a dozen or more mountains of about 20,000ft, most of which have not even been attempted. For a climber it is close to paradise, and the more so when on our previous visit it had hardly revealed itself through wraiths of autumnal sleet and snow.

The four climbers were organized to climb as two separate parties. This is the essence of 'alpine-style' climbing as it allows great flexibility of climbing arrangements and divergence in what climbers climb and in the timing of ascent. It contrasts markedly with traditional methods where fixed camps, fixed ropes and large numbers of climbers create great rigidity.

Jim Curran and Tony Riley aimed to climb the South Ridge of Barnaj 2 (20,990ft) while we had originally intended to try its West Face. In the first days of September a joint advanced base was set up at almost 16,000ft, eerily close to massive granite walls flung down from below the twisted spire of the Phallus of Shiva, a curiosity of Barnaj. At last on a cold, blustery morning, John Yates and I traversed the boulder slopes to reach the hanging valley below the West Face, which forms a Sanctuary cut off from any easy access.

The face offers a possibility, but of a most serious kind. A sharp green ice ridge soars up into hanging ice cliffs. If they can be passed, the upper wall of the Central Summit of Barnaj 2 can be climbed, though with some difficulty at those altitudes. Unfortunately after an hour studying the face from a massive rock prow below the Sanctuary, no obvious route through the cliffs could be seen. Even worse, the route to the ice arête was more threatened by hanging ice cliffs and rock falls than we had been able to anticipate from my photographs taken in 1977. Nor did the weather encourage us, two men rather than three as originally intended, to persist in this plan. There were few stopping places on the route to sit out the daily snowfalls. Thoughtfully and with some regrets we decided to consult the others and share the South Ridge Route. With only three weeks at base camp this appeared to maximize our opportunities, so late on 3 September we hurried back down the moraines to the green valley and base camp.

In the darkness as we arrived, Jim, Tony and Suthar were cooking a lordly supper. Suthar was a vegetarian and bit by bit, as we were primarily living on Indian food, we were being converted. Dahl (lentils), rice and a variety of suitable sauces were the staples. As we waded through a pressure cooker full of such food, arrangements were made. Both Tony and Jim had at various times

143

suffered some illness, and just then Jim displayed the classic symptoms of the sick white sahib in Asia – so while he recovered Tony decided to join us in our preparations for a push up the South Ridge. Should Jim fail to recover we agreed that he would accompany us.

In the next few days we were repulsed by bad weather, retreating after a damp night in an uncomfortable cave. Then we had the misfortune of attracting the attentions of a local wildcat, which was not content to raid the refuse. During our absence on the mountain it entered the advanced base tent and urinated on every square inch of our equipment and food. We spent some time clearing the mess and resting before the next attempt.

On the evening prior to our departure Jim arrived, cheerful and apparently near to recovery and we could revert to the much more efficient system with which we had begun. John and I were up at 3am and by dawn John was already climbing up ahead as we ascended the long slopes below the first ice gully of our route. After a hard frost came a fine morning.

Sunday, 9 September was auspicious. At a short steep section we put on the 300ft 'everdry' rope and I smacked the pick of my ice axe into the black ice. This time the adventure had really begun. In only a couple of hours despite heavy loads the couloir was climbed and an escape made on to the icy shelf of a hanging glacier which leads to the South Ridge.

Few stones fell on that frozen, fine morning. As we laboured across the shelf there were some crevasses to avoid as the sun crept over the shoulders of Barnaj 3. I hid behind black glasses and my floppy hat as the route lay up a steep ice slope towards the ridge. There was a steep step across the yawning hole below the slope, then the gasping routine of planting the ice axe pick, walking up the crampons on steep ice, planting the pick . . . while John rested in the heat haze, which soon dispelled the chill of night, in the basin below. Bit by bit, with John leading the next section, we reached a snowy shoulder.

It was a nostalgic moment – Jim Curran and I had spent four nights of storm with Geoff Smith and Tier here on our last attempt in 1977. The Himalaya shrug off such pinpricks with indifference. The very ground had changed. Our campsite was rent in half by monster crevasses. At midday we brewed lemonade as the effort and the altitude began to tell.

Beyond the nasty crevasses a steep slope of rock and ice led to the ridge. The old fixed rope helped a little, but it was frayed and suspect. The 600ft seemed endless, painful, and snow flurries began as I scraped my crampons up the steep and brittle ice, circumnavigating awkward rock steps. At last the single piton at the head of the rope appeared and above it a good bivouac place. At about 18,000ft we had done well and it was time to rest.

Once on the ridge we entered a different world. The basin of advanced base was so far below that the crevasses appeared as blue scratches in the shadow. In the distance the bigger peaks increasingly differentiated themselves. To the west the twin pyramids of the Brammahs lunged skywards and beyond loomed the massive double hump of Nun Kun (23,000ft). To the north an indescribable multitude of mountains reared out of Ladakh, while to the south and east not one of the shapes was familiar. As darkness fell snow swept in as we tried to rehydrate. John made coffee and a freeze-dried meal and I arranged my legs so that I could sleep straight. They projected out of the tent zip into my rucksack in the direction of sunrise.

Time is a stern master when you are limited by what you can carry in one rucksack with your own legs and lungs. We had food for four or five days, a minimum of climbing equipment, just enough gas fuel to provide vital water. Yet we could not rush at this altitude: everything must be done steadily, carefully, calculation first, whether it be lighting the stove, erecting the tent or 'front pointing' up an icy arête.

The sun rose on my horizon at 5.30am on 10 September. Ice covered all our equipment inside the blue and red bivouac tent. John remained inert as I began the chores, stuffing frozen snow and ice in the brew can. Gradually coffee brews pushed back headaches and lethargy, while a little porridge settled queasy stomachs. Yesterday's heavy effort was telling: today we must be careful to avoid overtiredness. It was necessary to gain height, but with the symptoms of some altitude sickness not far away in both of us it might be best to avoid too great a push for fear of preventing a greater effort tomorrow. Today was a day of technical climbing, mainly on rock up the pinnacles of the ridge.

With the sun on its east flank the ridge proved a pleasant surprise. Tower upon tower never failed in interest. Forays on the west side led into the icy shadows but we emerged time and again on its warmer side. John led, in control, carefully, with pleasure, and I enjoyed the position, the photographic angles, the views, the relative safety and security of rock. Now and then the remoteness asserted itself. A few miles to the east trapped between two north walls which dwarf the Eiger and the Matterhorn, the Hagshu La Pass (17,000ft) appeared as an obvious 'U', and I recalled that remote fastness from an exploration with Geoff Smith two years before. Beyond was the unclimbed Hagshu Peak, which has been tried several times without success.

At last, early in the afternoon, John had a tiring struggle with a short ugly chimney, where sacks had to be hauled, and we flopped onto the rock shelf above in tired relief. Beyond, open ice and snow slopes had already softened in the sun but there was perhaps 1500ft to the south summit. Cloud was crowding in again, with snow already on Brammah. Quickly, anxious to remain dry, we erected the tent behind a small boulder to keep off a hostile wind. Soon little was visible but the green icicles of a nearby ice cliff in a sea of mist and driven snow.

We ate and above all concentrated on liquid, even awakening at midnight for another warm drink. Ice again coated everything but the snowfall had ceased by then. Instead jagged lightning short-circuited the whole of the southern sky. It had been a poor, late monsoon – had the predicted second phase come to relieve the beleaguered Punjabi farmer? I prayed that it would be confined to the plains for our summit day.

John boiled the water at 5.15am and my head hurt, but it was time to go. Without fixed camps, sherpas, fixed ropes, relays and dumps of food all depends on movement. We ate porridge and fudge and stored almost all our gear under the boulder. Little food was left in any case, and only one can of gas. John led off unencumbered and I followed with a minimum of food and protective clothes in the sack. It had to be today. The summit slopes proved long, icy and arduous. We sought a little security in what rock we could find, and John led out repeated 'pitches' of over 300ft. The snow was firm and we made good progress, but a film of cloud swept over us as we carefully ascended a final few hundred feet of hideous loose rocks and ice. The last ice was steep, genuine ice climbing using two ice picks each. At 12.15, after six hours of climbing, we were at the South Summit (21,000ft). Mist blocked out the view and it had already begun to snow.

There was no procrastination. A few unneeded items were left in the sack and John led off along the ridge connecting the South and higher Central Summit. The latter remained unclimbed after a large Japanese expedition replete with camps and paraphernalia reached this point in 1975 after weeks of climbing. The ridge was surprising and potentially hazardous, knife edges of ice alternating with steep and awkward pinnacles.

More and more snow swept in on a cold and strengthening wind. After crossing one steep pinnacle my mental alarm clock chimed a warning. 'We can go on for another hour, I think,' I said to John as I emerged panting into the wind after heaving up a steep wall. Otherwise we must have a forced bivouac. The rapidity of John's reaction showed that in his mind alarms had sounded too. 'We cannot get to the Central Summit by then … OK, I suppose we go back then.' Both of us were aware that this ridge would be quite as difficult and time-consuming to reverse as to climb, while the weather worsened by the minute. Already I was setting off to reverse across the pinnacle. The main summit appeared momentarily then was swept away again in the mists.

It snowed incessantly for most of the five hours of descent, though once there was a tantalizing clearance. The upper slopes we treated gingerly, creeping from loose stone to loose stone, belaying wherever it was possible. With our few slings and rock pitons it was possible to abseil the lower ridge to the upper bivouac, tired and stumbling in the deep soft snow.

By then the wind was strong and the snow driving in everywhere. We slumped into our sleeping bags in the bivvy tent as quickly as we could, zipping out the bad weather and hoping for better. There followed several hours of uneasy sleep before thirst drove us to make coffee at midnight. I juddered awake and felt a desperate urge to drink, so we took turns to brew, reaching out bare-handed to collect the freezing snow, waiting an hour or more for the precious fluid. It was the usual menu – coffee, lemonade, coffee, dried beef bourguignon, when at last we managed to eat.

Dawn was grey, and it was still snowing. We escaped our cocoons with difficulty. Wearing all our storm gear we lumbered down the abseils and tricky little descents, double checking every anchor – we were on the way home.

By 9am we reached the first bivouac site and stopped for a moment to collect extra equipment which remained from the 1977 attempt.

During the descent to the lower basin a block shifted as I abseiled the rope;

I dropped a foot or two with a curse. In the snow basin the steep slope was avoided by a snowy circuit through seracs to reach the traverse. In the couloir stones began to fall from the slopes of Barnaj 3 and ropes jammed on the stones inset into the ice as we descended. A few additional anchor points indicated that Tony and Jim had been on to the upper glacier. The occasional pot shots turned into a cannonade of rock as we reached the rock buttress that protects the lower slope. Once on the glacier we were suddenly very tired, before going on down to advance base. There we packed, leaving Jim's and Tony's gear for another attempt, and staggered in the late afternoon on down to the glacier and base camp.

There was only a day of further good weather, when Jim and Tony made another attempt. As I watched from the west side of the glacier they reached the last slope to the ridge as snow and high clouds covered everything. Late next day they were back after a night in a snow hole in a crevasse. The game was over again.

As my timetable was extremely tight my friends allowed me to leave alone. In rain I walked in one stretch to a hut beyond Chisote. As I ate a plate of rice two equally soaked individuals of evident Britishness arrived. They were eking out even sparser supplies. It was my first encounter with Steve Venables and his brother. In my haste I had to leave early next day, too early for goodbyes. It rained throughout the hours of daylight.

Dr Pete Thexton

Memorial Service Address (Ealing 1983).

Few of Pete's present climbing friends knew him before 1977. Then he joined the ACG and had already done much rock climbing and some alpine climbs of a high standard. It seemed to go back, as he only gradually revealed, to fondly remembered family trips to Lundy. Cautious as he could be, he waxed eloquent whenever the island was mentioned.

Perhaps exams and the organization of hospitals weighed heavily on him. His first expeditions in 1978 look very much like a liberation. He led most of the first ascent of Thalay Sagar, and the long sad expedition to the North-West ridge of Latok – after the traumatic experience when Pat Fearnehough was killed by rockfall going into the Karakoram – left him older, still reticent and cautious, but with a smouldering energy and resolve within. He was a practical mountaineer, meticulous in preparation and execution of his aims, a streak that came out in some aspects of his medical work, and as a caring but unpretentious expedition doctor, knowing his own limits and those of an over-authoritarian profession. Very much his own man, he was privy to many others' secrets; the springs of his own motivation lay so deep that only a persistent enquiry came within the walls. Now and then, on Latok and elsewhere the volcano erupted.

Pete Thexton and Alan Jewhurst celebrate Christmas at Everest base camp, 1980.

Dave Wilkinson and Pete Thexton, Latok Glacier.

Though he could be very hard on himself, he did not always expect as much of less singleminded companions. He hated to lose an opportunity. On Latok, after a two-month siege and a last ten days on the mountain, we retreated with the autumn in a storm. All day we were in grey driving cloud, solo climbing down snow on a ridge so open that we could not protect it with the rope. There followed a narrow knife edge, which had taken a day to fix with rope to ease repeated passage. As we were going down we took off the rope and fled to a little safe notch to spend a night before the hazards of the lower slopes.

During the night an icy blast came from the north and the three of us shivered in sleeping bags. There was little food. Stars and frost came together and in the morning conditions were well frozen but very cold. It augured well to make the last descent safely. Pete sat thoughtful ... 'Shouldn't we go up?' He was outvoted, but who can say that he was wrong?

On Everest in winter (1980–81) he doctored us all as health failed in outrageous conditions. The mountaineering imperative loomed large to him, and he loved the West Shoulder so much at −25°F to −55°F that he stayed there alone for days at near 24,000ft until his coughing cracked a rib. Nevertheless he sacrificed immediate climbing to come down to base to treat Wang Chop, our cook, who had a haemorrhage. Pete had the inner fire but he climbed for pleasure. He did not blame friends for his own weakness or mistakes. He was

148

supremely steady, often unhurried while others betrayed their anxiety in too much rush. Yet he did extreme things, like climbing the North Face of the Midi solo in winter in a storm. He tested his powers and learned daily from experience. Under an unassuming exterior was immense inner strength, deep-rooted in his past, his will and intellectual and practical gifts. His pleasures were evident, in physical effort, sunbathing even at sub-zero temperatures, his enormous appetite for food for a small man, and the ability to increase his rock climbing standards in the last years far higher than he had formerly dreamed.

Pete made many friends, more, probably, than any one of them knows. His grasp on life was tenacious, and he was very happy in the mountains.

He died on Broad Peak in 1983, of altitude-related sickness, in which he was so interested, attended by Greg Child, porter Gohar and Don Whillans. Don thereby relived the nightmare of the death of Bob Downes on Masherbrum, so many years before. It was again the second major climb of the summer, after success on a new route with Greg and Doug Scott, on The Lobsang Spires.

MIRRORS ON MEN AND EVENTS

Involvement in *Mountain* magazine had begun long before at its inception in 1968. Ken Wilson had once suggested I become editor, and buy the magazine, around edition 35 or 40, but I declined, because I was busy elsewhere and had no money.

Curiously I happened to travel to London with Tim Lewis and Geoff Birtles when they took over in 1978. A year later I became part owner to expedite their necessary divorce.

I was unaware of the pleasures and the pains such close involvement would entail.

Angles on Reinhold Messner

'And what rough beast slouches towards Bethlehem to be born.'
(The Second Coming, Yeats)

In the 70s and 80s Reinhold Messner completed what must be regarded as the dream of Hermann Buhl, eventually climbing all the major 8,000m summits without oxygen, and many of them solo. Others tried, and some came near to comparable success on some peaks, though by 1986, when Messner completed his crusade, only the Pole Jerzy Kukuczka, Swiss Erhard Loretan and West German Michael Dacher were near. Many failed to stay the pace, and some died.

The Seventh Grade by Reinhold Messner. Kaye & Ward, 1974.

Mountain 39. (1974).

The title put me off, despite the interest I had in seeing what this remarkable climber would have to say. Only a few days beforehand, a good British climber had spent the whole of our wet Wales weekend wobbling into a flat spin about the ten-hour Eiger ascent that Messner accomplished. It was therefore to be hoped that this book would give some idea of how he ticks, but instead here was a technical title: it conjured up visions of the Elbsandstein mountains of East Germany, with would-be alpinists clawing out frustration on little, dizzy, rounded walls, or of the endless double-binded boredom of Drummondine grade f-spew six half-screw-and-a-rurp old-style Padarn Lake conversation.

Hence the relief when the 'dry technical' treatise breathed life:

150

I leaned my head against the wall and closed my eyes . . . when I opened my eyes again, I saw the grey Dolomite wall with fine moss lying in the cracks. The irregularities of the rock stood out, clear and lustrous, they became interwoven with the moss forming fantastic pictures.

Consideration of the 'seventh grade' is made to live in an episodic essay in autobiography, revolving round a relatively short and highly charged phase of a young climber's life: he is a student, ex-student, teacher at times, a climber more than anything.

Time is little respected within the few years covered. Instead, the author uses his life to point the direction towards an open-ended scaling of climbing difficulties. The events are sometimes gripping, once one sees past the precise, terse style. They should be, for they include a mass of exposed and difficult solo climbing on routes like the North Face Direct on the Droites, the Phillip/Flamm, the Sassolungo, and others in the Eastern Alps. It has not always felt easy, and the author admits he has encountered real difficulties: 'I thus found it hard to comprehend that things were not working out well and that the confidence which I had built up . . . had evaporated, leaving behind a sense of fear which prevented me from tackling this last impasse.' This contributes greatly to the sense of authenticity which pervades the whole book, and supports broader statements concerning the author's feelings about his chosen activity: '(The climber) sees things in a new light with a clarity and mobility which can for example be attained by meditation. Above all he sees himself in a new relationship to the world.'

The sincerity of the enterprise is also underlined by apparently eccentric observations: 'Experienced mountaineers, who take a severe climb as a matter

Clint Eastwood, Reinhold Messner, Peter Habeler and further unknown glitterati.

of course, when they are at home become startled out of all proportion if
something falls to the ground.'

Whatever the truth in this, the author exudes conviction and commitment on
every line. His exhaustive training goes far beyond that undertaken by any but a
few British climbers, yet this is not a narrow fanaticism. He assimilates the
alpine past, demystifies and redefines the present, and looks forward to the
future. To those who berate him as a child of death, he is scornful. Yet: 'There
was something that I still had to learn, to laugh at myself.' Though he loves the
mountains, a feeling inadequately expressed by the book's pictures, he also
knows that they can be 'neutral and indifferent as though man has never
existed'.

The episodes are not fully digested, and the book has a diary-like quality
which prevents the erasure of inconvenient and honest thoughts. For all the
problems of translation, there are not enough books like this.

Solo Nanga Parbat by Reinhold Messner, translated by Audrey Salkeld. Kaye & Ward (1981)

Mountain 79, (1981).

Stardom may be envied but it is rarely easy. Within weeks of Everest without
oxygen in 1978 Messner was in Pakistan heading for the 'German mountain'.
His life with Uschi had crumbled and the publicity machine worked inexorably
at making his life the common currency of mid-Europe. It is hardly surprising
that, 'This time I don't want to see if I will survive or fail, I just want to go.'

The epic tale of the ascent of the Rupal flank in 1970 is well known, but that
of a former solo stab in 1973 less so. How climbers nurse their plans and
schemes! One suspects few can be more assiduous than Reinhold in cultivating
that internal garden. Refreshingly this time he lets more out, rather than
stressing sensationalist 'Seventh Grades' or 'Death Zones' which can mean
much only to people who are ignorant. Solo, one has to face one's weakness –
there is no other excuse, but when action comes, 'There is time to do it but not
to think about it.'

After much agonizing, loneliness and fear Reinhold does, yet again, and the
book is pretty good too. Quite apart from bringing the author to life once more,
it summarizes Nanga Parbat's history and avoids the temptations to rehearse
once more the controversies of the 1970 expedition. It is less important to
pursue the blasphemies of extreme climbing than to know that the 'desperate
business of living can be transcended by sheer joy of being alive.'

High Ambition – A Biography of Reinhold Messner by R. Faux. Gollancz. 1982

Messner is an industry and further books about him need justification. But
Messner's success requires explanation, and Ronnie Faux tries to see his career

as being of a piece. Former Messner books tend to reflect particular ascents or experiences and sometimes create a fragmentary impression. Of course Messner has chosen his objectives with great care, and to this, as well as exceptional drive, his numerous 8,000m climbs must be attributed. He has not taken on objectives which would swallow him as some other very accomplished solo climbers have been prone to do.* Thus his greatest feat has been to both ascend and to descend more or less intact, and to carry through a plan of startling ambition. Despite great risks and epics he has survived, though he, too, seems sometimes haunted by those who have not. Faux tries also to make sense of Messner's ordinary life, but perhaps like Georges Bettembourg comes close to the conclusion that it cannot exist.

Restating Tradition – A Comment on Wilfred Thesiger's Desert, Marsh and Mountain

To survive always involved the nicest calculation. 'We know we must have at least one of the Saar with us, otherwise their tribe, blood enemies of the Rashid, might follow us into the sands and kill us. Everyone at Manwakh assured us we should in any case be killed by the Yam and the Dawasir.'

They survived, but only just, crossing 400 waterless miles and only just avoiding an encounter with raiding parties who were killing everyone they met.

Thesiger travelled in disguise and became steeped in Arabic language and custom. On a second visit to the Empty Quarter he asked one of his Arab companions, 'if on my first visit he had guessed I was a European' – 'No, we often wondered who you were, but it never occurred to us you were a Christian.' These Arab journeys were mostly accomplished between 1946 and 1950, but by then Thesiger had spread his wings into exploration in Kurdistan, the Madan of Iraq, a huge area of swamp, where he lived for long periods among warring tribesmen. He avoided the summer in that area by a number of visits to remote areas on the border between Afghanistan and Pakistan and his accounts of Hunza and Nuristan are of some interest. But most telling is not the subject, the people and places of these wild and remote regions, but the motivations of the man. Here is no casual visitor, no tourist with misted eye. Thesiger went as close as possible to his hosts, forming deep friendships of many years' standing; always the only European, hating the havoc which modernization wreaks, he has accepted the change that the social discipline of the hardest life can impose. Nowhere does it show more than in the feeling and sensitivity of his photographs.

Those climbers with aspirations among primitive societies particularly should read this book, for Thesiger is the desert Shipton.

*Nicholas Jaeger or Roger Marshall.

Eric Shipton. The Six Mountain Travel Books by Diadem and The Mountaineers' Seattle, 1985

Mountain *103. (1985).*

Collections and anthologies excite mixed feelings, and never more so than when they incorporate complete books that are already favourites. They risk the loss of the essential character of each original work, pages and illustrations ingrained into one's consciousness, appropriated. Reworkings can kindle resentment.

That is all very well for those in possession, but of less use to younger climbers, or those previously unfamiliar with the world of Shipton, Tilman and their companions. It is to the credit of Diadem and The Mountaineers that they have launched this, and its companion collection of Tilman's *Seven Mountain Travel Books.* Anyone can trek or climb in Nepal, India or Pakistan without their insights, and in consequence find themselves the poorer. Together Shipton and Tilman represent a high point of the romantic-individualist exploratory mountaineering and its literature at the point where the reality of Empire collapsed and the illusions of post-imperial Britain were speedily erected. Shipton and Tilman lived that collapse in flight from the 1920s failure of the Kenyan tea economy, and concentrated instead on lifelong adventure. They disciplined that by a shared constant detestation of humbug and pretence, and Shipton's deep aesthetic appreciation of mountains combined with an endless exploratory urge.

As Jim Perrin states in the introduction to this edition, 'For the span of their contents alone, Shipton's books are noteworthy', involving Himalayan first ascents, extensive explorations of the Karakoram, experience in China and Sinkiang, the intrigues over Everest's first ascent, and a search for another spiritual haven in the storm-swept territories off the tip of South America. Shipton was happy to explore until his health failed, he hit hard times and transcended them; he was both a renowned figure for much of his life and 'to all intents and purposes a professional pauper and a kind of international tramp'.

In the collection of his books and their joint issue there is a deep nostalgia, but though they formed the slender means that helped him survive from one expedition to the next, they convey a persistent enthusiasm and *joie de vivre* that makes their whole seem greater than their opportunistic parts. As mere memorabilia they would be remarkable, but their guts is in the inspiration, the wish to emulate that Shipton inspired in contemporaries and later companions, and which still shines from the pages. Surely few more recent Himalayan explorer climbers have not held him as model. Without his lightweight expeditions the peregrinations of the Collisters, Venables and Griffins would have been less likely, not because of their practical geographical results, but because of the spirit in which his ventures were undertaken. One cannot easily forget the enthusiasm with which the discovery of an old ski stick basket was greeted near Snowlake in 1971 – for it must have come from either Shipton's 1939 expedition or (perhaps) the Greenald expedition of 1956. Perhaps only

George Bettembourg leads off on the first
ascent of the North Ridge of Nuptse.
Photo by Doug Scott.

Rugged Bill Tilman. *Photo by W. G. Lee.*

those who have tried to emulate their travels, carrying their own means of survival for days on end in the glacial wilderness between China and Pakistan, will fully appreciate the energy, skill and enthusiasm that made the Shipton explorations such high adventure.

The books' texts seem unabridged; modern maps make such extensive travels more comprehensible and a good number of the original photographs have been revived to good effect, both dramatic and humorous. Modern photography has been used to give a somewhat updated feel, though it has been kept in check to prevent it overpowering the textual content which is the centre of interest. Costs make inevitable light paper, small print and the lack of an index. Appendices fill in much of the detail that Shipton must have thought of insufficient consequence to be embodied in his books, and a bibliography allows the most interested to go further. Finally, Jim Perrin's introduction acts not only as a focus for the books, but as a trailer for his forthcoming biography of Shipton. One hopes that will take the story further, as has his recent work on Menlove Edwards. Further clues to the motivations and inspiriting drive of Shipton the enigma, enlivening to activists and dreamers alike, can only be welcome.

Two Generations by Edmund and Peter Hillary. Hodder and Stoughton, 1984

Mountain *101*. *(1985)*.

Climbers are often better at describing their actions than at expressing their thoughts. Their enthusiasm enriches words describing ascent or descent into the teeth of a storm; they seem sadder, less adequate, when faced with society's complexities and evils, or with their own essential loneliness and thoughts.

Ed and Peter Hillary have written accounts of their recent lives, the themes touching, occasionally interlocking, but also separate. Dominating Ed's life and permeating his account are the tragic deaths of his wife Louise and daughter Belinda in 1975. The aircrash and its aftermath, and the breaking of the carefree chain of happiness and extraordinary adventure which it seemed to mark, left him to face sadness at a bad time, as greater age forced down mountaineering achievement. The story is about soldiering on, frenetically active, jet-boating up the Ganges, visiting the East Face of Everest, and still gambling with life as altitude hit back. It is a frank, even slightly brusque statement, but while it describes the pain it sketches out a personal strategy of survival and adjustment in the face of impossible loss and emotional hardship.

Peter Hillary is his own man, with many of the frontier strengths and virtues of his father. One senses that he sought to avoid the mountaineering road, but eventually succumbed despite discouragements and deaths on the way, notably in the accident on a new route on Ama Dablam. He has tales to tell of his early life, remote New Zealand faces, alpine ski descents and Himalayan adventures, culminating in the Himalayan end-to-end walk with Graeme Dingle and the attempt on Lhotse without oxygen with Fred From, Aid Burgess and Paul Moores. The latter is interesting for itself, while the account of Ama Dablam makes too little of the help the survivors of the accident received.

Father and son have a direct, engaging style, but both reflect on the world somewhat pessimistically. It may be that Ed became less optimistic as he saw too much, though his energetic hospital building and relief work fund-raising suggest that it is personal loss rather than hope for mankind that hurts the most. Peter sees himself as 'an insouciant character, born for the 60s but arriving too late to fill that mould ... misplaced, however, gregarious and somewhat stultiloquent sandy-haired dilettante with a passion for the salubrity of the hills'.

For all their travels and self revelations, it is a sometimes insular account, referenced back to a family badly mauled by fate, to the wild shores of New Zealand and to the mountains. Few of the other people engaged in the expeditions come alive, except when quoted in Peter's account of Lhotse. For all the interest in belonging, in humanity, in friends, for the most part they sink into the background behind the mountains themselves, the winds, the technical description. Perhaps that comes of too many diaries, the individuation of high mountain ageing, the wish to belong rather than its reality that should be recognizable to many mountaineers despite all the contrary claims.

Smythe's Mountains: The Climbs of F. S. Smythe by Harry Calvert. Gollancz, 1985.

Mountain 108. (1986).

The climbing career of Frank Smythe, meteoric in his own time, is less well known to many younger mountaineers today, even in the English-speaking world. It is rather as if his success as a climber, writer and photographer has faded with him. Yet any reader of Harry Calvert's book must marvel at his activism, at the verve and energy he dedicated to climbs in several continents.

The secret of his success seems to have been a single-mindedness unusual even among mountaineers, but equally an ability to spread his appreciation in his books to a large audience who remained devotees thereafter. He appealed not to the debunking and austere in his readers, as did his contemporary Tilman, but to a romantic yet optimistic and sentimental vision of mountaineering. Ultimately Smythe sold a much-simplfied, heroic and sympathetic picture of himself to a wide public, and was resented by some of those who thought they knew the 'real Smythe' better. The author claims that he writes for the same public of Smythe enthusiasts, fired by his straightforward ideals in their enjoyment of the hills, great and small. One can read the book and emerge more informed, but one questions whether this book is as inspirational as Smythe's own. Once removed from its subject, the spell seems to be broken. Surely Smythe should not be done the injustice of being taken at his own valuation after thirty-five years? When will the 'real' Smythe be resurrected, if ever? One may doubt whether the self-doubting Smythe behind the myth would have sought out a more evaluative biography in his own time, but the mountaineering posterity perhaps deserves one now, even if there is a general market which does not care.

To be fair, Harry Calvert probably chose a difficult subject. Smythe's introspective and obsessive character, and the severity of his conflict with T. Graham Brown early in his career, probably gave him a jaundiced view of many climbers and the world in general. That sits very oddly with his public and much publicized persona. The reconciliation of the two is probably impossible without a much more critical treatment. The author remains too much influenced by Smythe's self projection to find that possible.

The White Death by George Bettembourg. Reynard House Seattle, 1982

Fifty Years of Alpinism by Riccardo Cassin. Diadem, 1982.

Mountain 90. (1983).

In the past the most able climbers, if they were lucky, might visit the Himalaya once or twice in their lives. Myths grew out of slight experience of really high places and sometimes sheer lack of knowledge did not prevent the most exceptional feats like that of Norton on Everest when he exceeded 28,000ft without oxygen in 1924. But the stuff of much legend was heroic failure, whether in the English tradition from Mummery to Mallory and Irvine or in the German losses on Nanga Parbat. Since the Second World War and especially in the last decade, all this has changed.

As the major peaks have been climbed, adventure, in the form of small alpine expeditions, has been reasserted, culminating in Messner's solo ascent of Everest. But greater exposure to and experience of the realities of the high altitude environment has rubbed away much of the naïve romance. In some ways a more negative judgement of the pleasures of the highest altitudes is beginning to pervade. There is achievement and even pleasure in high places, in the harshest of circumstances, but as George Bettembourg intimates, 'To be so happy, one of these days you are going to get it behind the neck.' To climb well you must want to do it, but in the Himalaya the potential sacrifice whatever your experience includes yourself. Bettembourg, with his Chamonix and American experience is perhaps in a better position to convey feelings about this, and about the reasons to go on nevertheless, than most mountaineers. A relative of the famous guiding family, the Charlets, he is steeped in the Chamonix tradition which is marked at every turn by danger as well as mastery in the mountains. *The White Death* recounts a concentrated biennium of Himalayan experience, with ascents alpine style of Broad Peak, Kusum Kanguru and Nuptse North Face, and a vivid account of his expedition to Kangchenjunga with the British.

Khumbu Himal.

Distrustful of big expeditions Bettembourg admits to haunting feelings about self, past climbers, lovers and companions, the ghosts ever present in extreme experience, and emphasizes the greater intensity of such feelings as time passes. He has more to say about himself, his companions and the experience of high altitude climbing than has been revealed for a long time. Intensity compensates too for photographs and understandable francophone expressions.

Too few great mountaineers survive to very great age. Riccardo Cassin is one of Europe's great survivors despite active climbing well beyond his seventieth year. The doyen of Italian alpinism before and after the Second World War, he continued to make further ascents of considerable difficulty throughout his life.

Cassin's is a matter-of-fact text, reflecting a simple, honest pleasure in his achievements and in the feats which he helped to inspire in others. In his fifty-year retrospective there are few spectres – instead he repeats the North-East Face of the Piz Badile with a grown-up son, relishes his ability to organize the expedition to Gasherbrum 4 after what he regards as an unfair exclusion from the successful K2 Expedition, saves Jack Canali from falling to his death in the descent from the Cassin Ridge of Mount McKinley, using only an ice axe belay, and goes on to lead the ambitious but eventually unsuccessful attempt on the South Face of Lhotse. Nor is the afterthought from a rather wise old man amiss as young, brilliant mountaineers push themselves into ever more ambitious experiences – there is always a sense in which Cassin seems to see his achievements as something more than a mere expression of his individuality: '... my long experience in the mountains now enables me to evaluate both sad and happy events in a rather calmer manner'.

Which is as it should be, for he has experienced everything that the mountains can give and take, though the summits may be different from those ardently pursued by his spiritual successors.

In 1987, aged seventy-nine, Cassin returned and climbed the North-East face of the Piz Badile.

High Drama by H. MacInnes. Hodder and Stoughton

Mountain 76. *(1980)*.

The gory side of mountaineering has its own appeal, and the rescuer an aura often denied to the climber, who is often patient or victim. Yet it is climbers, stalwart hillmen and helicopter professionals who bear the brunt of rescues. Hamish MacInnes knows as much about this as anyone, and has lived in the firing line for more than two decades in treacherous Glencoe. After covering the more technical aspects in his *International Mountain Rescue Handbook* he has gone for the drama.

Hamish MacInnes ponders
the problem.

Many of the stories bear resurrection: though the death of Tony Kurz on the Eiger is well known, how many people knew that the great climbers of Munich had their own troubleshooting rescue squad in the 30s? Other tales range from the Tatras to Scotland, The Grand Teton and New Zealand to the high wastes of the Himalaya. If there is a message it is probably hidden in 'Self-help on the Ogre'; for whatever the expertise of the rescuers ultimately it is individual judgement that counts, before the potential accident.

The Next Horizon by Chris Bonington. Gollancz, 1973.

Mountain 26. *(1973)*.

Maybe in mountaineering as well as in the rest of British society the cult of the stony-faced, quick-fisted hardman is at last on the way out. If it is, then perhaps the opaque mystique-building of the climbing idols will also disappear – or at least become less prominent. That, at least, is the impression gained from this second volume of Chris Bonington's memoirs. From beginning to end, the clash between the individualistic traditions of British climbing and the need for co-operation in larger scale projects is apparent.

160

A much mellowed Bonington is revealed. Not that competition is eschewed. Indeed its terminology persists throughout the book in the frequent references to the healthy spirit of competition (is it part of the dance of our chromosomes?); but the reader quickly realizes that in the face of truly formidable questions of success or survival there is scope for profitable alliance with the opponent or with competing teams (as occurred in the Winter Direct on the Eiger). Competition, as the author implies, can be afforded and is stimulating within the bounds of gamesmanship, in the search for new British climbs or the snatching of some first ascent abroad. But it is not worth a single life, as indeed it is dubious whether any mountaineering feat is worth that high a cost. In this context the playful competition of Tom Patey is remembered, though the extent to which this was a direct response to the author's own highly developed competitive spirit is not. Yet just as Patey was prepared to poke fun at himself, so, in a more serious manner characteristic of his personality, the 1973 Bonington reveals far more of himself than before.

The 'thruster' has travelled the road to success, despite some bleak troughs and most intense personal tragedy. From his privileged position he can more readily debate mistakes, fears and loves. Self-revelation is unusual in post-war climbing literature, and greatness does not thrive on revelations of human frailty. But Bonington steps from the pedestal, reveals major conflicts and fears, philosophizes on nuts but admits to his guilt, sees many of his climbing

Chris Bonington's next horizon. *Photo by Tony Riley.*

strengths and weaknesses, and enters into the debate on commercialization of which this book is an aspect. Yet he admits the unforgivable, the enjoyment of some of these commercial situations. After all, what could have been more pleasant than that week on Hoy? And the pleasure came across to the viewers. For a professional there can be no better defence. Armchair mountaineers and sturdy, never-reveal-the-pain climbers may see these as the confessions of a climber grown soft with family toils and fat on the spoils of war. The rugged may dislike a nature romanticism, which can cloy and certainly cannot match the translated naïvety of Kurt Diemburger's *Summits and Secrets* (Allen & Unwin, 1971), They may wish for more do-or-die drama, and distrust the quick shifts into the present tense which doubtless fall flat on occasion. But perhaps this is because they lack such feelings themselves or distrust their revelation. Maybe they should be glad to find that the pressure to get the book finished, the financial worries and the family ties cannot stop the real enthusiast, and that the loss of close friends cannot kill the spirit for ever.

Photographs are numerous, but they suffer inevitably by comparison with the magnificent Annapurna book, and include relatively little that the addict will find entirely new; there is little such climbing photography. There are a few fine colour plates.

For those with broad interests the story is interesting enough. It says a good deal about some of the most lively spirits of advanced mountaineering in this era, and much too of the atmosphere of a period when Britain developed her climbing as an export product. Bonington's progress from individualist-alpinist to entrepreneur-organizer requiring co-operation in the fulfilment of his plans is symptomatic of the responses of a vigorous and adaptable personality. Whatever the 'next horizon', those who wish to climb so widely and to survive in our society are going to be forced into similar traits.

The rest of the story is well known, with Chris's leadership of the successful Everest South-West expedition in 1975, the Ogre ascent and epic in 1977, success on the first ascent of Kongur in 1981 and loss of Pete Boardman and Joe Tasker on Everest's unclimbed North-East Ridge in 1982. Reflected is his relentless energy, but also a strategic tidiness which ensured that Chris had to climb Everest in his fiftieth year, not least because his whole public believed he had already done it.

The Shining Mountain by Peter Boardman. Hodder and Stoughton, 1978.

Crags *16. (December 1978).*

After Everest South-West Face in 1975, it was by no means inevitable that the most capable and bold climbers would switch to small parties seeking out technically difficult Himalayan objectives. Most Himalayan climbing continues to be done by the big guns; large parties with large resources are still the norm, despite the impression sometimes given in the Anglo-Saxon world. Meanwhile some leading mountaineers, and particularly Messner, have come to concentrate on the biggest peaks, seeking to climb them without oxygen or a large support party. This 8,000m Munro-bagging tends to cut against a concentration on that other ideal of big mountaineering – intrinsic and sustained technical climbing. The success on the West Face of Changabang represents a different strand in big mountaineering. At 22,520ft it is a small mountain by Himalayan standards, and the West Face is of similar size to the biggest in the Alps. But it is a very difficult compact rockface, plastered with ice and low enough to allow technical climbing as hard as that achieved on the most difficult alpine climbs. Like Trango Tower, it must appeal immensely to any ambitious climber bred on the technical concentration of hard West European climbing.

Certainly it was an obvious objective to Joe Tasker after his brilliant, hazardous and truly alpine ascent of Dunagiri with Dick Renshaw in 1975. The West Wall looked harder, but still an alpine-style ascent was initially planned, involving hammock bivouacs and a tortoise-like movement up the wall. In face of weight and mere survival problems it was eventually abandoned for a mini-expedition approach involving, of necessity, a line of fixed rope.

Possibly this came as a 'moral blow' to these able practitioners, for ethically (or emotionally) alpine style has great appeal as an ideal and in practice. Nevertheless, after a recovery at base camp and an autopsy of the first attempt they stuck with it, and after forty days and forty nights broke through to the summit.

Pete Boardman.

They retreated safely, only to suffer one of those sad quirks of fate which are part of the fabric of mountaineering experience. A few days after their success, they had the lonely job of interring four corpses of fallen climbers in the glacier below Dunagiri.

The Shining Mountain is one man's book* – refreshingly, after those Himalayan compendia from everybody's diaries. Despite the huge role Joe Tasker played in the ascent and the dialogue that comprises so much of the text, it is the author's story. Both climbing and writing seem to involve a strong reaction to the threat imposed by Boardman's status as public property after the ascent of Everest. An impression of heightened personal isolation permeates, but fortunately the reader can travel in the spaceship.

Sympathy is established from the outset – to face the grief and endless inquiry after Mick Burke's death and the ascent of Everest, all under the spotlight of maximum publicity, could have been a withering experience for anyone, particularly when it was linked to a public office in the British Mountaineering Council (BMC). In the event Changabang West Wall was climbed and public office abandoned. From the genesis of the idea to the revealing 'We wanted to be home', the story is engagingly and sensitively told. The narrative is deepened by its generosity in including not only an insight into the earlier experiences of these highly motivated and able people, but in its location within the long literary tradition of mountaineering, with echoes of Longstaff and Shipton that might be scarcely comprehensible to those insensitive to mountaineering's roots.

These climbers take with them not merely their techniques on rock and ice, their gear and their music. Their culture may be that of bisyllabic conversation, but they can read away their bad memories and fatigue at base camp; diarize and photograph endlessly in the causes of posterity and paying for the trip; admit to their climbers' neuroses about the state of the head, guts and capillaries, and even to that regime of Valium and Moggies which seems to be in such contrast to the external world of indifferent or plainly hostile, yet overwhelmingly beautiful mountains. One wonders a little at the authenticity of some of the language (does anyone ever say 'effin' hell'?) in a book so dependent on direct speech for its life, but it's a change to write a review which turns to the illustration so late in the day. The publisher has allowed a reasonable amount of colour, together with a fairly conventional layout and an allocation of black-and-white photographs.

A dozen or so colour pictures is probably the minimum that the climbing world expects these days, fed as it is on the lavishness of the West Coast American publications and the British magazines. Yet the layout is classical and pleasing, and two fine little line drawings add an air of tradition, as well as useful information on the line of the route for those who wish to climb another route on the face! But this is not just a picture package – it is a young man's book, modest

*Though Joe Tasker saw his role in it as very large and a stepping stone to his own *Everest the Cruel Way* (Eyre Methuen, 1981) and *Savage Arena* (Methuen, 1982).

in form but written somehow from a position of confidence and strength, which belies surface humility. For all that, it is healthy and honest, not least in its ever-ready admission that sooner or later a pin might pull or the last 8mm rope break.

Everest: The West Ridge by Thomas F. Hornbein. Diadem and The Mountaineers Seattle, 1980.

Mountain 79. (1981).

This is a timely reissue of a handsome book recording a great epic of 1963. The ascent and its presentation still retain a telling modernity, while the pictorial update improves the classic story. Now Unsoeld and other protagonists have died, but, as Doug Scott says in his foreword, the values and the commitment involved in great ascents change less than some would wish to believe. The ascent was an outgrowth of a very big expedition, but in many ways this conspired against success on what may have seemed an eccentric sideshow to

Everest and Makalu. *Photo from the Boardman Collection.*

Mirrors on Men and Events

others in the party. That it became the highlight speaks reams. There was still a long way to go to the oxygenless solo ascent but it was a step on the way, back towards earlier and forward towards future ideals.

Tim Lewis, Editor of Mountain (d. 23 August 1984)

During his editorship the magazine developed its international scope to match a rapidly evolving climbing world. Its style also changed, the news features becoming scrupulously functional and unhistrionic, yet balanced by frequent essays of a discursive or philosophical nature. The magazine reflected a more artistic character both in photographs, captioning and titling and particularly with artwork and line illustration.

Timothy Ifor Morgan Lewis was born in Aberystwyth in 1944, the son of two teachers. The family subsequently moved from Wales to London. He was educated at Dulwich College, and Jesus College, Oxford where he took an honours degree in Modern History in 1967. He also represented his college on the TV panel game University Challenge. *He continued with postgraduate work at University College, Bangor. Between 1972 and 1977 he lectured in General Studies at Derby College of Further Education.*

Tim made me laugh for twenty years. His death in 1984 made memories flood. Not everyone knew him as a climbing activist. Many recall him slim, tall, red-haired, fiercely decisive on rock and ice, in mountain storm or caving flood. As thunder rolled up the valley of La Bérarde we made a rapid series of abseils down the North-West Face of the Ailefroide in 1975. Others will recall an epic in the crumbling depths of the Gortani Cave when an earthquake shook it while the party were deep underground, or other incidents spread between many people and places over two decades. It was an active commitment concealed by his sharp individualism, defended by his acute sense of privacy and an essential modernity which recognized the loneliness of self.

Even recently he had climbed in Corsica, among warm and witty friends in Czechoslovakia, in the Peak. But he was much more than a climber. Intellectual sharpness made him self-critical to a fault. It was turned outwards in brilliance and a near unanswerable wit which delighted so many of us – and could be so acid that it drove the faint-hearted into their bunkers. The targets were either deeply liked or deserved the Exocet missiles. Charlatans, fools, knaves and the spokesmen of entrenched and ruthless interests deserved the fire and brimstone of his anger. It had a 'chapel' quality. Unfortunately there were occasional casualties among innocent bystanders, a possibility which makes most of us mealy mouthed.

Motivated to heady academic feats in his youth, he eventually questioned their validity. Unresolved ambitions produced fluctuating moods, periodic

166

crises. Distaste for conformity, mediocrity and bureaucracy drove him to abandon college lecturing when he had already found doctoral research on the administration of Anglesey by Cromwell's major generals too arid and narrow. He took to magazine production (*Rocksport* and the CC *Journal*, pioneering in that field, to photography and a flirtation with many worlds. In the mid 70s he made a clutch of new friends and descended some of the world's deepest caves. Ever moving, restless, he became Editor of *Mountain* in 1978.

His wide knowledge of mountaineering, ideas on photography, fluency, and ability to meet new people and generate loyalty in them made this seem a good berth. As Ken Wilson always testified, it could be an unholy grind. The magazine grew in circulation and extended its international coverage as the times changed. Tim aimed to make it more the property of its readership than had sometimes been the case before, and less a vehicle for his personal views. Editorial histrionics and self-glorification he held in profound distaste for over thirty issues, and whatever the inducements he was ferocious in defending the integrity of his product. Self-inflation, star cults and over-exposure of particular interests and issues were all resisted.

Editing exposed him to other dangers. Prickliness disguised deep, heartfelt and unresolved personal contradictions. Surface hedonism ('more than enough is insufficient' was the motto of one brilliant era) disguised deep moral convictions and a vulnerability even greater than his friends suspected. His mother's death closely followed by that of many friends and especially the deaths of Al Harris and Alex MacIntyre, cut him to the quick, and made his job of reporting a sport replete with alarms the more difficult.

Under pressure he returned to essentials. One was a deeply held moral code and greater closeness to his intimate friends. Another was his Welsh identity. Never lost, his Hiraeth (longing to return to Wales) strengthened, as did a desire to hear and speak the language. When not there he found strength on the even more solitary western shores of North Scotland among volcanic and sandstone rock, Pictish forts and moody mists cluttered by fewer people. Each visit made it harder for him to tear himself away. This seemed to represent a reassertion of the core of his being.

Unresolved intellectual ambition masked feelings poetic, romantic and backward-looking as came out in his best photography. At heart he was in exile wandering a wasteland less warm than his Celtic roots. His long journey sharpened his wit and elaborated his knowledge. It fuelled his confidence and pushed him to pack in so much, but while stirring us to laughter he made his life a chain of hard thoughts.

In primitive human belief only kings, poets, chieftains and magicians were privileged to be reborn. Countless less distinguished souls wandered disconsolately in the icy grounds of the Castle, uncheered by modern Christian hopes of resurrection. Tim was both spiritual and a secularist, but his presence could be uplifting, his person mercurial. Where can he have gone but to Caer Arianrhod, the place beyond the North West Wind, if not into the blaze of the sun itself, the Celtic Heaven.

167

Abode of Snow. A History of Himalayan Exploration and Mountaineering from Earliest Times to the Ascent of Everest. Kenneth Mason (1955 1st Ed). Foreword by Doug Scott. Diadem and The Mountaineers' Seattle, 1987.

In 1955, Kenneth Mason chronicled the whole of Himalayan exploration and climbing until that time. It was a remarkable achievement for which he was well qualified. It has never been superseded. Most other histories are partial, regional, related to particular expeditions or mountains. History is thrown in as colourful background, uncritical and naive at worst.

Even relatively sensitive writers can rarely hope to equal Mason. Why is this? As a former Superintendent of the Survey of India, working there for most of two decades from 1909–1931, his experience was vast. Subsequently he was Professor of Geography at Oxford University. The book was written in retirement, buoyed up by the recent successes on Everest, Nanga Parbat and K2 in 1953 and 1954. What had long been promised had at last come to pass.

Abode of Snow is already an old work, but it remains essential. Hugh Ruttledge said of it years ago, '. . . the scope is vast; historically from the 17th century to the present, geographically from the Indus to the Bramaputra. Clarity on this enormous canvas is achieved by an ingenious arrangement of chapters, in which time, place and sequence are in proportion and continuity is never lost.'

Mason meanwhile is modest in his Preface: 'Though I had been a member of the AC since 1914 I was never an expert climber in the modern sense. During the 1930s there was so much activity in the Himalaya that most of my spare time was taken up in editing the Himalayan Journal.' He gave this as the reason for not writing such a history three decades before, when contemporaries had urged him to do it.

The book opens with a compact description of the main areas of the range. In 40 pages of words and maps this is completed, for the enlightenment of anyone but the greatest expert. Short sections introduce each major area from the Punjab to Assam. For brevity and clarity it can have few rivals. Part one ends with the weather, where suitably dry humour emerges: 'Dr de Graaf designed a portable lightning conductor which was effective, but on the whole I found by experience, that it was pleasanter to come down.'

'Early travellers' until 1885 are dealt with in Part Two. Though written about in detail elsewhere by John Keay and others, this is a masterly précis. By 1862, 37 summits over 20,000ft had been ascended, and five over 21,000, mostly by Indian Pundits and Surveyors. All the most important mountains had been fixed in their positions and many heights had been measured. On the Northwest frontier Muslim Pundits often suffered death.

For Mason, 1855–1918 marked the beginning of modern mountaineering. From Younghusband's journeys onwards the exploration and climbing are described. Separate sections examine developments in Punjab, Kumaon, Nepal,

Sikkim, Assam and the Karakoram. Little that is important is omitted, despite short space.

In 1910 Mason's personal experience enriches the text, as he supervised the triangulation north of Gilgit which eventually met the Russians working down from Osh north of the Pamirs in August 1913. He is unstinting in praise for the discipline of surveyors, Gurkhas and Hunzas who often had to remain at Survey stations beyond 17,000ft for a week or more to do the work. They added major West Karakoram peaks to the map, like Disteghil Sar (25,868ft). When they met the Russians, inaccuracy proved slight. Their use of stereoscopic photography in the Taghdumbash Pamir for exploratory purposes was another scientific novelty. After this epic, Mason obviously had experience of the area rivalled only by Indian army field officers like C. G. Bruce.

The subsequent sections cover some well known ground, including the Everest Expeditions between the wars, the Germans on Nanga Parbat and elsewhere, Nanda Devi in 1936 and K2. Invaluable are accounts of the numerous explorations, including his own in the Shaksgam, as these are not so easily dug out of a large literature. As an individual Mason regretted that 'the old friendliness of the mountain brotherhood had received a shock. Men who had met among the mountains of the world had fought as enemies and learned to hate ... men's names had been expunged from the membership of their Alpine Clubs. Friends had been killed or maimed, especially those in the prime of life.'

He, Bruce and others, had wanted to set up an Alpine Club in India, as had others before them. They wanted hill men to become guides in the alpine sense. Also they talked about trying Everest, had ideas about acclimatization, and found increased difficulty with the British and Indian Government authorities in travelling near frontiers after the Russian revolution.

Again the developments in the different areas are carefully described, as is the founding, in 1927, of two mountaineering clubs, one in Simla and one in Calcutta. Within a year they merged to form the Himalayan Club, of which Mason was journal Editor for so long.

Thus the roots of modern climbing were encouraged in the sub-continent, with the express intention from the outset to encourage Indian participation. It is interesting too to see that Mason is careful to avoid exaggerated reaction to the German tragedies on Nanga Parbat in the 1930s. 'It is easy to look back and criticize. But it must be realized how little was known at the time about the rapid deterioration of strength above 23,000ft, especially under storm conditions.'

Perhaps he knew the Germans too well, and had reason to respect them. Karl Wien and Peter Aufschnaiter were at different times his guests in Oxford while seeking permission to go to Nanga Parbat. For Mason 'The War was like a giant avalanche that sweeps everything before it.' Nevertheless, after it the 'spirit of kindness' which Mallory had begged for on Everest, was at last displayed by the world's greatest mountains. True, Art Gilkey died on K2 in 1953, but Everest and Nanga Parbat were at last climbed, and K2 in 1954.

This completed a project dreamed of by Bruce and Mason many years before.

His emotions rarely show. He comes over as a practical man, a little like Noel Odell. Only that systematic practicality made this exhaustive study possible. A more arty or purely imaginative soul would have found it hard to stand the 40 years of grind that went into its making. Yet the 80 black and white photos betray the *joie de vivre* of the man and his friends. Verve, joy in the wilderness and energy burst from those of the author and his fellows. So, like many good things, this indispensable work grew from personal enthusiasm and commitment, the memory of past joys and hardships. For a post-imperial generation it is an 'eye opener' as well as an essential primer in the physical character and exploration of the Himalayan peaks. Perhaps most refreshing of all is Mason's profound unwillingness to indulge in speculation on beliefs and culture, about which the author was presumably more informed than those who so often insist upon appropriating them for fashionable western consumption, after a few months trekking in Nepal.

FILM ILLUSION

In the mid-70s there was a revival in making films about climbing in Britain. It was partially rooted in the television outside broadcast (OB) tradition of the BBC, going back to documentaries and live broadcasts involving Joe Brown and Clogwyn d'ur Arddu in the early 60s and subsequent efforts at Kilnsey, Anglesey, The Old Man of Hoy and Anglesey again in 1970. Hamish McInnes and BBC Scotland also branched off into a series of programmes in the 70s, and other film projects. Expeditions after Annapurna South Face (1970) and Everest also needed films to be made, and apart from company crews Mick Burke and Leo Dickinson made names by 1975 for their specialized craft.

My involvement in early OBs was incidental, at Kilnsey in 1965 and Anglesey in 1970. The emergence of Tony Riley and Jim Curran with the independent *Trango* and *Menlove Edwards* films, and *The Bat* in 1979 changed my interest, which nevertheless remained hybrid – I always seemed to do some organizing, some safety, some finance and a bit of camera work, but arguably never enough of anything for my own or other people's satisfaction. There was thus some pleasure in working on a full feature, directed with subtlety and intelligence, as there was later, behind the scenes on The Old Man of Hoy in 1984, and in mountain camera work in the Himalaya.

Fred Zinnemann's Five Days

Fred Zinnemann seems to have harboured at least one dream. (In the industry of dream palaces I am sure it cannot have been his only one.) In 1981–2 it was realized: throughout the summer he and his film crew laboured among the Bernina and Bregaglia peaks near Pontresina. What was he trying to achieve?

Mr Z has a long list of films to his credit since *The Wave* in 1934. They include *From Here to Eternity, High Noon, Oklahoma, The Nun's Story, A Man For All Seasons, The Day of the Jackal* and *Julia*. He claims to avoid élitism, 'to entertain people at large'. His modest bearing, gently persuasive ability to make effective working relationships and avoidance of film-tycoonery are endearing. For the climbers who participated in the project such feelings became paramount, outsiders as they were and unable to fall to conventional film industry hierarchies.

Yet Fred, as we knew him to the horror of film professionals, was born in Vienna in 1907, took a bachelor's degree at twenty, went to the Paris Technical School of Cinematography, then back to Germany as assistant cameraman, before Hollywood in 1929. There have been fewer more revolutionary times or places to be in film-making. Compared to contemporaries in late Weimar, he has been conventional. Yet alongside modern Rambomania and Special Effects obsession he is radical, steering between the Scylla of esoteric experiment

Fred Zinnemann directs the mafia.

The end of the affair.

without audience and the Charybdis of the crassness of much modern (especially but not exclusively) American cinema. Many of his films can be read to convey coded political messages, subtly, sceptically, with guarded ambiguity. That extraction of the message is left to the viewer, might make films like *Julia* or *A Man For All Seasons* the more subversive in a political climate less liberal than that of the 60s.

At least this makes more sense to me of this sage of Mount Street, who in humour and background had so much in common with my old Viennese professor.

From the first, in a couple of weeks spent helping Sean Connery in the practicalities of climbing, and talking to Mr Z and Peter Beale the producer, this enabled me to make sense of a film with a 'light' script. It seemed very special to Fred. There were dramatic possibilities in the near archetypal roles of Dr Meredith, recently returned from India and Everest, his niece Kate and the handsome guide Johann. The outcome was tragedy, death for the guide, melancholy, one feared, for the doctor enamoured of his niece. In her freedom from childhood fixation, Kate became free, or more nearly so. There were no human heroes, though there were dangerous antics. So it seemed to me, as the summer slipped by, rising at 4.15am, make-up at 5.45am, with bacon butties to follow while Martin Boysen and I waited for the helicopter. It was a personal reading. Not even Sean Connery could make his fallible role seem heroic. He played a doctor and romantic and therefore fatally flawed man of his generation, and so supposedly did I, in doing his more serious climbing.

Who, then, did Fred celebrate? About that he was clear. The guide was virtuous but ill-fated. The doctor flawed and compromised, Kate struggling like Johann with her past affections and possibilities of future escape. All else was common and various humanity, of differing sexes and nationalities. It was the mountains that came to speak and adjudicate over lives fated by the imperfections of humanity. Johann and the Doctor seemed precipitate in their mountaineering, a little too pushing, competitive, naïvely brave in face of a potentially overpowering adversary. The mountains reached out from the screen, enticing, beautiful, sometimes threatening, occasionally heartless, implacable. Despite the beauty it ends in tears. Surely this is Vienna before 1914, articulated via the neutral territory of Swiss mountains in 1931, for an audience of the 80s.

Mr Z always claimed that Kay Boyle's story 'Maiden, Maiden' on which the film was based brought back acute memory of the Austrian Alps in childhood:

I can tell you how I came to make the film. I've always wanted to make a picture about climbing as I remembered it from my youth which of course is totally different from the way it's done today. The reason I wanted to do that was because I wanted to get the sense of adventure that existed in those days, which now is very rare among ordinary people. Except for the great climbers it's no longer an adventure because if you want to go on Piz Palu there are fifty people ahead of you. A lot of the mountains are wrapped in cables and made to look like spider webs. What I was trying to show was the mountains as they were in those days, when there were relatively few people and the huts were very small and you had this enormous feeling of being very tiny against the majestic, mysterious, very silent kind of landscape that you were in. And in order to get that across we had also to use the equipment of that period and people had to learn how to climb in those terms.*

Martin Boysen and I launched out from the helicopter on to the fine ice arête of the Central Rib of the N Face of Piz Palu, climbing together in the Alps for the first time since the 1963 accident on the Civetta. We had climbed often in Britain since, but never abroad. Mr Z liked Martin who had a more difficult job than I, helping Lambert Wilson to become guidelike as I helped Sean who had been to sea, and could spend a little time just concentrating on getting the rope and ice axe handling to look right, without embarrassment or real difficulty. As Mr Z said:

Lambert was a stage actor from Paris who had never climbed in his life and had no time for preparation. When he came to Switzerland to start shooting he had great problems with all the technical parts, rope management and all that. And, the Swiss guides who were excellent in themselves were no help because they laughed at him, more or less openly, and the poor boy got more and more rattled. And then Martin took him under his wing and it was really a miracle to see that in two weeks, Lambert managed to look like a credible mountain guide. And though he did not do any of the really hair-raising bits that we have in the film he did quite a lot of it himself.

Mr Z was also steeped in the Trenker movies of the 30s, and some of our scenes were dramatic remakes of takes from his classics. This connected the action closely to images that older Europeans would know well, even if this was alien to Anglo-Saxons. Thus we found ourselves springing across and falling into yawning crevasses, chopping steps with long axes up steepish ice, rock climbing in fine-nailed Robert Lawrie boots on Bregaglia granite and swarming up steep faces with oldified ropes to simulate those of 1931. It was exhilarating but serious, bringing back the classic abseil (burns and all) using about one rope sling per rope length, relying on straight ten-pointed crampons. Though we had done many of these things in the 50s, and had as good a back-up team as has ever been assembled led by Hamish McInnes and Joe Brown, it could be more exciting than intended, especially associated with numerous, sometimes dodgy, helicopter flights.

I was thankful to work with Mr Z and Peter Beale. Somehow the older man's urbanity protected us from pressures for more speed, cost-cutting or other threats lethal in this environment. As a result the climbers and local guides were

*Quotations based on Geoff Birtles' *High* interview. *High* 6. (December 1982–January 1983).

able to get to know one-another and work well. The film crew were well protected and there were no serious accidents despite the odd near miss. When one of these involved an ice block hitting Mr Z and a camera he caught the camera and shrugged it off. His philosophical approach to the whole thing was totally consistent, ever trying to get it right, inveighing another take, standing in baking heat or freezing cold without flinching, in his seventies, when everyone else wilted.

There must have been weary moments for him, but it hardly showed. Instead boundless enthusiasm and encouragement came over. Always 'Very good, very good', followed a take as Pepigno, Fellini's cameraman, looked at his band of assistants anxiously. Somehow, nevertheless, there was another.

My conviction that there was most emphasis on the female role was enhanced by Sean's parting comment, as he sweated it out with the close up scenes as I left. 'There's more of you than there is of me in this.' I think there was more of Kate (Betsy Brantley) than anyone, that ultimately the mountains freed her, whatever the fates of the doctor and Johann. Meanwhile the film freed Fred Zinnemann. Technical demands led to a short return, with a few of the climbing Mafia and film crew after Christmas. After finishing the location material in high cold places and winter temperatures, Fred chose to go with Martin and Joe Brown to the wintry summit of Piz Palu. Though the day was bright it was not a place to linger too long, and after a little time Joe gently suggested descent. Fred Zinnemann replied, 'Is it really necessary to go down?'

BACK TO THE HILLS

Between 1982 and 1987 I visited the Karakoram three times and the North-East Ridge of Everest once. All were highly adventurous but unsuccessful expeditions in the sense of summit bagging. There were illnesses and injuries, but no one in our little companies died. At the same time elsewhere among my climbing friends there was attrition. This makes its mark, and throws one back on one's friends, reassertion of deeply felt values and of old verities. Primitive sources of inspiration can restore some peace of mind as can a memory of advice given glibly to others.

Fortunately this remains possible. The touch and texture of rough gritstone, the finger biting edges of Gimmer and Pavey Ark, the thrill of swinging on straining arms up walls too smooth-looking to be feasible, the pleasures of a good nut or ice pick placement, and above all the laughs, their seemingly endless regeneration. Why mountains and irreverence go together I do not pretend to know, but for me their twinning is inescapable, as axiomatic as the foreboding in Llanberis or Glencoe.

Into the Gasherbrum Cockpit – The Scottish Expedition to Gasherbrum III (1985)

A rucked seam of the world's highest peaks rears along the borders between Pakistan, China and India.

The Karakoram range is dominated by K2 at 8,611m the world's second highest summit. Impressive retainers are Broad Peak (8,047m) and the Gasherbrums. Though arbitrariness exists in league tables, Gasherbrum 1 is reckoned to be sixteenth (8,068m), Broad Peak eighteenth (8,047m), Gasherbrum 2 twentieth (8,035m) and Gasherbrum 3 (7,980m) twenty-fourth highest mountain in the world.

Today climbers are interested more in the technicality and in the element of discovery involved in their adventures than in height alone.* Most of the highest Karakoram peaks have been climbed several times, and we sought the challenge of a little-known peak by a less-known route. Edinburgh statistician Geoff Cohen, thirty-seven, searched the records, and came up with the idea of doing a new climb on a totally unclimbed side of Gasherbrum 3, initially with his Edinburgh climbing partner Des Rubens (thirty-two) a school teacher. The mountain had been climbed only by its easiest route in 1975 by Alison Chadwick and the Poles Janus Onyszkiewicz (Alison's husband), Wanda Rutkeiwicz and K. Zdzitowiecki, a powerful team. Wanda succeeded on Everest, but Alison died on Annapurna.

*This becomes more true now that the race to be first to climb all 8,000m peaks is over.

176

Geoff's route was much more mysterious than that done by the first ascensionists. They had taken an obvious gully which could be reached from the usual route up Gasherbrum 2. As the latter is reasonably frequented, and had other Polish climbers on it in 1975, the original route is not too isolated from other climbers, camps and fixed ropes, a lifeline in storms or other emergencies. Our alternative shared that approach from a base camp on the Duke of Abruzzi Glacier (5,400m) only to camp one (6,000m). Then it struck off towards a huge icefall of 900m which spilled from an upper choire between the giants Gasherbrum 3 and Gasherbrum 4 (7,925m). Like the Western Cwm of Everest this choire looked dangerous to reach and extremely isolated once occupied. Its floor was close on 23,000ft. More than 10 miles (16km) from base camp, it could only be reached by long toil on a seemingly endless glacier. It had been used for serious approach to a climb once only, by the illustrious Italian group led by Riccardo Cassin in 1958. Walter Bonatti and Tony Gobbi, two of Italy's finest climbers, took two weeks to find a way into the inner 'cockpit' *en route* to their ascent of Gasherbrum 4. How long would it take us? Geoff asked Clive Rowlands and myself to join the party, as the route looked very serious for a two-man party.

Arriving at base camp on 11 July we used a spell of good weather to set up our lower camps and to acclimatize to 6,000m. At these high altitudes excessive speed of ascent is likely to lead to altitude sickness, a rapid killer, which claimed Dr Pete Thexton among others, despite his earlier medical research on aspects of the problem, on Broad Peak in 1983. Then from camp one Geoff and Des

Gasherbrum III.

Rubens made carries into the jaws of the icefall, aiming for the 'cockpit'. Clive Rowlands (forty), the proprietor of the Inverness mountaineers' shop, and myself, a lecturer from Sheffield Polytechnic (forty-two), were plodding slowly up the endless slopes of the lower glacier in the glare of mid-morning when we saw the tiny dots on the lower slopes of the great icefall. What a monster it was, frilled with a near-continuous overhanging ice-cliff nearly half a mile in width across its exit and protruding with layer on layer of ice towers squeezed up by the endless motion of the ice below. We knew that we would have to spend time under the towers, not minutes but many hours, and maybe days. It was an uneasy prospect.

Later that day in mid July we arrived wearily at camp one (6,000m) meeting our friends there. They had carried up supplies to the shelter of an overhanging ice wall perhaps a third of the way up the fall. Des had the misfortune to be suffering from a tooth abscess – these things worsen at altitude, with changes of air pressure and the cold as well as unfamiliar diet and the general deterioration of physique which ensues above 5,000m. Reluctantly he and Geoff went down to try to get dental help from another expedition sharing the base camp site. Clive and I did not envy them, especially Des and the relentless jarring of his dental nerves.

At 3am next morning we set off up, at first skirting the base of the 2,000m wall of Gasherbrum 2, keeping well out on the glacier in the hope of avoiding avalanches. Here, in a tiny tent, we met Renato Cassarotto, who after climbing Gasherbrum 2 with his wife, Goretta, now had hopes of a similar new route before embarking on an extremely ambitious traverse. He decided that he did not feel well, gave us his excellent food, packed and set off for the long lonely descent of the crevassed glacier. Sadly, he died on a very similar descent coming back from K2 in 1986.

A steep snow slope led towards the icefall, with a few big crevasses but good frozen snow bridges as yet unsoftened by the sun. Still walking in deep shadow Clive struck out a little ahead following the scratches in the hard snow made in previous days by our companions. At last the snow chute narrowed to a gully, with the awesome ice cliffs crowding to peer down on us from 500m above. It was a case of grinning and ignoring them, though their detritus lay all around. As soon as possible we struck out into the middle of a subsidiary ice chute, still threatened by spectacular green leaning towers which reeled drunkenly over our route. Some day soon some must fall. Oh, that we will not be here!

It became a race against the sun, which had already struck the towers above. The last few hundred feet involved a gasping climb upwards as the surface snow softened. At about 9am we emerged where a little shelf was tucked under a great ice arch. At its extreme right hand Geoff and Des had left the dump, at the far point of their progress.

It was not a healthy place, for there is no security in an icefall of this scale, almost too big for human comprehension. It required faith, patience, a certain blanking of the critical faculties. We decided to excavate an ice cave, a retreat under the very wall of the ice cliff. Missiles from above might fly past outside while we skulked within, and we would at least feel safer in this cubby hole. Much of the day went by in excavations shovelling out the snow, ice, and picking away at the harder glacial material. A domed ceiling became a pretty feature of the interior. Absorbed and satisfied with our handiwork, it was easy to get soaked, and we tried to dry what we could in the midday sun, ferocious even at 6,400m. Tea was made at frequent intervals while we recovered breath and strength to go ice mining again. After about six hours it was finished, all the gear was stowed inside and the sun slipped round the nearest of the leaning ice towers.

By 5pm it was freezing hard, and we geared up for our first quick exploratory stab into the upper reaches of the fall. A rounded rib of ice swept down above, cut like ham with huge crevasses. We prospected up, making a trail on the hardening show, to stop at a vast hole where the only way forward involved a traverse to the right and steep short descent. There, with only half an hour of light, we called it a day.

Next morning the high point was reached early in bitter cold, and a rope fixed to descend before we climbed up into an ice maze of awful complexity with holes disappearing in every direction, hotel-sized towers leaning on all sides and the great ice whirls and blocks of the upper cliff looming over it all. Neither of us liked it, and we emerged under the upper frill with the prospect of several shaky crevasse bridges followed by long exposure to the upper cliffs with no sure way of getting past. To make it worse the daily roast had begun, and the bridges we had already crossed would be falling to pieces.

'I've had enough of this,' Clive opined, in deep Yorkshire, despite ten years in Inverness. I agreed, and we scuttled back to our cave as fast as our legs would carry us.

When the evening freeze came we were off again, probing the left edges of the giant fall. One crevasse crossed the whole width, but to our joy we came to a bridge on to steep ice leading into an upper corridor. The way had been hard work, hip deep snow each step, but the die seemed cast – it was the left corridor. Next day a patch of bad weather drove us down right to base but a few days later we were back again, all four at the ice cave. Clive felt a bit off, but when I had frightened myself on one route round a vast hole, Des led another, steeper but safer and more logical, into the upper corridor. Then Geoff struck off strongly up a vast slope descending from Gasherbrum 4, skirting the fall line of the upper ice. After a long time cramponing up the slope in a great diagonal we reached a little gully by the innocuous left end of the great ice cliff. My altimeter read 6,900m. A couple of hundred feet more and we could traverse right round a snow rib, and the basin stretched ahead. It rose 2 or 3 miles gently with most crevasses covered, the polished ice of the East Face of Gasherbrum 4 to the left, and, filling our view east, Gasherbrum 3. It was a mass of rock slabs and complex ice slopes, with a great pinnacled ridge to the right, and a vast granite bastion on the frontier with China. We had arrived, in the 'Cockpit of the Gasherbrums', a sight and sensation granted to only a handful of the best climbers before. We could not establish ourselves that day, but we knew the way and had made steps to help future travels through the upper fall.

Next morning it was my turn to feel odd; for whatever reason I could hardly put one foot in front of the other. The others picked up a substantial amount of gear and supplies and set off to colonize the Cockpit. I rested in the ice cave awaiting revival.

That day and the next they camped in the upper choire; Geoff and Clive went on to weigh up the various possibilities on our mountain. Geoff reached the col on the North-East Ridge of Gasherbrum 4, but his view, both of our route and of K2 and Broad Peak was obscured by cloud; with darkness coming he had to return.

Next morning I had recovered, and plodded happily through the upper fall in good conditions. At the big crevasse we had a fixed rope, and the ice wall was climbed by kicking in the crampons and clamping up the rope. Once up the long diagonal slope I rounded a corner and could see the blue tent about ¾ mile away. A stiff very cold wind blew up the valley.

When I arrived everybody was still in bed after the previous day's efforts. Cramped conditions did not help. After some tea I set off towards the ridge which seemed to offer the best chance, intending to make a nearer and more comfortable camp. Another ice cave seemed best. A crevasse offered ideal snow, not too difficult to dig, and soon Clive came up to help. Later in the day we carried everything into the lee of the crevasse, setting up the tent close by. More steps were made in the packed crust leading towards the ridge. It was Des's turn to feel weak, but he and Geoff joined us camping near the cave entrance.

Before the end of the day snow swept up the Cockpit in a curtain, and persisted throughout the night. Much of it got into the cave, with its too short entrance. Next morning things still looked bad, and were possibly getting worse. Realizing that there must be a price for a long period of good weather we set off down. To remain would merely entail eating all our food and using fuel carried up laboriously. It might also mean that we would not be able to escape.

Retreat in a 'white out' took a day and a half. Clive led almost all the way, and we remained in one long rope. The descent of the icefall proved nightmarish, the steps had all disappeared and we could not see more than a few yards. Safeguarded only by our own ice axe and crampons, we gingerly groped our way down to the ice cave. After tea the lower slopes were descended in deep soft snow. To make things more fearsome, ice towers had fallen recently, opened huge runnels, destroyed bridges on crevasses and buried our bit of useful fixed rope. Lower down the debris of a huge recent fall extended over ¼ mile. On top of this chaos were 3ft of new snow, through which we crawled on hands and knees, just managing to keep a sight on the person ahead. Most of the crevasses were covered, but with snow too soft to give support. Eventually, after about seven hours we reached camp one. There no one stirred, though a few tents were visible in the blizzard. After eating whatever was convenient from our tent there we roped up and staggered on down, with Clive always in the lead and me as anchor. All tracks were obliterated and we barely made the half-way dump by dark and almost went past it. There we camped, and made an equally confusing descent of the South Gasherbrum icefall in continuing storm next day.

The storm lasted from 2 August to 7 August. Deep snow threatened to break tents even at base camp. Members of other expeditions to other mountains seeped in daily, battered and delayed by the weather. One large group did not reach base camp until the 6th, though they had been little higher than us when the storm broke. Clive decided that conditions would take too long to improve again, even after a weather clearance, for 6ft of snow had fallen at 6,000m. He went down with Naseer, our liaison officer, and Fhidah the cook. Perhaps he was forewarned of a mystery illness, which hit him before Concordia.

On the 10th the weather was better, and we struck off in trio up the icefall, leaving very early. An Italian expedition to Gasherbrum 1 had tried to reopen the route, and got beyond the half-way dump. In two hours we passed that, but then ran into abominable deep snow. It took twelve hours in all to reach camp one.

There followed a day of poor weather, which did little to improve matters. Plans were made to continue nevertheless, and Geoff and Des set off before dawn for the icefall. Perhaps I had seen too much of it, and I went down, leaving very early in the dark to get down the crevassed glacier before the bridges softened. I was tired, but soon strengthened as height was lost. The Gasherbrum 1 party had not moved when I passed their tent *en route* to base camp.

With much effort Geoff and Des regained the ice caves at camp two and then camp three. At camp two a huge ice cliff collapse had come near to burying the cave and its invaluable supplies. They crawled through the fallen blocks to get into the amazingly preserved interior. Camp three in the upper choire was intact in the cave, though the tent was buried and had to be excavated. Still feeling confident they pressed on to the ridge next day solo climbing a ramp and using the rope to climb a series of tricky rock and ice pitches. That night they bivouacked close to 24,000ft, on a poor ledge. Next day Des recalled,

At 5am Geoff and I started getting ready. In our little cramped bivouac bags it took an hour to heat the water for a small brew of tea. The wind tore at the fabric of the bags, secured to the ledge with slings and ropes.

At 7am we started up the ridge, still in the shade though the sun had risen, lighting up range after range of peaks. Only harsh jagged mountains and glaciers could be seen, or enormous glaciers, as the nearest villages were two weeks' walk away. No greenery alleviates the savagery of the scene, as in the Alps. It was bitterly cold.

We made steady if slow progress. The gale whistled across the ridge freezing exposed skin in minutes. Completely encased in down suits we were engrossed in the climbing, which was continuously difficult on the upper section of the ridge. Unroped we climbed over slabs and pinnacles, with awkward snow on steep shelves overlooking the vertical drop to the distant glacier. Anywhere on this ground a slip would be fatal, although there was a need to concentrate on every movement and every breath which would have made use of the rope an extra burden. If one of us was injured there would be no hope of rescue, and little chance of the other being able to get him down. We were totally on our own.

We had the satisfaction of steadily gaining height and from over 25,000ft were able to look down over the ridge of Gasherbrum 4 to the Abruzzi Glacier 10,000ft below. To the north straddling Chinese Sinkiang and the Soviet Union were the snows of the high Pamirs. Nearer at hand Hidden Peak and Gasherbrum 4 were being blocked out by rapidly moving clouds. Progress was slow and we used the rope on difficult ground. Still several hundred feet below the summit there was a complex of rock towers, making assessment of the remaining time required almost impossible. We had set a pre-determined return time of 4pm. To go on was undoubtedly very difficult, with the summit defended by a steep rock tower. The wind howled round us and the visibility was only a few yards. After weeks of high altitude and of constant physical struggle we had now come close to our limits. So many mountaineers have continued at just this point, and many have not returned. Our decision was not a difficult one and we began the long slow dangerous descent . . .

After more than five weeks of constant activity above 18,000ft it was a remarkable effort. Here there is none of the psychological easing which comes of mixing climbing with alpine resorts. Almost everything is dead, brutal remote and inhuman. The decision to retreat was a wise one. Des Rubens suffered frostbite in several toes. One is mindful of Leslie Stephens's acerbic but appropriate comments on the original exploration of the area in 1892, '. . . these huge, frigid images of death and stagnation were a little overpowering, and required some association with the land of the living.'

POSTSCRIPT
At base camp, of the eleven expeditions of the summer two remained when I descended. I tried to secure an already deteriorating base, ate well with two old Italian support climbers and walked next day almost to Urdokas. Next day, I dined with a large group from Karakoram Tours at Paiju, then caught my French friends, Benoit Renard and his party, with whom we had been in the Pamirs eleven years before. I finished my descent to Dusso with them in two days.

AROUND EVEREST

Chengdu Hotel, Peoples' Republic of China, Rules   August 1986

'Be polite and graceful. Liproars are not allowed. The guest shouldn't walk out of the room with his upper part naked. Its not allowed to drink wildly in the room. Gambling as well as other dirty games are not allowed.

Guns and bullets should be sent to the local arsenal or police station for keeping.'

Kingdoms of Experience: Everest The Unclimbed Ridge by Andrew Greig. Hutchinson, 1986.

Mountain *114. (1987).*

In 1984 Mal Duff boldly seized the permit surrendered by the Norwegians when the 'hot shot' Hans Christian Doseth died with his companion, falling after climbing a mighty new route on the Trango Towers. The result was the Scottish-Pilkington North-East Ridge Expedition pre-monsoon in 1985.

Kingdoms of Experience refers to the variety, wealth and complexity of the individual reactions of the expedition members to the immense pressures, both physical and psychological, which very high mountains can generate. It is a thoughtful, introverted, unironed text, seeming to let the individuals speak for themselves from their diaries or reminiscences, without the writer imposing too harsh a standardization on their endless calculations, worries, gripes, illnesses

Everest, advance base camp, Seligman-Harris North East Ridge Expedition, 1986.

and joys. Though the lover of a smooth narrative might find it hard to follow, it comes over as authentic, multi-faceted, human, evoking sharp memory of some of the individuals, and some thoughts about this expedition among others.

For everyone it was the biggest expedition, biggest budget, biggest objective yet. Organizationally it had to be relatively large scale, and compared to the quixotic smallness of the first attempt when Pete Boardman and Joe Tasker disappeared, it was. Yet in practice the logistics of the megaroute, and the weight of even limited oxygen for use very high, together with some difficult weather, wore out ten climbers and some very game ancillaries. They ran out of health and push only a little before running out of time, but did well to avoid serious consequences in repeated sallies up the ridge to near 26,000ft.

Andrew Greig portrays this attrition in severe detail, with its consequent splitting of climbing partnerships and material hardships more or less unique to the very highest peaks. The endless effort comes over as deep seriousness, a sense of isolation in individuals as they strive to survive, 'Himalayan thuggery' as Jon Tinker called it. The repetition, hauntings from dead climbers in fevered imagination, desire for human warmth in totally unforgiving thin air, makes the trip sound dire and Calvinistic when not relieved by adolescent swings of mood or base camp festivity.

The insidious weakenings resultant on too long at, or above, an advanced base around 21,300ft are all too familiar. In truth, though, this seems to have been a good expedition despite its hardships and disappointments, sufficiently so in itself and in the expertise of its chronicler to merit an attentive read. Even relatively young expeditions split into 'Boy Racers' and 'Old Farts' it seems, but time at high altitude tends to swell the ranks of the latter. There are some interesting observations about the Kurt Diemberger-Julie Tullis film team in action, and a sad little account of the Basque accident on the 'easy' North Col Route which seems to claim lives annually. Always too there is the topographical problem of this ridge as summarized by Jack Longland of the 1933 British Expedition: 'Well, have you got up to our route yet?'

In 1986, I spent August to October on the North-East Ridge of Everest, a member of the Seligman-Harris expedition. In the bad weather of September and October that year we reached 26,000ft (Trevor Pilling and Harry Taylor) but no further. Notable was the sight of Erhard Loretan and Jean Triollet reaching the summit after a fast ascent of the North Face as we were establishing advanced base camp (28 August 1986).

K2 Tragedy – A Postscript

Mountain *113. (1987).*

Recently the British domestic mountaineering magazine *Climber* usefully published an interview with Kurt Diemberger. This clarified the facts on a number of details about the process which led ultimately to the deaths of Julie Tullis, Al

Rouse, Dobroslawa Wolf, and the two Austrians, Weiser and Imitzer. As usual the facts do *not* speak for themselves. In an editorial comment three contributory factors were emphasized alongside the bad weather which struck the party high on the mountain.

1. If the camp four gear stashed by Diemberger and Tullis had not been removed it might have eased the overcrowding at camp four and allowed Rouse and Wolf to make an earlier attempt, or the Koreans to get away sooner.

2. The sudden arrival of the Poles who had climbed the South Pillar made a crowded situation worse.

3. Diemberger undoubtedly points the finger at the Austrians for their astonishingly selfish and dangerous behaviour. If the agreement was as Diemberger says (*that they should spend one night in a Korean tent, make an attempt and go right down to camp three*), then the Austrians were the prime cause of what followed. This contrasts strongly with the Koreans who seem to have been bullied out of their rightful place . . .

The piece went on to stress, correctly, that Al Rouse throughout conducted himself well, a contributing factor to his ultimate death.

As an attempted explanation of the tragedy, Kurt Diemberger's account seems informative factually, but incomplete analytically, while the editorial comment gives insufficient attention to the really important factors in this disaster, and inadvertently misses the real lessons which may be learned from the whole pattern of accidents on K2 this year. The question of why Julie Tullis, Al Rouse and the others weakened so much at camp four is no mystery, as this piece concluded, though overcrowding doubtless would not help. Stated simply, they stayed at great altitude too long, and tried to rest too high. The Austrians did likewise, as did Maurice and Liliane Barrard earlier in the summer. This was the conclusion of the latter's companion, Michel Parmentier, who was himself caught in a storm and barely survived coming down (relatively quickly) from above 8,000m. Not only did he suggest it at the annual meeting of the French Fédération des Montagnes on 5 November 1986, but he appeared to gain the agreement of virtually all the most informed high altitude climbers and doctors there. After all, for the experienced, that has been the logic of the very fast ascent without oxygen for nearly a decade, as practised so successfully by Reinhold Messner, Kristof Wielicki, Jerzy Kukuczka or Erhard Loretan, and by Jean Afanassieff, Eric Escoffier or Benoit Chamoux, who were at the meeting above and appeared to agree. For them, and for most successful fast, light ascents, a relatively 'safe' climb demands that climbers do not stay much more than *thirty-six hours* at the highest altitudes, and that descent is as fast as possible. There is no real question of acclimatization much beyond 7,500m, and a longer stay invites rapid deterioration.

With this logic, it follows that the fifth day's rest, at camp four, was an error, extending the stay at around 8,000m for too long. When this was compounded by bad weather which trapped the climbers there in descent, and by a fall and forced bivouac in the case of Diemberger and Tullis, then a weak position became untenable. This was practically similar to the Barrards' descent, when they had climbed the top section of the mountain in extremely short stages, with inevitable deterioration which most likely contributed also to Tadeusz Piotrowski's fall, despite its initial cause being a lost crampon.

One other factor needs to be stressed. Lightweight oxygen-free ascents really need good weather on the highest peaks so that the way, the tracks of others, fixed ropes or camps can be found quickly, and body temperature maintained. There seem to have been suggestions of the advent of bad weather on the summit day (6 August), but who has not taken their chances more than once when the summit seemed near? After two nights at camp four it seems that the summit parties had already been too high too long as they set out, with consequent dehydration and other critical effects, a situation that left almost no reserve for bad weather and further delay.

Of course there are a number of examples of Himalayan climbers staying beyond about 7,000m for longer periods without artificial oxygen, than the thirty-six hours or so which had become the yardstick on very fast ascents; notably on K2 in 1953, where a seven-man party stayed around that level for the period of 1–9 August in mostly mixed or stormy conditions. There is little evidence that their chances of success or survival were enhanced by this long and partially involuntary sojourn. Apart from Art Gilkey's subsequent embolism, others seem to have suffered serious altitude effects, even before the famous fall, Peter Shoening's near-miraculous belaying of the whole group, and the eventual safe retreat of all but the unfortunate Gilkey himself.

K2 – The Savaged Authors

High. *(November, 1987)*.

In the aftermath of the multiple deaths on K2 in 1986, volleys of newspaper articles, magazine features and eventually books and film burst on us. Much of the content was painful and perplexing, though perhaps less unexpected to those who have been on many recent expeditions than to the wider public. As a compulsive reader and friend of many of the surviving climbers as well as the dead, I read everything. Each exposure reopened old wounds, but contained less that was new. It is not a pretty literature, and forced me into innovations in method. Each new book was read usually within twenty-four hours of receipt. Post-midnight hours allowed the agonies of the carnage to be tolerated, lubricated by whisky, calibrated in quantities which were intended to anaesthetize. This usually worked – next morning the book was finished, its content assimilated. Feelings took longer, but could at least begin with a new day.

On 18 August 1986 at 17,400ft at the Everest base camp below the snout of the Rongbuk Glacier, Patrick Green and Sam Roberts were performing miracles

Jean Afanassieff and Kurt Diemberger. *Photo by Terry Tullis.*

Walter Bonatti and Julie Tullis. *Photo by Terry Tullis.*

in the big frame tent which was our kitchen. A few yards away we sat around a small table in another family frame tent. A cold wind blew down the alley between, from the Lho La and the Everest cirque. Paul Moores patiently fiddled with the radio for the BBC World Service, which could be found on the high Tibetan plateau, though less easily than Moscow. Then came the news. 'Alan Rouse, the leader of the British K2 Expedition, is missing on the mountain. He is thought to have died high on the peak. There are numerous other fatalities.' In our circle of grizzled mountaineers, some of the eighteen taking part in the Seligman-Harris Expedition to Everest North-East Ridge, Al's death struck like lightning. It was to be a long time before the names of a long list of other casualties registered. From our British perspective Al was among the most accomplished of UK high altitude climbers, having achieved arguably more than any other living British mountaineer except Doug Scott or Joe Brown. Many of us had climbed with him. He had been leader of the winter attempt on Everest in 1980, of which I was deputy. The core of his K2 team, John Porter, Brian Hall and the Burgess twins, was from that same group, with the addition of John Barry, Phil Burke and Dave Wilkinson among the climbers, and Jim Curran, Jim Hargreaves and Bev Holt in specialist functions. On return to Britain in late October, the other accidents seemed less surprising, with the possible exception of the Poles Tadeusz Piotrowski, Andrez Wroz and Dobroslawa Wolf. Julie Tullis was less experienced, though very strong and determined. I suppose we knew too little about some of the other casualties.

Autumn a year on is publication time, another Karakoram season past, another North-East Ridge of Everest attempt afoot. The winds blow no less cold in the limbo of the living. Julie Tullis's autobiography *Clouds from Both Sides* (Grafton, 1986) appeared after her death, and a paperback edition followed close behind in 1987 with a quickly cobbled additional chapter by journalist Peter Gilman. Then come the two books 'about' the British Expedition. Reading them all led me to contemplate the writing K2 has engendered since its first exploration. Of course '. . . what does the mountain care?' as John Barry opines early in his *K2*. Surely if it does not, cannot, then people must. Somehow those who have written about climbing on K2 have seemed at times to take on themselves the monstrous temperament assumed in that black pyramid. The literature of K2 includes at least one of the greatest tales of survival ever told, in Houston's account of the death of Art Gilkey and the retreat in 1953. But some of the writing inclines to rancour, of which I would like at least to consider the causes.

Had all mountain writing fallen in acrimony, one might accept that from Aleister Crowley and Oscar Eckenstein in 1902 to John Barry there was a specificity of genre. But no great mountain could alone produce a particular species of writing. Everest, the most written-about mountain of all, has not produced much work in the 'tell it as it was (or as I wish it had been)' school. There has been mountain writing like that: the use of people's confidences to stab them in the back, and the use of humour without the sympathetic symbiosis, which differentiates it from verbal bullying. Generally it has been seen for what it was, while the mainstream of mountain writing has stayed nearer to Scott of the Antarctic's apologists than Apsley Cherry-Garrard or Roland Huntford. Malcolm Slessor's *Red Peak* (Hodder and Stoughton, 1964) was an exception, but not really about an expedition and essentially nationalistic in its orientation. In general, British 'big mountain' climbers have retained faith with one another, even when ambitious individuals bent the facts to fit their future plans or forgot enough to be highly selective about the past.

In inclination I am little opposed to those who wish to tell it as it was. Nor am I very nationalistic, and thereby inclined to lie or omit to defend honour in the mountains or elsewhere. This means that I perceive the framework of operation for any expedition book writer differently from that of post Everest in 1953 or 1975, in the UK context, and likewise for Americans after failures on K2 in 1953 and 1975, and success in 1978.

In what way is the context different once it is not national honour that is to be defended? One chooses to climb with particular groups, and should within reasonable bounds defend the integrity of the group once joined, for which one shares a degree of responsibility. To join at all implies that in any big mountain venture, as is well illustrated by the whole tone of Joe Tasker's *Savage Arena* (Methuen, 1982). If that is not accepted one should not have joined, or should suffer a share of deserved guilt.

Galen Rowell's *In the Throne Room of the Mountain Gods* (Allen & Unwin, 1977) and Rick Ridgeway's *The Last Step* (The Mountaineers' Seattle, 1977) both recorded acrimonious expeditions. Bitterness from the successful expedition still emerges in Cherie Bremer-Kamp's *Living on the Edge* (David & Charles, 1987). The major difference seems to be that Rowell rejected the unpleasant personal relations as unseemly, while others perhaps saw them as inevitable. Which comes to the root of the question whether or not to reveal all an expedition's conflicts and pains to the world, or indeed whether or not to do so in the aftermath of other climbs.

Presumably writers who feel they have to do so, have suffered the consequences of conflict and feel their integrity would be threatened if this were not reflected. Does this justify their laying bare the weaknesses of their companions in the process, whatever the literary technique used to achieve that? If so they also should be aware of the difficulties revealed by Virginia Woolf: 'But since dialogues are even more hard to write than to speak, and it is doubtful whether written dialogues have ever been spoken or spoken dialogues have ever been written, we will only rescue such fragments as concern our story.'

It is the case that since the Crowley expedition, British and American expeditions to K2 seem to have been riven with dissent. The exceptions were 1938 and 1953 and for the UK, 1978. If the 1939 Fritz Wiessner expedition was not so affected at the time, it became so after the deaths of Dudley Woolf and the three Sherpas who tried vainly to save him. Italian success in 1954 plunged non-summit climber Walter Bonatti into gloom and eventual great feats, and there seems to be some disappointment between Pakistani climbers and Japanese after the 1977 and 1981 successes.

John Barry.

Jim Curran.

Renato Casarotto.

Al Rouse, centre, at Kumjung with David
Breshiers and Alan Jewhurst.

John Barry is doing nothing new in being critical, using humour and other people's dialogue to pass judgement on others, and in trying to disarm by mild self-denigration. That many of the comments seem to have been of the nature of confidences might not look good in court but is unsurprising. The humour is typical of British climbers, though its best practitioners understand that it is essentially a verbal medium, dependent on the intended victim being able to give as good as he gets, and also on a certain commonality of values and sympathy. Reproduction of such badinage to a seemingly serious purpose is both to devalue it and to invite crass misunderstandings in a general reader. In particular in cold print it looks inhumanely cruel, as there is no sense of context.

K2, Savage Mountain, Savage Summer (Oxford Illustrated Press, 1984) is a self-confessed personal view by one of the climbers who agreed to write the expedition book. That can be a chore, despite a little cash in the end, and in this case likely notoriety. It combines an attractive clean-looking package and some reasonable photos and diagrams with a personal narrative and diary of events.

It is not an expedition book in the Lord Hunt or Chris Bonington sense. Its stance is too partisan, its account too incomplete and disjointed. Only a slight obeisance is made in the 'useful' direction with a few appendices, largely of the type that sponsors like. It is closer to Joe Tasker's *Everest the Cruel Way* (Eyre Methuen, 1981) which used the narrative form in a polemic to further his own future, again for the most part at Al Rouse's expense.

Despite language more literary and at best very evocative, it is less controlled than Joe's writing. While he was disciplined and self-aware, striking out selectively and probably along sincerely believed lines in both the *Everest* and *Savage Arena* books, this K2 book shows no such economy. The text swipes first this way and then that, hitting almost everyone eventually, and particularly Al Rouse. One could come away with some very odd impressions. The team is represented as disunited and relatively weak. It may not have succeeded, but the route chosen was very long and hard, and forced on them by permission vagaries. Most of the members had climbed in the Himalaya before on high peaks. The hope was that John, Phil Burke and Dave Wilkinson would make it stronger still. Reading into the barely concealed agenda it appears that John had difficulty understanding how to integrate into an ethos less authoritarian than the military and, despite the leadership role he was supposed to play with Al Rouse, acted disruptively. A brooding frustration seethes below the considerable literary flair of the author, even at his most readable and evocative.

Thus from the playing up of minor and inevitable faults to the emphasis on the errors of almost all his companions, blow on blow falls on those unfortunate enough to have been in his way. Mistakes were made, but this welter of innuendo and damnation by omission and inclusion seems incapable of doing any good. All books seriously written deserve at least one sympathetic reading, but does this? What is it for? Contracts once made need to be honoured, pages to be filled. Much of the K2 saga happened after the British party had gone home, despite the revealingly disordered list of the dead on the rear cover of John Barry's polemic. (Brits first, ladies before gentlemen, then Americans,

French, Italian, Polish, Austrian and last Pakistani.) Was the author satisfied with his own performance, as climber, as one-time leader? The book retains a curious fascination, as a mirror into which its author will have to look longer and deeper than any other reader.

K2. Triumph and Tragedy (Hodder and Stoughton, 1987) is about the series of events which made up such an awful year on K2. Though still a personal memoir, Jim Curran's book is of a different genre. It details the strengths and weaknesses of the British team, acknowledges many of the problems, engages in personal response, amusing anecdote, some inevitably drawn from the same events. Evidently whatever other problems Al's leadership faced, his worst was one member who did not accept him in that role and made few bones about it. At a vulnerable and exhausting time there was unproductive sniping, encouragement of an atmosphere of philistinism and verbal bullying, which tended to weaken effort when resources were modest and the objective difficult. When that British effort ended Curran stayed on filming and maintaining a base camp support for Rouse, and thereby went through the immense trauma of the multiple deaths that followed. His different priorities enabled him to stand back and write a book that does some justice to the people who were there, living and dead, of whatever nationality.

These are reflections on K2 from two different worlds. though both authors have drunk from the same pots and walked the same interminable paths. One is almost entirely self-centred, hiding thwarted ambition and incomprehension at the seemingly greater abilities and achievements of apparent weaklings and 'lefties' behind style, satire and pseudo sympathy. Curran tries to take in the horror, pity and seemingly inevitability of tragedy, nearly chokes at its immensity, but goes some way towards the resolution that any sensitive reader deeply needs. Its broad humanitarianism may not be fashionable, especially among the ruder Visigoths and dishonoured Samurai of England, but it has lasting value.

POSTSCRIPT
Harsh as these judgements seem, little has happened to persuade me that they should be modified, though there has been much more mountaineering since 1986, including yet another attempt on Everest North-East Ridge, and an international attempt on K2 organized by Andreij Zawada, the first in winter.

Conquistadors of the Useless

Impression. *(1971).*

Climbers treat the question 'why' as nonsensical. For those involved it is self-evident. Regular weekend drives to Wales, the Lakes or Scotland are enlivened by long-standing friends and a flow of new acquaintances. One climbs in beautiful scenery and remote places. The challenge of fierce icy wind is much

Rick Ridgeway making some of his last steps towards K2 Summit, 1978.

the same on wintry bens or Mont Blanc. Physical rewards and satisfactions, beauty and matey darts evenings in pubs, mid-week, winter and summer, go to provide a way of life sharply differentiated from city existence.

Such a quirky subculture reinforces climbers in their daily lives, whether they are regular weekenders or occasional performers. With their own literature, songs, jargon, and mythology most need only a modest recharge which may even be vicarious to offset the inner gnawing restlessness which results from mountains or at least rocks. Yet it is a persistent nagging need which pulls climbers back to the hills, as wives and companies know, after fruitless attempts at re-education.

A lunatic activity usually has some rationale. Why do people begin? How do they enter the priesthood of experts? Memory allows slight signs of motivation to seep into the open. Distant rosy-hued cliffs are translated by adolescent eyes into visionary experience. There is a wilderness of possibilities and a ruthlessness with self in early morning yawning starts, with ambition boiling up and the rare promise of dry rock as the stars fade into a blue and perfect dawn.

There are warm friendships too with people who share fearful escapades, rock and human falls, motorcycle and car crashes, celebrations of triumph and rescues of the living and the dead.

The appeal for us was that of a lifestyle outside the sterilities of engineering shop or examination treadmill, beyond cities but a reaction from them. An exhilaration also pervaded the classlessness of post-1945 climbing. Its heroes were plumbers whom the battered echelons of the traditional leisured showered with condescension. Climbing youth fled from town smoke, parents and musty social relationships into hitch-hiking, motorcycles, cave dwelling and other residences in tents, under boulders, in swimming-pool verandas, cricket pavilions, park shelters and under bridges. Always there was a place to stay, a sustained social life, freed of trammels, costing little, and so beloved of adolescence that every habitué loved to introduce uncomprehending friends. Whatever he could climb, the sign of the true climber was that he 'went away' regularly.

The climbing pales into insignificance in this account of early motivation. To some it was merely an excuse to get out of the cities – they might have sailed or cycled or now would to to pop festivals. But climbing is strenuous escape, taking strength, skill and nerve beyond what some would sustain. Its specific technologies demand efforts of mastery and for years the sign of the end of a climber's career was 'selling his gear', usually before marriage.

Most important of all is the cohesiveness of climbing social groups, tight networks whether formal or otherwise which endure for five, ten, fifteen or more years. Climbers live together for long periods as well as occasionally dying together; hundreds of journeys, dark exits from storm-bound summits and grim descents; long nights in bivouacs or remote huts. Often their debts to one another are incalculable, payable only in attachment.

All the monstrosities of personality development sprout large in such a fraternity. Individualists claim that they are little influenced yet insist on recognitions, attempting unceasingly to justify themselves. Many social groups are fiercely competitive yet friendly in their internal relationships. From the exterior they are often clan-like and remote. The very names given to climbs indicate the seriousness of their discoverers' views of their role. One can progress through the beauties of the Lake District, via 'Totalitarian' to 'Funeral Way', continue to 'Post Mortem' and end with 'Rigor Mortis'. Beyond that can be found (suitably) 'Valhalla'.

Mountaineering has differentiated itself into multiple activities, ranging from outcrop climbing and winter bogtrotting to escalated versions of the same in Wales or the Lakes, bigger problems in Scotland, sea-cliff climbing, sea-stack climbing, coast traversing, winter mountaineering, alpine climbing and expedition climbing further afield.

The motivation of individuals involved in a multitude of activities could be expected to display little uniformity but there are common denominators. Climbers at all levels of proficiency and commitment must feel a twinge of affinity for Nietzsche's 'The secret of knowing the most fertile experiences and the greatest joys is to live dangerously.' Whatever the handbooks recommend, or the educational vested interests claim, mountains remain deadly dangerous to all who frequent them. If they were not so the most ardent mountaineers would not climb. The extreme individualists and the tight-knit groups would not exist, nor would the mystics and visionaries who make explicit what lies behind most mountaineers' motivations. There would be the merest sport, with its teachers, occasional practitioners, organization men and promoters with cash-register eyes. Fortunately the range and risks of the activity remain so great as to resist the threatening exploitative element. The ethos of mountaineering, if it exists, is too nebulous to be defined, indelibly marked with escapism, anarchistic tendencies and a joint romantic and aesthetic appeal to the spirit.

Yet the pure physical joys cannot be discounted. Of 'danger sports' few have the appeal of mountaineering in the unique range of demands made of human beings combined with unusual satisfactions. Fear of heights seems to be fundamental in modern man yet it is overcome against the climber's better judgement.

The combination of technology and self control makes climbing near incomprehensible yet visually spectacular to the sober citizen. It is a gamble with the risks of Russian roulette and no apparent prize. The climber knows the pleasure of pulling his body up apparently impossible and dizzy walls, the relief of overcoming truly fearful obstacles, sharp contrasts of day and night, cold and extreme heat, pain and exhilaration. Fear is essential to him as it is inhibiting to the layman, and the value of the activity is determined by the possibility of crumpled corpses combined with the acutest sense of being alive. Thus the appeal to the emotions is strong, deep and in a sense wholly 'primitive'. 'I am the enemy of gravity ... he who will one day teach men to fly will have moved the boundary stones, all boundary stones will fly into the air with him. He will baptize the earth anew as the weightless.'

Climbers rarely reject their society. Climbing appeals to emotions repressed

195

Ed Drummond plus poem performance pole.

in the role-playing, visual vulgarity, indignity and antlike forms of order in our cities. From them most climbers come, especially from the uglier northern towns where climbing is near, the pull compounded by hills just beyond towns' drabness.

Again to many, climbing, like the European hiking movement of the 30s, is seen as a source of potential freedom, as indeed it may have been in the middle-class mountain activities before 1914, in the tradition of nude tarn bathing and mixed alpine sleeping quarters. In the mountains, first restless middle-class elements and later working-class young people found the sexual freedoms that were impossible amid the family houses of city existence. It was a permissiveness predating by decades that mythologized in the 60s while elements of danger in the sport served only to intensify the immediacy of situations and the blindness of patience in face of danger.

People who tear up the M1 to Wales or the Lakes from London and make a mass exodus from the northern towns on Friday evenings do so partly because once a pattern of behaviour is established even the restless tend to remain creatures of habit. But whether they get their kicks from pushing themselves to the limit on an easy or a hard climb, or have gone so far in their needs as to regard such activities as mere preparation for the 'real' tests of Mont Blanc, the brittle ice of the Eiger Nordwand or the Himalaya, it is not enough to see motivation simply in terms of competition or gymnastics.

These people are in reaction against the disunities of personality forced on them in city life. Few climbers are death lovers. The opposite is the case. On Stanage and on Everest they seek the Holy Grail of self unification, a unity combining the mind and body in the achievement of a single purpose, a purpose with aesthetic as well as physical appeal. Only this can explain the sensation familiar to so many climbers after travelling far in an alien country. As the mountain valleys open up and the distant snows glisten, on a winter night in Scotland or early summer in the Soviet Caucasus, one feels that one is coming home.

'What we sought was the unbounded and essential joy that boils in the heart and penetrates every fibre of our being when after long hours skirting the borders of death, we can again hug life to us with all our strength.'

Forward Communication

Everest Base Camp
Rangbuk
Shigatse
Via Lhasa
Tibet

28th July, 1986

Dear Paul

I received a letter from the Embassy of Pakistan, London, on Saturday, 26th July, saying that we had got Latok II. The main bit was as follows:

'We have been informed by the Ministry of Tourism, Islamabad, that permission has been granted to your party for scaling Latok II via route – Rawalpindi – Sakardu (by air or road) – Shigar – Dassu – Diano – Gomboro – Chahgo – Askole – Drinsong – Biafo Glacier – Baintha Gurpar Glacier – Latok No. II Peak, for the period from 23rd May 1987 for 90 days. Formal permission letter will be issued accordingly.'

Enclosed is a list of the team members as a start to 'getting to know each other' and of course, how to contact them.

I would like to arrange for us all to meet in the near future to get the show on the road and introduce members to each other, North Wales would preferably be suitable to all. If you could let me know when you are, and are not able to go, I may well be able to sort out a date when we all can.

I'll be in contact again as soon as I have your replies and dates, or with any further information available.

Yours sincerely,
  Ted.

INDEX

Note: page numbers in bold type refer to illustration captions

Abalakov, Anatoly 130
Abalakov, Vitaly **121**, 132
Adjudicator Wall (Peak Dist.) **20**
Afanassieff, Jean 118, 185, **187**
Ahmed, Captain Javed 134
Aigulle des Grands Charmoz (Alps) 116, 117
Albigna (Alps) 118–20, **119**
Allen, John 9, 47
Allen, Nat 8, 14, 24
Aman, Ashraf 133
Alpha Club 2, 9, 65, 70, 71
Alpine Climbing Club (ACC) 46, 94, 169
Alpine Climbing Group (ACG) 118
Alps 2, 67, 92, 94, 103, 106–20, 163, 173–4
Amatt, John 9
Am Beachaille **100**
Annapurna (Himalaya) 114, 171, 176
Anthoine, Jackie 138
Anthoine, Mo 137, 142
Asgard (Baffin I.) 125–8, 130
Aufschnaiter, Peter 169
Austin, Allan **56**, 57, 64, 70, 71

Bachelor's Buttress (Peak Dist.) 1, **3**
Baffin Island 125–8, **126**, 130
Baintha Lukpar Glacier (Karakoram Himalaya) 134, **139**, 140
Balcombe, F. G. 55
Bancroft, Steve **26**, 26
Banks, Mike 92
Barker, Bill 116
Barnaj (Jammu Kashmir) 141–7
Barrard, Maurice and Liliane 185, 186
Barry, John 188, **190**, 191
Bastion Route, High Tor (Peak Dist.) 11–13
Bat and the Wicked, The 76–82, **78**
Baxter-Jones, Roger 116–18, **117**
Beale, Peter 173–4
Beeston Tor (Peak Dist.) 9, 22, 23, 24–5
Behemoth, Miller's Dale (Peak Dist.) 10–11
Ben Nevis 46, 67, **74**, **76**, 92, 94; The Bat 76–82, **78**;
    Observatory Ridge 73–6
Bettembourg, Georges 118, 153, **155**, 157–9
Big Plum (Peak Dist.) 20
Birkett, Bill 70
Birkett, R. J. 57
Birtles, Geoff 18, 150, 174
Black Wall (Gwynedd) 31
Blanc, Mont 108, 110, 112, 116, 118, 194, 196
Boardman, Pete 162–5, **163**, 184
Bolger, Terry 3
Bolger, Tom 23, 24
Bonatti, Walter 177, **187**, 189
Bonatti Pillar (Alps) 108–10
Bonington, Chris 71, 96, 98, 112, 137, 160–2, **161**, 191
Borrowdale (Lake Dist.) 64, 82, 84
Bower, George 57
Bower, the (Suicide Wall, Cratcliffe Tor), 6–7
Boysen, Martin 25, 26, 70, 90, 96, 106–7, **119**, 120, 173–5
Braithwaite, Paul ('Tut') 71, 117, 120, 125–8, 130, 131
Bremer-Kamp, Cherie 189
Bridge, Alf 57
British Climbing Society (BCS) 95
British Mountaineering Club/Council (BMC) 63, 164
Broad Peak (Himalaya) 2, 176, 177, 180
Brown, Joe 9, 14–15, 38, 41, 96, 130, 142, 171, 174–5, 188
Brown, Les 65, 70, 71, 106, **108**

Brown, Peter 69
Brown, Rod 8, 69
Brown, T. Graham 157
Brown, Valerie 142
Bruce, C. G. 169
Buhl, Hermann 2, 106, 150
Burgess, Aid 156, 188
Burgess, Derek 8, 188
Burke, Mick 114, 164, 171
Burke, Phil 90–1, 188, 191
Byne, Eric 7, 14, 15, 67

Cairngorms 91–2
Cairn-mor-Dearg 73, 79
Calvert, Harry 157
Canali, Jack 159
Carrington, Rab **74**, 77, **78**, 79–82, 116, 118, 120
Cassarotto, Renato 178, **190**
Cassarotto, Garetta 178
Cassin, Riccardo 157, 159, 177
Caucasus **121**, 122–5, 130, 197
Central Pillar (Esk Buttress, Eskdale) 57–8
Chadwick, Alison 176
Chamoux, Benoit 185
Changabang (Himalaya) 163–4
Cheedale (Peak Dist.) 19–21
Chee Tor Girdle (Peak Dist.) 8, 9
Child, Greg 149
Cioch Club 17–19
Civetta (Alps) 106
Clarke, Alan 8, 31
Clarke, Sid 57–8
Climbers Club (CC) 2, **30**, 48–9
Clogwyn d'ur Arddu (Gwynned) 33–8, **35**, 79, 171
Clough, Ian 114
Cluelow Cross (Peak Dist.) **1**
Cnoc a' Mhadaidh (Scotland) 86–91, 97, 102
Cohen, Geoff 176–81
Col Roseg (Alps) **119**
Colton, Nick 117
Connery, Sean 173–5, **172**
Conway, Sir Martin 132–2
Craig, Bob 129, 131–2
Cram, Geoff 69–72
Crawshaw, Christine 97–9, **100**, 101–2
Craig Ddu (Gwynned) 31–2, 194
Creag Meaghaidh (Scotland) 83, 94
Creation, Raven Crag, Thirlmere **62**
Crew, Pete 25, 31, **35**, 36–8, 43, 57, 70
Crowley, Aleister 188, 189
Cunningham, John 73
Curran, Jim 61, 77, 80–1, 143–4, 147, 171, 188, **190**, 192

Dablam, Ama 156
Dacher, Michael 150
Dark Angel, Sheagra **100**
Dead Banana Crack, Stoney Middleton **3**
Dearman, Bob 8, 17, **20**, 24–5, 90–1, 122
Devassoux, Christine 118
Dewhurst, Alan **148**
Dickinson, Leo 171
Diemberger, Kurt 2, 162, 184–6, **187**
Dingle, Graeme 156
Dionard 96–102
Dolphin, Arthur 70
Doseth, Hans Christian 183
Dovedale (Peak Dist.) 22–5

Index

Downes, Bob 90, 149
Downfall Ravin, Kinder Scout (Peak Dist.) 28–9, **28**
Droites, Les (Alps) 72, 116, 151
Drummond, Ed **196**
Duff, Mal 183
Dunagiri (Himalaya) 163–4

Eastwood, Clint **151**
Edwards, Menlove 63, 155
Eiger 114–16, 145, 150–1, 160, 161, 197
Eissenschmidt, Eva 131
Elliott, Frank 7, 14
Emerald Gully (Beinn Dearg, N. Highlands) 84–6
Engineers' Slabs (Gable Crag, Great Gable) 55–7
Escoffier, Eric 185
Esk Buttress, Eskdale (Lake Dist.) 57–8
Everest 114, 125, 148, **148**, 154, 156, 158, 162–6, **165**, 168–9,
   171, 173, 176, 177, 183–92, **183**, 198
Extol (Lake Dist.) **56**, 67

Faux, Ronald 152–3
Fawcett, Ron **62**
Fearnehough, Pat 66–9, **68**, 70, 73, 75–6, 109–10, 133–7, 138–9,
   147
Fell and Rock Climbing Club (FRCC) 46
Foinaven (Scotland) 86–91, 96–102
Fork Beard Glacier (Baffin I.) **126**
Fraser, George 90
From, Fred 156
Fuller, Angela (Soper) **62**
Fuller, Brian ('Fred') 85, 88, 89, 109

Gable Crag, Great Gable (Lake Dist.) 55–7
Gardyloo Buttress, Ben Nevis 73, **74**
Gasherbrum 1 (Karakoram Himalaya) 176, 181
Gasherbrum 2 (Karakoram Himalaya) 176–8
Gasherbrum 3 (Karakoram Himalaya) 176–82, **177**
Gasherbrum 4 (Karakoram Himalaya) 177, 179–80, 182
Gilkey, Art 169, 186, 188
Gimmer Creag (Lake Dist.) **62**
Gippenreuter, Eugene 130
Gobbi, Tony 177
Goodwin, Dave (Spud) 87, 88
Grand Capucin, The (Alps) 110, **111**
Grandes Jorasses **115**, 116
Gray, Dennis 63, 122
Great End Crag (Lake Dist.) 59, 60
Great Gable (Lake Dist.) 53–7
Green, Patrick 133–7, 138, 140, 186
Greenbank, Tony 72
Gregory, Dave 15, 26
Greig, Andrew 183–4
Griffiths, Brian 91
Grindley, Ed 63
Guillard, Mick 23, 24, 109
Gwynedd 31–49

Habeler, Peter **151**
Hall, Brian 77, **78**, 79–82, 118, 188
Hargreaves, Jim 188
Harris, Al 71, 167
Haskett-Smith, W. 53, 54, 69, 70
Hassall, Bob 23
Haston, Dougal 76, **78**, 79, 82, 114, **115**
Hayes, Geoff 29–30
Helyg (Gwynned) 48–9
Hen Cloud (Peak Dist.) 1, 3; Central Climb 5–6
Henderson, Brian 82
Hennek, Dennis 125–8
High Tor (Peak Dist.) 11–13, 14, 16, 19, 67
Hillary, Edmund and Peter 156
Himalaya, the 2, 92, 115, 118, 121, 132–47, 154, 156, 157–9,
   160, 162–6, 168–70, 171, 176–92, 197
Himalayan Club 169
Holt, Bev 188
Horbein, Thomas F. 165–6

Howard, Sheila 97, 101
Howard, Ted 97–102, 105, 137
Howard, Tony 8
Howell, Malcolm 61
Hunt, Lord 130, 191

Jackson, Chris 8
Jammu Kashmir (Himalaya) 141–7
Jardine, Ray **45**
Jewel, Jimmy 47
Johnson, Dave 15

Karakoram **68**, 69, 132–41, 147, 154, 169, 176–82, 188
Kellett's Left Hand, Gardyloo Buttress, Ben Nevis **74**
Kelly, H. M. 46, 70
Kentmere (Lake Dist.) **56**
Kenyon, Ron 70
Khumbu Himal (Himalaya) **158**
Kinder Scout (Peak Dist.) 7, 27–9, 82;
   Downfall Ravine **28**, 28–9
Kipling Groove, Gimmer Crag (Lake Dist.) **62**
Kirkus, 36, 37, 63
K2 (Himalaya) 118, 129, 141, 159, 168, 169, 176, 178, 180,
   184–92, **193**
Kukuczka, Jerzy 150, 185
Kurz, Tony 160

Lake District 2, 4, 50–72, 192, 195, 196
Lareton, Erhard 184
Latok 1 (Karakoram Himalaya) 133
Latok 2 (Karakoram Himalaya) 147–8, **148**, 198; 1977 132–7,
   135; 1978 137–41, **139**
Latok 3 (Karakoram Himalaya) **139**, 140, 141
Laycock, John 6
Lee, Guy 130
Lewis, Tim 91, 150, 166–7
Lhotse (Himalaya) 156, 159
Limelight, High Tor, Matlock **3**
Livesey, Pete 60, 61–4
Llanberis (Gwynedd) 31, 33, 73, 176
Llyn d'ur Arddu (Gwynedd) 44
Lochnagar 103–5, **104**
Longland, Sir Jack 1, 184
Loretan, Erhard 150, 185
Lowe, Geoff 131
Lukan, Karl 112

McHardy, Alan (Richard) 2, 3, 4, 31, 47, 53–4, 70, 71, 73, 106,
   122, 125, 130
McHardy, Barbara 122
MacInnes, Hamish 71, 92, 94, 103, 108, 122–4, 130, 159–60,
   160, 171, 174
McIntyre, Alex 118, 98–102, 167
McLean, Big John 73
Macnaught-Davis, Ian 130
Maiden Stacks, Whiten Head, Sutherland 86–91, **93**
Makalu (Himalaya) **165**
Manifold (Peak Dist.) 22–5
Mason, Kenneth 168–70
Medlar, The (Lake Dist.) **52**, 96
Messner, Reinhold 150–3, **151**, 158, 163, 185
Metcalfe, Eric ('Matey') 57
Miller's Dale (Peak Dist.) 9, 10–11
Millsom, Len 16
Minks, Pete 142
Mohmed, Ghulam 142
Moores, Paul 156, 188
Moorhouse, Denny 91
Morgan, Jeff 23, 24, 25
Morin, Yves 131
Morrison, Don 69, 133–7
Moseley, Ron 15
Moss Ghyll **68**
Murray, Al 70

Nanga Parbat (Himalaya) 133, 136, 152, 158, 168, 169

200

Nanga Parbat Pilgrimage (Buhl) 2, 54
Napes Needle (Great Gable, Lake Dist.) 53–4, 69
Needle Ridge (Great Gable, Lake Dist.) 53–4
Nicolson, Ian **119**
Noyce, Wilfred 130
Nunn, Hilary 84, 119
Nuptse (Himalaya) 71, **155**, 158

Odell, Noel 170
O'Hara, Mike 90
Old Man of Hoy, The 92, 95, 162, 171
Old Man of Stoer, The 82, 92
Oliver, Geoff 72
Onyszkiewicz, Janus 176
Owen, Mike 57

Pamirs (C. Asia) 129–32, 169, 182
Parker, Alan 10, 31, 33, 50
Parker, Terry **52**
Parkin, Andy 116, 118
Parmentier, Michel 185
Patey, Tom 82, 84–6, 87–9, 91–6, **93**, 114, 125, 161
Peak Climbing Club 67
Peak District 1–4, **1**, **3**, 5–30, 67
Peak Lenin (Pamirs, C. Asia) 129–32
Peascod, Bill 70
Peck, Dave 2
Perrin, Jim 154
Petites Dru, Les (Alps) **108**
Phipps, Pete 101
Pic Schurovski (Caucasus) 123, 130
Pietrowski, Tadewz 142, 188
Pilastro de Rozes 106–7
Pilling, Trevor 184
Pinnacle Club 46, 49
Polyphemus Gully (Lochnagar) 103–5, **104**
Porter, John 188
Proctor, Tom 8, 18, 24, 60

Raven Crag, Thirlmere (Lake Dist.) **62**, 96
Ravenstor (Peak Dist.) 9, 26
Read, Steve 8
Renard, Benoit 182
Renshaw, Dick 115, 163
Ridgeway, Rick 189, **193**
Riley, Tony 77, **78**, 85, 133, 135–7, 143–4, 147, 171
Ritson, Will 50–3
Roberts, Sam 186
Robertson, Brian 82, 92
Roches, the (Peak Dist.) 1
Ross, Paul 64, 70, 71, 109
Rotatiev, Paul 123
Rouse, Al 37, 116, 118, 119, 184, 188, **190**, 191–2
Rowell, Galen 189
Rowlands, Clive 9, 31–2, 65–6, 84, 88–9, **93**, 97, 130, 137, 177–81
Rowlands, Steve 65, 84
Rubens, Des 176–82
Rutkeiwicz, Wanda 176
Ruttledge, Hugh 168

Sabir, Nazir 133
Scafell Pinnacle (Lake Dist.) 64–6, 70, 71
Schoening, Pete 129
Scotland 73–105, 192, 195
Scott, Doug **3**, 8, 118, 125–8, 130, 137, 149, 165, 168, 188
Scottish Mountaineering Club (SMC) 46, 49, 79
Seeds, Pete 122, 130
Seligman-Harris North East Expedition (Everest Himalaya) **183**, 184, 188
Sheffield University Mountaineering Club (SUMC) 8, 65, 70

Shipton, Eric 128, 133, 153, 154–5, 164
Shoening, Peter 186
Sirplum, Cheedale (Peak Dist.) 19–21
Slesser, Malcolm 130, 189
Smith, Geoff 145
Smith, Robin 65, 71, 77, **78**, 79–80, 130
Smith, Speedy 130
Smith's Gully, Greag Meaghaidh **83**
Smoker, Paul 54
Smythe, Frank 157
Snowdonia 2, 4, 50
Soviet Mountaineering Federation (SMF) 123, 129, 130
Soper, Jack 37–8, 57, 64, 65, 69, 70
Steep Ghyll, Scafell (Lake Dist.) 64–6
Stephens, Leslie 182
Stoney Middleton (Peak Dist.) **3**, 9, 13–19, **16**
Street, Jack **3**, 8, 9, 18, 23, **26**, 26
Streetly, John 33, 71
Suicide Wall, Cratcliffe Tor (Peak Dist.) 5, 6–7
Suthar, Hanuman 142–3

Tasker, Joe 115, 162–4, 184, 189, 191
Taylor, Harry 184
Thesiger, Wilfred 153
Thexton, Dr Peter 138–40, 147–9, **148**, 177
Thor, Mount (Baffin I.) **126**
Tilman, Bill 154, **155**, 157
Tiso, Graham 129
Tofana, Pilastro de Rozas 106–7
Toogood, Bob 42, 89–91, 98, 101–2, 103–5
Triallet, Jean 184
Tullis, Julie 184–6, **187**, 188
Turner, Jack 141

Ullin, Jon Gary 131
Ushba 122–5

Venables, Steve 147, 154

Walker Spur 71
Ward, Willis 65
Wasdale Head (Lake Dist.) 50–3
Webb, Barry 8, 15–16, 71
Wein, Karl 169
West, Gray 8, 15, 20, 22
Western Gully, Ysgolion Duon 39–43
Whillance, Pete 58, 70
Whillans, Don 15, **56**, 71, 149
Wielicki, Kristof 185
Wiessner, Fritz 189
Wilkinson, Dave 116, **135**, 138–40, **140**, 188, 191
Wilkinson, Revd Frank 125
Williams, Pete 8, 22
Wilson, Ken 19–21, 37–8, 39–43, 53–8, 64–6, 73, 84–6, 103–5, 150, 167
Wilson, Lambert 174
Woodall, Chris 122–4, 130
Wolf, Dobroslawa 185, 188
Woolcock, Oliver 10, 65, 70, 71, 82
Woolf, Dudley 189
Wright, Allan 64, 97
Wroz, Andrez 188

Yates, John 139, 143–6
Yorkshire Mountaineering Club (YMC) 46
Ysgolion Duon (Gwynned) 39–43, **40**

Zawada, Adreij 192
Zdzitowiecki, K. 176
Zinnemann, Fred 171–5, **172**